For the Sake of Argument

For the Sake of Argument

A Life in the Law

A Memoir

Joel Jacobsen, Esq.

PUBLISHING

New York

© 2009 Joel Jacobsen

Published by Kaplan Publishing, a division of Kaplan, Inc.
1 Liberty Plaza, 24th Floor
New York, NY 10006

Printed in the United States of America

10 9 8 7 6 5 4 3 2 1

Library of Congress Cataloging-in-Publication Data

Jacobsen, Joel, 1959–
  For the sake of argument : a life in the law / Joel Jacobsen.
    p. cm.
  ISBN 978-1-60714-085-6
  1. Jacobsen, Joel, 1959– 2. Lawyers—United States—Biography. 3. Practice of law—United States—History. I. Title.
  KF373.J33A3 2009
  340.092—dc22
  [B]

                                                                    2009014498

Kaplan Publishing books are available at special quantity discounts to use for sales promotions, employee premiums, or educational purposes. Please email our Special Sales Department to order or for more information at *kaplanpublishing@kaplan.com,* or write to Kaplan Publishing, 1 Liberty Plaza, 24th Floor, New York, NY 10006.

To my mother,
Eloise Tittle Jacobsen,
daughter of two lawyers
and mother of two more.

CONTENTS

PART IV: PRACTICE MAKES...?

Variations on a theme.

INTRODUCTION

I ONCE TAPED A quotation from Supreme Court Justice Oliver Wendell Holmes, Jr., to the door of my office:

> ... what a profession the law is! ... what other gives such scope to realize the spontaneous energy of one's soul? In what other does one plunge so deep in the stream of life—so share its passions, its battles, its despair, its triumphs?[1]

One of my colleagues wrote beneath the quotation, "What drugs was he taking?"

A life in the law means making the trip from Holmes's rhapsody to my colleague's cynicism and back again, sometimes several times a day.

My legal career has been old enough to drink for several years already. When I look back, I'm struck by the near-randomness of its course. I mainly have my ignorance to thank for the way things turned out. From the decision to apply to law school to the most recent decision to switch jobs, my life in the law has been a series of big choices based on little information.

There were lawyers in my family, but none I could quiz for an insider's insights as I entered the profession. My mother's parents, both lawyers, died before I finished elementary school. My older brother was two years ahead of me in law school, but two years isn't nearly long enough to provide the necessary perspective. Without a network of family or friends to pass along the wisdom of the ages, I made choices about my education and career—choices that determined my life course—based on whatever scraps of information reached my ears, fortified as neces-sary by unwarranted assumptions. In writing this career memoir, my guiding principle has been to include the things I know now that I wish I'd known then.

Law, medicine, and the church are the traditional learned profes-sions. But while no one doubts the social utility of medicine, the phrase "social utility of lawyers" sounds like a setup waiting for its punch line. And even in the wake of much-publicized scandals, comedians don't get laughs by comparing members of the clergy to sharks and hyenas. Lawyers occupy a unique position in our society: necessary, respected, trusted, even (in their incarnation as judges) revered—and ridiculed and despised.

Many young people start law school idealistically only to learn the profession has its own plans for them. For example, those who plan to "do environmental law" may discover upon graduation that the only jobs available in the field involve working for polluters—who, after all, are the ones needing guidance through the regulatory maze. Is it a sell-out to take such a job, or does helping corporations comply with the law provide more practical protection for the environment than any number of protest marches? Or both?

In our courts' zero-sum system, every winner is paired with a loser. That means lawyers work in a system of built-in frustrations. They need to learn to be careful in the way they define victory. Their pro-fessional lives require that they constantly adjust their expectations, confining their hopes and ambition within the limits of the probable while recognizing the many things beyond their control—clients, wit-nesses, judges, opposing lawyers—that can prevent the probable from coming true. Those learned attitudes can easily carry over to one's life away from the office, too. Numerous studies show that lawyers suffer from clinical depression at rates between two and three times that of the general population, although you wouldn't know it from attending any gathering of lawyers once they start swapping their funny stories.

Lawyers are great storytellers. But you might notice how the alcohol flows. It turns out that about 20 percent of us are problem drinkers, twice the national average.[2] A high level of unhappiness seems endemic in the profession, but is it inherent in the work?

It's not possible to understand either lawyers or the world they inhabit without first understanding what it's like to be one of them. Lawyers are people who've gone through the unnecessarily weird and harrowing experience of law school. They find themselves cast in professional roles that require them to act in ways that frequently don't feel entirely genuine. It does something to a person to belong to such a profession.

For the Sake of Argument isn't a memoir of trauma or of history in the making, but of a career, something much closer to home for most of us. It's an account of triumphs and fiascos and of stupendously bad decisions made after the most careful deliberation. Sometimes the practice of law can be deeply satisfying. Even when it's no fun at all, it frequently compensates with a wealth of ironies and incongruities, although it's often not possible to laugh about them until the first (and sometimes the second or third) wave of anger has passed. But eventually the anger is over and only the sense of absurdity remains. Some of it remains in this book. If, as I believe, the only appropriate response to pomposity is laughter, lawyers are rarely without a reason to laugh.

PART ONE

Learning to Want to Think Like a Lawyer

Launching a legal career.

CHAPTER I

The Decision to Apply

M Y DECISION TO apply to law school was shrouded in such ignorance about the legal profession that I find it hard to reconstruct
what was going through my mind. I bought one of those guide-to-the-
law-schools books and remember sitting cross-legged on the floor of
my bedroom in my parents' house with the oversized paperback open
to an outline map of the United States decorated with a couple hundred little dots scattered over it like crumbs on a table. I'd be going
to one of those dots, but my imagination refused to give me a picture
of what it was going to be like.

Today's applicants have the luxury of much-better-informed ignorance. They can go online and see what the campus buildings look
like in bright sunshine (even if the sun never once shines during the
academic year), look at the smiling mug shots of the professors (even if
they never once smile in class), and take virtual tours of the libraries.
But all that information still won't tell them what it's like to attend
the place.

The book was crammed with information that refused to assemble
itself into any recognizable pattern. Trying to make sense of it was
like reading a novel after the pages had been shuffled—there was a
story there, but it wasn't telling itself. I learned how many volumes
each school's library had. To a literature major the numbers seemed

very small, in the mere hundreds of thousands—and that was a full generation before the Great Age of De-acquisition brought about by the proliferation of electronic resources, which have done to historically interesting law books roughly what synthesizers did to studio-based musicians. But knowing one law school had 400,000 volumes and another had 400,001 didn't tell me which one to apply to.

I also read numbers representing student–teacher ratios, average entrance-exam scores, percentage of applicants accepted, and tuition. (Seen in retrospect legal education was virtually free in the early 1980s, though it didn't strike any of us that way at the time.) And, above all, I read numbers representing each law school's ranking.

Or, rather, RANKING, because ranking is the single most important datum about any law school. The meaninglessness of the ranking doesn't detract from its importance. Lawyers are trained to accept arbitrariness (we'll get to the why and how), and numbers don't get much more arbitrary than the annual rankings of law schools. A top-ten list with the usual ivied suspects wouldn't be a big deal—everyone already knows the brand-name private universities that would inevitably dominate it, if only because their alumni are the ones invited to vote. But the law school lists go far beyond the top ten, and they do so with a precision that dares you to find it spurious. You can discover who's number 50, and 75, and 100, and even 203. And you can sit on the carpet of your childhood bedroom and wonder how to relate those numbers to yourself.

I suppose prospective students are meant to ask themselves something like: Do I feel like a top-ten Harvard–Yale–Stanford sort of guy? Or a middling, Seton Hall–Missouri–U.C. Davis man of the people? Or a low-self-esteem Widener–Willamette–William Mitchell dork? (Coming late in the alphabet is a poor strategy for law schools ranked in *U.S. News and World Report*'s lower tiers, where institutions are listed alphabetically. And what's with names like William Mitchell, anyway? How come I'd never heard of it before? I learned there are also law schools called John Marshall, Roger Williams, Thomas Jefferson, Thomas M. Cooley, and my favorite, La Verne.)

But I didn't interpret the rankings that way. My reaction was more like; are people at Harvard–Yale–Stanford going to be rich, snobby, climb-over-corpses strivers? Will they devote their energy to playing mind games, or, worse yet, be so imbued with the status competition of prep-school life that they don't even realize they're playing mind games when they talk about Daddy being called down from Wall Street to consult with the attorney general (or whatever it was, exactly, that high-powered lawyer-daddies did to confirm their importance)?

My impression that high ranking equals unpleasant experience was seemingly confirmed by Scott Turow's *One-L,* his classic memoir of the first year of Harvard Law School. I was particularly struck by his description of the effect law school had upon his and his wife's sex life. Harvard Law: the anti-aphrodisiac. Who would have guessed that Harvard's law school, rather than its psychology department, would run the experiment that proved Freud right about sublimated urges?

As for Turow's descriptions of the dynamics of his study group, I couldn't make out what that was all about. What was a "study group"? It sounded like an oxymoron. Why did Harvard require its first-year students to participate in a group activity that seemed both so stressful and so ultimately pointless?

As I was to learn, "stressful" and "pointless" are two of the cardinal principles governing legal education. Not that either is necessary or even useful in learning the law. But tradition is important in the conservative institutions devoted to instruction in this most conservative of professions. And, although I didn't know it at the time, those law school rankings embody the true spirit of the tradition. The numbers themselves are pointless: they tell prospective students absolutely nothing about the education they'll receive. But they contribute to their stress by imposing upon them the burden of trying to get into the "best" possible law school. They also contribute, I would learn, to the stress of professors working their way up through the ranks. The career ladder of one of my professors went from the University of Puget Sound to Notre Dame to Northwestern, in strict conformity with *U.S. News and World Report* rankings. (Me, I'd have preferred the view and the salmon. Some people don't know when they have it good.)

So as I sat cross-legged on the floor and tried unsuccessfully to visualize myself inside each of the dots on the outline map, I wondered not so much where to apply as how to choose where. Twenty-seven years have passed and I still don't know a good way to make that choice. Instead, I've learned that my original contradictory impressions, which I thought at the time so uninformed, were correct all along: it makes no difference where you go to law school; it makes all the difference in the world.

SOME PEOPLE GROW up knowing they're going to go to law school. They're the ones who rule the debate-team roost in high school. They devote their undergraduate years to that mysterious major called pre-law, which isn't listed in most college catalogues (apparently, you just have to know about it) and sounds like a description of barbarism: "Before Justinian imposed his code, the life of man was short, nasty, brutish, and pre-law." Those born-to-practice-law types are easy to spot during the first days of the first semester of law school: they're the ones already networking with the professors.

I wasn't one of them. Applying to law school felt like defeat. It was an admission that I couldn't think of any better alternative. I'd had a strange academic career, dropping out of high school to start college early at the College of Creative Studies of the University of California, Santa Barbara. CCS admitted me without a diploma on the basis of "proven ability in the arts"—writing. It billed itself as a graduate school for undergraduates, allowing its students to design their own curriculum. I ate up my literature classes, taking huge course loads, and wound up graduating at age 19.

Nature had obviously designed me to get a PhD in English and a faculty position someplace with a pleasant grassy quad, but in this as in so many other respects, environmental conditions of the 1970s frustrated nature's plan. All the colleges and universities had gotten giddy with new hires in the 1960s as the baby boomers passed through the system like a goat through a python. But by the late 1970s enrollments were falling, and they were falling fastest of all in fields such as English as uncertain economic times drove students into marketing and other majors that promised a job to go along with the degree. Meanwhile, the newly tenured baby boom English profs were decades from retirement. The word among students was that there were 50—no, 100!—job-seeking English PhDs for every academic opening. There might as well have been a million.

In English departments around the country, grad students, gypsy professors doing part-time gigs for janitor money, and assistant professors clinging to three-year contracts all went batty with the need to please their thesis advisors and/or impress hiring and tenure committees. The pressure to conform was immense, and took the form of unquestioning devotion to "theory"—the appropriately generic term used to describe what struck me as a toxic mix of narcissism (celebrating the cultural centrality of the critic) and ass-kissing (especially of you, O my master, and those you in turn adore). Even I, immature creature that I was, understood that people who actually believed in the meaningfulness of their work wouldn't insist on it as relentlessly as the theorists who always claimed to be subverting some paradigm or another, not that the paradigms ever noticed.

A few years later I had a kitten who, in her gentle way, disagreed with my decision to pay so much attention to books. She would climb up to a comfortable purring position on my lap, between the book and my eyes. While petting her I would bring the book to the other side of her furry body. She would walk around the corner and re-position herself higher up on my torso, and I would bring the book still closer to my eyes. We would keep going that way until the book was too close to read or my face was full of white fur, when I would set her down on the floor and hold the book once more at arm's length and she would return to my lap, purring with undisturbed equanimity as she settled down once more between the book and my eyes ...

Literary theory, as I saw it, aspired to the condition of my kitten, but it did so with none of her cuteness and still less of her affection. Theory was something that sought to insert itself between the reader and the read. So graduate school in English was out of the question. But what was in it?

I had picked up the contagion of economic anxiety that so characterized the era. One source of my worry was all the business majors who wondered, not always smugly, what I was going to "do with" my literature degree. It took me the better part of 30 years to come up with a satisfactory answer: I'm going to spend my undergraduate years reading great books because I'll never have so much time to read so intently again, while you're spending the last years of your youth practicing to be a middle-aged schlump.

However, the decision to attend law school was made before I had achieved the philosophical perspective of middle-aged schlumpness. In truth, I more than half-believed I needed something to "do with" my degree. I didn't want a job, but could see I needed a career. Another good fit would have been journalism—I liked to write, and I've always written quickly—but my personality unsuited me for it. I wasn't shy, exactly. That is, I wasn't afraid to make myself do new things, like going to college at age 16 and then spending my junior year abroad at 18, which incidentally is a fabulous year to spend in Dublin, especially if it's 1977–78 and the music scene is bursting like a flowerpot falling from an upstairs window. It wasn't ordinary timidity that held me back but a sensitivity to anticipated rejection that worked like an emotional stutter in my personality. Whenever a connection was about to be made, the needle would hit a scratch and start repeating. If the heavens had listened and delivered a girl into my bedroom, there to strip seductively to the sound of a sultry saxophone, I would have been tense with the certainty that she was leading up to "You're nice, but I'm really not interested in a relationship right now." I don't think any girl ever actually said that to my face, but then they didn't have to: I heard it anyway.

It's not as if I have the excuse of an abusive childhood, except in the sense that I grew up with three older brothers. Santa Barbara, as it happens, is an excellent environment for learning how to feel uncomfortable in one's own skin, since everyone else is so beautiful in theirs. So I finished college at an impressionable age, deeply impressioned. The thought of working as a reporter, calling up people and knocking on their doors, made me mentally cringe. (Many years later I found the perfect physical representation of that cringe in my current semi-Siamese cat when she's not in a mood to be petted.) I reviewed movies for a weekly alternative paper, the long-since-defunct paper-and-ink *New Mexico Independent* (not the modern website with the same name). That was the only type of journalism I could do alone in the dark, but it paid like something that was fun to do.

So what kind of career can a person who likes to write, but doesn't have the option of becoming an English professor and doesn't want to become a reporter, look forward to having? Teaching the stoned and the armed in a high school? Preparing technical handbooks for a manufacturer? Writing novels about obtusely hypersensitive English majors? Law school?

That explains the decision adequately, I believe.

LAW SCHOOL PLAYS a vastly more important role in the careers of lawyers than medical school does in the careers of doctors. That's not because of the knowledge imparted. On the contrary, I'm certain that most of the information imparted in medical school actually pertains to the practice of the profession, which can't be said of law school. Yet after a doctor has practiced medicine for 30 years, no one cares where he or she went to medical school. A lawyer, by contrast, will always be judged by the brand name on his or her diploma. When the second President Bush nominated Harriet Miers for the Supreme Court in 2005, she was widely deemed unqualified, and one of her disqualifiers was that she had gone to law school at Southern Methodist University (#46).[1] After she withdrew her name the President substituted Samuel Alito, a graduate of Yale Law School (#1), and he sits on the Supreme Court today.

All of the justices on the United States Supreme Court attended either Harvard or Yale with the sole exception of John Paul Stevens, who was allowed in despite having attended Northwestern (#9). Ruth Bader Ginsburg began at Harvard Law but for family reasons transferred to Columbia (#4) for her final year and degree. That was acceptable, too.

Presidents might think they have freedom to choose who gets nominated to the Supreme Court, but they're working from a list that has already been drastically culled by the people who wield the greatest influence over the Court's composition and the future direction of the nation: law school admissions directors. The admissions people make the first cut, and it goes deep, eliminating from serious consideration a good 95 percent of lawyers.

Or, rather, a good 95 percent of 22-year-olds contemplating law as a career. If you want to serve on the Supreme Court you have only one chance at making the list, and the chance comes and goes half a year before you even begin to study law.

That's just one way in which a prospective student's choice of law school (and a law school's choice of prospective students) makes all the difference in the world. It takes less ink to explain why it makes no difference at all: the education is exactly the same at every law school. The same textbooks are read in the same sequence. The professors teach their classes the same way. The professors themselves are often the same; I'm confident the class I took at Northwestern was no better for its location than the same class taught during my professor's earlier stops at Puget Sound and Notre Dame. Widener, Willamette, and William Mitchell provide everything Harvard does except membership in the alumni club.

Over the years I've come to believe that lawyers, law professors, and—especially—law school administrators fixate on the rankings and the prestige they bestow (or withhold) because without an arbitrary distinction between law schools there would be no way to tell them apart but the architecture.

I WOUND UP applying to half a dozen law schools around the country, all of them public and therefore (a) presumably unpretentious, and (b) comparatively cheap. Cheapness is important for reasons beyond the obvious. A lot of people take out massive student loans to start law school, confident graduation will give them the paycheck necessary for payback, then discover that they hate the study of law but can't afford to drop out. Law school can be an academic form of debt peonage.

One law school above all others could promise both lack of pretension and cheapness: my hometown University of New Mexico. From age 11 I'd grown up in the university neighborhood, attending a junior high that abutted the campus, so close that squad cars full of riot-geared police officers patrolled the streets by the school's front lawn when the university's students were protesting (I think the occasion was the Christmas bombings of 1972). Filled with the spirit of a time when phrases like "youth movement" were used without reference to a marketing campaign, I flipped off one such squad car and remember the open-mouthed shock of the officer who saw me. I'm sure he received much worse random abuse from the college students, but how much sharper from a 13-year-old. (Sorry.)

CHAPTER 2

Laid-Back U.

I TOOK THE LAW School Admission Test, or LSAT, but don't remember anything about it except that I was sitting next to Robert Hardi, a Hungarian émigré doctor. He was then working at the University of New Mexico's cancer treatment center. His presence in the next chair was far more memorable than the exam itself, although I can no longer remember his reason for taking it. Perhaps his experience as a dissident had taught him to appreciate the value of familiarity with the ways of those in power. At that time the LSAT contained a couple of sections testing students' mastery of English grammar and usage. I suggested those might be particularly difficult for someone whose first language had so little in common with English. He said that, on the contrary, he found those sections easiest because, unlike native speakers, he'd studied the rules of the language in a formal, systematic way.

Dr. Hardi's wife, Katalin Hardi-Lakatos, was a brilliant pianist I'd heard play on a couple of occasions. Political exile had been cruel to her musical career. For years running she hadn't even had consistent access to a quality instrument. I asked Dr. Hardi whether she contemplated returning to the life of a touring professional. He said she couldn't realistically launch an American career from New Mexico: "It would be like emerging from the dark side of the moon."

That was the shady spot where I began my legal education. The University of New Mexico School of Law's incoming class of 1985 consisted of about 110 students, almost all of them local—although the word "almost" in that sentence might understate the matter. UNM ranks in *U.S. News and World Report*'s "first tier" at #68. While that's pretty respectable for a public institution, there's no particular reason to go there unless you plan on practicing law in New Mexico. But if that's your plan, there can be no better place. It's the only law school in the state and most of the graduates stay within the huge rectangle of its borders, so your classmates of today will be the cohort of your career. For as long as you stick it out, they'll be your colleagues, opponents, and the people you call upon for favors. After ten or so years they'll start being your judges, too.

The same, I'm sure, is true of the public law schools of any state. For that reason, as well as the money angle, the local public law school is almost always the best option for any prospective lawyer who has no desire to move elsewhere. A degree from a brand-name law school is more valuable only if you want to (a) practice in a snobby firm or somewhere so far away that prospective employers are unclear about the language of instruction at your school (though that problem might be unique to New Mexico); (b) become a professor (law schools themselves take the rankings *very* seriously); or (c) serve on the Supreme Court.

UNM's law school was founded in 1947, financed by the GI Bill—all but two members of its first class were veterans. Its current building opened in 1971 and is architecturally of its time, all concrete slabs and glass at unexpected angles and as many short staircases as its architect could squeeze into a compact floor plan. It's difficult to give directions to rooms within the law school because there are no stories, only levels, and a dozen or more of those, none of them with names. (Since 1971, the school's physical plant has more than doubled in size. Luckily, the Americans with Disabilities Act went into effect before the most recent round of construction.)

The law library, which occupies one whole end of the building, is spacious and beautiful, with a huge wall of windows giving a view of the Sandia Mountains across the sixth hole of the university's nine-hole golf course. (It used to be an 18-hole course, but then the law school was built.) Big expanses of lovingly tended, overfertilized, and wastefully watered grass are rare in New Mexico, even if not quite as rare as they should be, making the view from the library particularly restful to a law student's eyes.

I didn't look up from the books often enough, though—after years with the same prescription, my glasses got thicker during that first year of law school. Studies have documented that damage to the eyes is a typical outcome of legal education.[1] That's something else they don't tell you on the websites: law school changes your body. Besides getting thicker glasses, I began cracking my knuckles. I'd never done that before, and even hated the sound, but now I found it necessary. Also, I'd never had backaches before the law school acceptance letter. Prospective students: beware.

One thing UNM had going for it, which I didn't appreciate at the time, was a very approachable, even friendly, faculty. The professors kept their office doors open and didn't mind chatting with students. They cracked jokes in class. The classes were generally taught as seminars, with students encouraged to speak up but not compelled to participate. No teacher ever selected my name from the roll in order to subject me to a public grilling. The largest classes had 55 students (half of the incoming class), and our legal research and writing classes were one-third of that. Not only that, but research and writing was taught by full professors, not by underpaid staff. So complete was my ignorance that I didn't realize these features were all highly unusual in an American law school of the era.

And, indeed, UNM has since fallen back to the pack by turning over research and writing—by far the most practical first-year subject, and for that reason the least prestigious to teach—to underpaid staffers.

LAW SCHOOLS TEND to be extremely conservative places. The conservativism generally doesn't express itself in the faculty's voting preferences. On the contrary, one study showed that law school professors who contribute to political campaigns overwhelmingly confer their favors on Democratic candidates. At Harvard, the Democratic lean is 91 percent, and at Yale, 92 percent. Then you get to the extreme cases, such as Stanford (94 percent).[2] Law schools aren't conservative in their politics but in what might be termed their institutional culture: the unspoken rules that govern conduct and establish expectations and make the first weeks so stressful to newcomers trying to intuit them. And yet law schools are new units in our universities. Not as new as, say, the television studios, but brand-new in comparison to traditional departments such as literature, history, and the sciences.

Until the 19th century, law was understood as a practical rather than academic discipline. Aspiring lawyers "read the law" in the offices of established practitioners, which meant they labored as apprentices, assisting in the real-world practice during the day while poring over instructional books at night. Blackstone's four-volume *Commentaries on the Laws of England,* which appeared around the time of the American Revolution, reigned in America for a full century as the foremost manual for aspiring lawyers. Apprentices read about what a lawyer was supposed to do and then watched a master do it. They were admitted to "the bar"—literally, allowed to pass unaccompanied through the gate in the low barrier that divides most courtrooms to this day—following an informal oral examination by the local judge. The ability to function effectively as a lawyer was the only skill that counted. Book-learning beyond the minimum allowed you to function *elegantly,* and elegance was always appreciated, but it wasn't essential. It was the whipped cream on the pumpkin pie.

The age-old practice of "reading" the law didn't die out until recently. In the early 1950s, after my lawyer grandfather had a debilitating heart attack, my grandmother read the law in his office and qualified for the bar, taking over her husband's small-town practice and eventually becoming a police judge. Nowadays that wouldn't be permitted—she would be required to leave her home and husband and spend three years in residence at some distant law school.

The expression "die out," which I used in the preceding paragraph, isn't quite right. The practice of reading the law didn't gently expire. It was killed. Law schools stamped it out as they acquired a monopoly on the training of lawyers.

The invention of the law school was partly a product of urbanization. In a small town, a bright boy might hope to win the attention and patronage of the town's outstanding lawyer, but a boy growing up in boomtown Chicago would have had a hard time even getting through the door of a downtown law office. That's why Union College of Law was originally founded in Chicago as a commercial institution where bright city boys without connections could pay for their legal apprenticeship. Only years later did that vo-tech school get absorbed into Northwestern University.

The semi-disreputable commercial origins of law schools are one reason why, to this day, they are so often physically isolated from the universities to which they are administratively attached. That's true even of many Johnny-come-latelies, such as the concrete slabs erected on UNM's golf course, divided from the rest of the university by a freeway-busy arterial street. Northwestern is a more extreme example, with its downtown law school an hour's ride on the El from the main Evanston campus. Such remote locations are physical reminders of the way in which law schools were only gradually overgrown by the groves of academe.

The modern law school curriculum dates from the late 19th century, and responsibility can largely be assigned to a single man: Christopher Columbus Langdell, the long-bearded, over-energetic dean of Harvard Law from 1870 to 1895 who standardized the "case method" of academic legal education. To most outsiders, the term "case method" is today associated more with Harvard's business school than its law school, but the only thing the two methods have in common is their name. In business schools, students study real-world "cases," meaning instances or examples of businesses that thrive or shrivel in the marketplace. In law school, the "cases" are judicial opinions. Adding to the ambiguity, the word "case," which already had too many meanings before the contributions of the legal world, can have several distinct meanings for a lawyer. An appellate court's written decision might wrap up a "case," meaning the entire years-long proceeding that began when the lawsuit was initiated in the trial court and including all the wrangling that led up to trial and the subsequent appeal. But the appellate decision is itself called a "case" when it's printed in a bound volume. The latter usage, by which the published tip of the iceberg is described by the term for the whole, was the usage employed by Langdell and his disciples. Their case method involved the intense reading of appellate judges' written opinions in cloistered environs as far from the real world of clients and courts as possible.

Americans (like all the ex-colonists) inherited from England a common law legal system, so called because it was theoretically common to all social classes. The distinctive feature of the system is that judges enforce a customary law—law that is based not on legislation but on prior judicial precedent, which in turn was based on prior judicial precedent, and so on backward through the ages until you reach what common lawyers called "time out of mind." Langdell's concept was that by studying the opinions of appellate judges, students would master the customary law. Better yet, they would get it straight from the judges rather than having it filtered through the interpretations of Blackstone and other commentators.

The case method curriculum pioneered by Dean Langdell, universally used in American law schools today, introduces law students to "the leading cases of the common law." The phrase refers to cases that altered the settled course of the customary law, diverting it into new channels, which makes it very nearly a contradiction in terms. Learning the law by studying leading cases is like trying to understand genetic transmission by studying only mutants. As we'll see, the case method pioneered by Langdell has itself altered the customary law in ways the dean couldn't have foreseen and, I'm pretty sure, would have abhorred to the depths of his conservative lawyer's soul.

LAW PROFESSORS HAVE long said they teach students to "think like a lawyer." But first the students have to want to learn to think like that. The first year of law school is designed to instill that desire. In many respects it's indoctrination. Its goal is less to teach the students about law than to put them in a receptive frame of mind. Even a low-pressure place like UNM accomplished that task by putting the squeeze on students.

The first-year student's day was carefully scheduled, beginning at 8:30 A.M. Students had an hour of class, then an hour off to prepare for the next class, then lunch, a third class, another hour off, and the fourth class of the day. Our four courses were Property, Contracts, Criminal Law, and Legal Reasoning (though I think the last was given a less self-evident name), and they met four days a week. One reason for the whole-day-consuming schedule was to discourage outside employment. Another was to build in time for study between classes. We needed that time—the study of cases is very time-consuming for a beginning law student.

Trying to read a judicial opinion for the first time isn't like reading a foreign language. It's hard, but not *that* hard. It's more like sitting in a theater for the first ten minutes of a Shakespeare play, or reading a random passage from *Paradise Lost:*

Made horrid Circles; two broad Suns their Shields
Blaz'd opposite, while expectation stood
In horror; from each hand with speed retir'd
Where erst was thickest fight, th' Angelic throng,
And left large field, unsafe within the wind

You recognize most of the words, and the sentence structure is generally familiar, and yet the meaning doesn't soak in. It floats near at hand, almost within reach, like a fluff of down pushed away by the air currents stirred up by your hand each time you reach for it.

We were taught to "brief" the cases we read. I recall feeling baffled by the very assignment. Our teachers talked about "briefing" cases as if it were self-evident what that meant, and as I glanced surreptitiously at the self-confident faces of my classmates it seemed apparent that I was the only student for whom its meaning *wasn't* self-evident. In retrospect, I'm not sure how I failed to register the frequency with which their sidelong glances intercepted mine—nerves, I guess.

"Brief" is another of those simple English words given an endlessly receding series of modulating meanings by lawyers. This particular usage (which is pretty much confined to law schools and paralegal studies programs) means to prepare a written summary of a case by filling in the blanks of a form. As with so many other things in the law, there was nothing difficult about the concept except the way lawyers talked about it.

But that didn't mean it was easy to learn how to brief a case. We were supposed to isolate the pertinent facts of the case, boil the legal dispute down to a one-sentence question, state how the judge answered the question, and then summarize the judge's reasoning. Only gradually did I realize that most judicial opinions follow the same four-part structure, at least roughly, which I suppose was the point of the exercise. Preparing "case briefs" quickly proved tediously burdensome and as soon as our teachers stopped collecting them I stopped preparing them, developing instead a coded method for defacing my textbooks (which consisted mostly of collections of cases). I would put three distinct types of brackets in the margins to indicate the pertinent, the important, and the very important passages, and use a yellow highlighter for sentences more important than those—the things I needed to memorize. Maybe a third of the text would be marked in one of these ways, but that meant that as I prepared for exams I could safely ignore two-thirds. This system worked well throughout my law school career and I continue to use a simplified version of it to this day.

In those early weeks I would use the entire hour between classes to extract the meaning from a single case. Today it would take me just a couple of minutes to accomplish the same thing, and not because I'm any smarter now. Fluency followed from practice, depending not so much on learning the words—legal jargon, while renowned for its impenetrability, is no harder to pick up than any other slang—but the way judges have of presenting their rulings. Over the centuries judges have developed customary ways of telling the reader "now we're getting to the important part." And competent judges always make an effort to wrap up their ruling in a takeaway phrase or sentence designed to be quoted, exactly in the style of a politician's packaged sound bite. With practice one learns to spot those key phrases and ignore the rest. As with skiing, it requires only a little practice to acquire a basic facility. But, also as with skiing, the first attempts are frustrating enough to make you wonder why you ever thought it was a good idea to start.

I used the word "ruling" twice in that previous paragraph. It describes the most important thing about learning to read judicial opinions. They look like literary texts, and often they read like narratives, but they're exercises of political power. It requires an adjustment in attitude to recognize that what you're reading isn't any kind of literature but a bureaucrat's stamp translated into prose. The opinion is like the computer code responsible for the design on your monitor. What's important isn't the code but the appearance of the webpage. In the same way, the important thing about a judicial opinion isn't the thing the judge describes, but what the judge does. A working lawyer doesn't read a judge's opinion to understand the real-life dispute that was the occasion of the judge's ruling, but to understand the ruling. *The judge* is the important character; the parties are mere props.

That's not the way our high school civics teachers describe the judicial process, but it's not cynical, either. Some years after I graduated from law school I read a biography of Roger Taney, the white-supremacist Supreme Court chief justice who devoted the final years of a very long career to sabotaging Abraham Lincoln's presidency and the Union war effort. The biographer was in love with his subject, in the way typical of biographers, and ended the book by describing admiringly how Taney left behind at his death opinions declaring unconstitutional the Union's conscription and currency legislation, even though those issues had never been raised by any case before the Court. The chief justice, who publicly suggested that God had extended his life for the divine purpose of thwarting Abraham Lincoln and the Republicans, wrote his opinions first, then waited like the spider he had come to resemble for cases to come along that would give him an excuse to publish his resolutions of them.[3]

Taney, in his shamelessness, was an extreme case, but he illustrates something first-year law students only gradually realize: resolution of the parties' dispute provides the occasion for the judge's ruling, but not its purpose.

UNM LAW SCHOOL was a student-friendly place, relatively speaking, although I didn't perceive it that way. Among the signs of friendliness that I failed to recognize were the "shadow exams" we took midway through the first semester. These were conducted like real exams but consumed less time—we wrote them during our regular class periods. Instead of names we wrote assigned numbers on our first pages, making our answers anonymous except to the office staffer who kept the key. The teachers read and critiqued our answers but no actual grades were assigned.

That's how we discovered that the typical law school exam consists of a narrative problem: a little story, a couple of paragraphs long, followed by one or two questions to be answered with essays scribbled into flimsy bluebook pamphlets or typed in a hall cacophonous with many typewriters (not a sound today's law students will ever have the chance to get used to). The story problems were usually absurd, because they compressed as many possible legal issues into the fewest words, and the questions were usually along the lines of: who can sue whom, with what chance of success?

When as a 16-year-old I took the ACT college entrance exams, my highest grade was in science, which was peculiar because I had (thanks to an unconventional high school career) managed never to complete a science course in my life. I scored high on the science exam because it took the form of narrative descriptions of experiments and observations followed by questions designed to measure how well the test-taker understood what he or she had just read. They were, in short, just like law school exam questions, except for the topics, which in both instances were more or less arbitrary anyway.

It came as something of a shock to me that the shadow exams were so easy. I had felt deeply ambivalent about attending law school and was, halfway through my first semester, still far from convinced it had been a good idea. I was studying hard with little subjective sense of understanding what I studied. And yet all my professors demanded of me was to read silly little stories and then improvise little essays relating them to our assigned readings. Only three skills were required: remembering the assignments; making connections between them and the silly stories; and describing the connections in writing under time pressure. The first and third skills were things I had long since mastered, and my inborn associative way of thinking made the middle part easy enough to make me distrust the facile connections I made. It turned out I had no reason for the distrust.

The shadow exams gave me a lot of confidence, which I suppose was their purpose. The real exams came at the end of the semester. They were physically grueling, being each four hours long, the same number of hours we spent in each class per week. I took a break in the middle of each marathon, eating a snack and walking around a bit, and was a little surprised that no one else did the same. I figured it would be easier to deal with the time pressure if I was relaxed and not distracted by hunger. Our semester grades were posted a few days afterward. To show how innocent the age was, grades were printed next to our Social Security numbers on a sheet pinned to a bulletin board. The semester grades were based exclusively on our exams, or almost exclusively—a couple of teachers claimed to include a class participation component in the grades. Maybe that was just a carrot to provoke discussion, but if they really took class participation into account it held me back because I essentially never spoke in class. I had noticed that if something was puzzling me, it was usually only a matter of time before someone else asked about the same thing, so there really wasn't any need to raise my hand. (Years later I became a part-time instructor in the paralegal studies department of Central New Mexico Community College, paying off my karma debt to my old professors as I try to egg my students into speaking.)

One thing I discovered when the grades came out was that they provided yet another expression of the law school obsession with rank. Next to our grades were numbers indicating our class ranking, from 1 to 110 (or, rather, 105 or so—we had several early dropouts). I was 3. I was actually *good* at what I was doing. It made me begin to wonder what it would be like if I got past my resistance and actually devoted myself to the study of law. What if I allowed myself to discover that this was what I was made to do?

IN THE SPRING semester we had a class in legal advocacy that had us writing briefs (a different sense of "brief"—these were written arguments) and arguing in front of a panel of three judges. The first-year students were all paired off into teams, and by the luck of the draw my partner and I were selected to argue first. That meant that at 8:00 A.M. we showed up in our suits or (in my case) our brother's suit. All the other first-year students, who would be arguing later that day or on successive days, were naturally eager to discover what they could expect when their time came, and so every seat in the law school's moot courtroom, the size of a real courtroom (and in fact sometimes used by the New Mexico Court of Appeals), was occupied. Closed-circuit TVs were set up to allow the overflow crowd in the lobby to listen and watch. How did I feel when I saw the huge crowd gathered to observe my first courtroom appearance? Poe expressed it well: "True! nervous, very, very dreadfully nervous…" My nervousness approached the condition of an out-of-body experience. My psyche was self-protectively dissociating itself from the spectacle I was about to make in my ill-fitting gray flannel.

And then I got up to speak. My panel of three faux-judges consisted of one of my professors; a distinguished old emeritus professor, Henry Weihofen, author of a treatise on legal writing; and a third-year law student. I launched into my prepared remarks, the judges interrupted with questions, the give-and-take was intense … and nothing else existed. I experienced a kind of tunnel vision. There were the judges, there was me, and everything else had gone away. I entirely lost awareness of the hundred or more people watching me.

I have no idea how I did. We either won or lost, but I don't recall which. For me, the revelation was the intensity of the moment. I can't say it was exactly pleasurable, but it certainly wasn't the reverse. It was something to be measured on a scale other than pleasure/pain. On one end of the appropriate scale would be "total concentration," but I don't think English has a word for the opposite end, unless it's "boredom."

I've since argued before appellate courts many dozens of times. I'm sure I'm closing in on a hundred arguments, if I haven't passed that mark already. I no longer get nervous. In fact, it disturbed me the first time I glanced up at the clock and saw it was a minute until the argument was scheduled to begin and realized my heart wasn't even beating hard. But I've never lost that tunnel-vision sense of utter raptness. There's nothing else like it.

IN THE SPRING semester the first-year students were invited to try out for law review. "Law review" is an extremely peculiar institution. Every American law school publishes at least one magazine, and some publish half a dozen. The magazines are edited by students under the eye of faculty advisors, just like an undergraduate literary magazine—except the feature articles are written by professors, not students. Tenure and promotion decisions are heavily influenced by the number of articles a candidate has published in these student-edited magazines. The higher the ranking of the law school, the more prestigious the magazines edited by its students, and so the more desirable an outlet for publishing one's scholarship. That makes *Yale Law Review* the legal equivalent of *Lancet* or the *New England Journal of Medicine,* and makes its annually rotating corps of student editors the makers of academic careers. But it also means that, unlike *Lancet* or the *New England Journal of Medicine,* the scholarship engaged in by legal academics isn't peer-reviewed; it's *student*-reviewed. The editorial decisions are made by people who haven't qualified even to practice the profession, much less judge the quality of high-level scholarly inquiry into it.

It's not a system any rational person would have designed. It was self-organized, like the reproductive organs of slime mold. But then the same is true of many institutions in the legal world. As I mentioned, although law schools themselves are relatively new academic institutions, legal academia is extremely conservative. The persistence of such a spectacularly irrational system for evaluating the fruits of legal scholarship is only Exhibit A.

At traditional law schools, positions "on" law review are meted out to the highest-ranked students. It's an academic honor, like the dean's list, but with obligations attached—there's a magazine to get out four or six times a year, after all. The staff members get to share a newsroom-style open office, which is typically located in or near the library. Members are selected at the end of the first year. During the second year they do production work on the magazine. At the end of the second year, they choose from among their number the editors for the following year. Being selected editor-in-chief can confer long-lasting professional advantages. When Barack Obama was selected the first African-American editor-in-chief of *Harvard Law Review,* he got a book contract out of it. Then he got to be President. So you can see what's at stake.

UNM was nontraditional, though. It didn't award places on its two law reviews based on academic standing. (Since my day the school has added yet a third journal, although its student body remains small.) Rather, students won their positions in a writing competition. The competition, like our exams, would be anonymous. I didn't plan on competing, but as the deadline neared a friend persuaded me to give it a try. I figured it would be fun to work on the magazine with him. My attitude was cocky. I was then still reviewing movies for the alternative newspaper and knew my writing was at least professional, and was pretty sure the same couldn't be said of all my fellow students.

The application consisted of 50 or so pages of legal materials—cases and articles, though I don't remember the topic. We were told to write an article discussing the provided materials without doing any additional research. I had left myself only a couple of days to write my article. Thinking I should try to get some sense of what law reviews were all about, I went to the library and pulled down a couple of bound volumes at random, opening them to articles that I found very hard slogging indeed—which should have been a warning that I was attempting a genre I didn't understand. But the rumor among the students was that no applicant had ever been rejected by either of the two law reviews.

That may have been true before I turned in my application, but it certainly wasn't true after I received back two identical rejection letters, one from each magazine.

It's strange how much it hurts to be rejected for something you don't particularly want. During my year in Ireland I was invited on a car tour with three American girls. I got along well with the two who were my fellow visiting students at Trinity College, but the third girl was a friend of one of theirs who had just flown in over spring break. This one, who knew nothing about Ireland and the Irish, was full of loud and confident opinions. Maybe her presence explains why the clerk at the car rental place told us Killarney would be a fine place to visit that weekend. And, indeed, the lakes were beautiful beyond imagining. Unfortunately—Irish humor is sometimes cruel, particularly when directed against Yank tourists—it was the weekend of the annual Killarney motor rally and every hotel and guesthouse for miles around had been booked for months. We drove from place to place, becoming increasingly desperate as the long Irish spring twilight settled around us. One nice lady told us she had only one bed and I facetiously said we could share it. The Ugly American girl announced loudly, "I don't want to sleep with you, boy."

Well, I certainly didn't want to sleep with her, either, but in some peculiar way that made it *worse*. Getting shot down by someone you aspire to leaves you where you began, but being shot down by someone beneath you ... When I received the dual rejections from the law reviews the feeling was shattering in the same unexpected way. Specifically, the rejections shattered all the confidence the first-semester exams and gaudy class ranking had given me. The law school was giving me an ultimate mixed message: I was among the best; I was among the worst. Indeed (if the rumor was true), the historical worst.

The only really meaningful thing about all this, I can see from the distance of a quarter-century, was that it was so meaningful to me. I didn't actually want to be on law review; I just wanted not to be rejected. I experienced both the semester grades and the rejections as judgments—not just on my exam essays (for which I had prepared diligently) or my law review application (which I had thrown together), but on my decision to enter law school in the first place. And more than that: on me. I had, without realizing it, bought into the law school system of values, accepting the law school evaluation of my worth, with its insistence on precise numerical rank. I'd been suckered in by grades, sucker-punched by law review.

Losing a stable sense of self is the signature effect of the first year of law school. If it isn't quite a universal experience, it comes close. The findings of the social scientists who study law students are almost preposterously dire. One 1986 longitudinal study followed a group of entering law students. During the summer before entrance, their level of psychological distress closely mirrored that of the general population. In fact, they scored slightly happier as a group than other graduate students, perhaps because they were looking forward to the academic adventure. Within two months of matriculation, rates of depression soared. As measured at different times during the six semesters of law school, between 17 and 40 percent of the students were seriously depressed. To put those numbers in perspective, a massive 2006 survey found a national depression rate of 8.7 percent, which is just half that of law students at their most cheerful. Nor does the story end with depression. Of the law students studied, "20–40% also [displayed] symptoms relating to obsessive-compulsiveness, interpersonal sensitivity, anxiety, hostility, and paranoid ideation in addition to social alienation and isolation."[4]

It seems I wasn't the only first-year law student to find his self-image unexpectedly challenged. (Could *this* be the explanation for Scott Turow's sex life?) But UNM was too laid-back, too considerate of its students, to give me the opportunity to explore the dark side of law school in depth. I transferred out.

CHAPTER 3

The Bogs of Prestige

I T WASN'T A writer's vanity that made the law review rejection so painful. I had no shortage of that commodity, but I'd already armored it with a writer's high tolerance for rejection letters. Upon being given a lifetime achievement award, Evan S. Connell, among the greatest of living American writers, told an interviewer he never encouraged anyone to become a writer: "It's mostly disappointment, mostly rejections."[1] He wasn't exaggerating. His great Custer book, *Son of the Morning Star,* became a bestseller and the basis of a TV mini-series only after being rejected by numerous publishers. Repeated rejection is the writer's lot. The fact that I've persevered long enough to publish this paragraph tells you that I'm not easily discouraged about writing.

But my vanity as a law student—my smugness about having figured out this law school thing—was shattered. Smithereens.

Once the passage of time allowed me to acquire even the tiniest amount of perspective, I had to admit that my rejections were well deserved. My application had too-faithfully reflected the carelessness of its preparation. But even that much perspective was a long time coming.

In the meantime, here I was, four-fifths of the way through my first year of law school, and I had only two data points with which to measure my value as a law student: the first-semester grades and the law review rejection. Averaging them produced . . . nothing. They canceled each other out. My year from August through April had been a long slog of study and stress, but all I could say for sure was that law school reciprocated my ambivalence about it.

The absence of feedback is a large part of what makes the first year of law school so stressful. The student makes a huge commitment in money and years. He works hard through the fall and the winter and into the spring, but his teachers seem intent on withholding information. (Even at comparatively student-friendly UNM, my first-year Contracts teacher liked to say: "Clear as mud? Good. That's the way I like it.") Until the semester grades come out, a student has no solid information with which to refute the insistent interior voice that tells him that submitting to this treatment was a mistake he'll regret for the rest of his life. (I do, in fact, rather regret taking that Contracts class.)

At Northwestern University School of Law, my next stop, first-year students didn't receive grades at the end of the first semester. Their first real grades were for their spring-semester finals, which they didn't receive until after their school year was over. They lived the entire academic year in an information vacuum, making the school's self-designated acronym, NULS, dismally appropriate.

There are many things that make the first year of law school a psychological crisis for such an eye-popping percentage of students. This is the first: the schools demand much and return little. The law schools' traditional withholding of recognition is felt especially keenly by students used to recognition—that is, by the very students most likely to be accepted into the most competitive law schools. Such students experience acceptance at a prestigious law school as the latest in a long series of academic triumphs. But the strategies that delivered them to the law school's front steps cease to work once they pass through the door. If law school were a lover, your therapist (and you'd need one) would be introducing you to concepts such as "withholding affection" and "passive-aggressive."

Here's a second reason why the first year of law school produces a psychological crisis for so many (and these aren't my jaundiced words—they were written by a law professor and published in a law review published by a prestigious law school): "Increasingly, faculties of elite schools and aspiring elite schools consist of professors who have not practiced law, who have little interest in teaching students to practice law, and who pay scant attention to the work of practicing lawyers."[2] (It is, perhaps, needless to say that I omitted two footnotes from that sentence. Law professors are nuts about footnotes. The more, the better.) Students go to law school to learn how to be a lawyer, but the professors aren't interested in teaching that. Frequently, they can't. The bright student senses the disconnect but rarely recognizes the source. It takes a student of exceptional self-confidence to recognize that the only inadequate person in the lecture hall is the hyperarticulate, imperious, intimidating figure in the front.

That second reason reinforces the first: a law professor can most easily disguise his or her ignorance about the real practice of the law by refusing either to correct or validate the student's understanding. Withholding provides intellectual camouflage.

Here's a third reason: "learning to think like a lawyer" really *does* require learning a new way to think. Or, rather, an old way. While reading a book on a topic wholly unrelated to the practice of law I came across this pithy encapsulation of the legal method:

the proper way of knowing involve[s] syllogistic demonstration—deduction from universal first principles or premises taken to have self-evidential status.[3]

Among 21st-century American lawyers, "universal first principles" are the pronouncements of superior courts, with the U.S. Supreme Court being the ultimate, unfailing font of new first principles. Every pronouncement of a superior court must be accepted as true by every inferior court, and therefore (at least for purposes of argument) by all lawyers who appear before those courts. All legal reasoning proceeds by syllogistic demonstration from the premises established by superior legal authority.

The quotation is from David C. Lindberg, who was describing the characteristic mode of thought of medieval philosophers, who had yet to relinquish "the Aristotelian fundamentals"—the philosophical methods developed in the fourth century before Christ. Learning to think like a lawyer means entering an intellectual time warp, sloughing off centuries of intellectual history, returning to the mind-set of the Scholastics who built their formidable logical system on the unquestioned verities of faith.

The ideal preparation for law school is close study of the first part of Saint Thomas Aquinas's *Summa Theologica,* not for its spiritual insights but for the rigorous logic, proceeding from profound first principles, that led the 13th-century genius to his conclusions about the nature of angels. Aquinas was the master of the closed-system way of thinking that, today, so frequently leads judges to technically justifiable but ridiculous rulings.

NORTHWESTERN UNIVERSITY'S PROFESSIONAL schools are located on the north side of Chicago's downtown, near the John Hancock building. The neighborhood is called "Streeterville" on maps of Chicago neighborhoods, though I don't recall ever hearing anyone use that name. It's unusually posh for a university neighborhood, which meant it was safe to walk around at night but short on comfortably run-down student hangouts. The campus stretches from Northwestern Memorial Hospital to Lake Shore Drive and includes the medical, dental, and business schools, too. When I arrived in 1983, the entire law school, with twice the student body of UNM, was stuffed into a building of approximately the same size. But Northwestern, being a far more traditional law school, had nothing like UNM's vertical concrete slabs erected at arresting angles on a golf course. It occupied a gray stone neo-Gothic building in the shape of a hollow square that, I'm pretty sure, was supposed to resemble an Oxford or Cambridge college, without the breathtakingly beautiful back gardens.

A building program, which got started about the same time I arrived, has since tripled the law school's physical plant. In practical terms, all that meant for me during my first semester was that as final exams approached, workers with pneumatic drills and sledgehammers were hard at work in the library. The racket they made was less of a hardship than might be imagined, because the library was such an unappealing place to study even when it was silent. *Especially* when it was silent. The stacks in the basement could have been the set of a horror movie. Each row of books had its own cobwebbed fluorescent fixture. You had to grope around in the dusty dimness until you found the dangling chain. You'd give a yank and there'd be a loud buzz, then a hesitant flicker, and then you'd see just how claustrophobically close together the shelves were spaced. The sudden flood of sickly yellow light would plunge the rest of the basement into deeper darkness—a cue for the pipes to start creaking and banging. Or *was* it the pipes? From time to time you might turn a corner and be surprised by the sight of a lone graduate student, invariably male and usually foreign, hunched over a carrel, breathing in the mold spores, going slowly mad. But by and large students avoided the place.

The new library was finished in time for my final semester in 1985, and it spectacularly corrected all the defects of its predecessor, being bright and airy with lots of natural light and big, inviting tables with views over the lake. My timing was such that I arrived on the scene at the worst possible moment, facilities-wise.

Northwestern was my second choice of transfer target. I was also accepted at Georgetown, which appealed to me as the most prestigious of D.C.'s multiple law schools. I'd been active in Jeff Bingaman's first campaign for the U.S. Senate and thought I'd enjoy hanging around the fringes of political life, but the Georgetown admissions officer I talked to on the phone told me I'd have to repeat first-year Criminal Law. I had earned four hours' credit at UNM, but Georgetown required five. Since Georgetown offered no one-hour criminal classes, this person told me over the phone, I would have to take the entire five-hour course. That meant I couldn't graduate on time unless I took five hours of classes more than any of my fellow students—not a terribly alluring prospect. So I went to my second choice instead, arriving in Chicago at the height of the "Council Wars" between Mayor Harold Washington and corrupt / racist / reactionary machine aldermen. That provided more of a political education than I would have gotten in Washington, anyway.

I probably drew two columns on a yellow legal pad to analyze my reasons for transferring out of UNM. I don't remember doing so, and for that matter I don't know why legal pads are customarily yellow. But, assuming I did, my first reason—sad to say—was that I'd absorbed the spirit of the law school rankings. I'd bought into the idea that a higher-ranked school would be a better school. I thought I would be going from the minor leagues to the majors. That was dumb.

A second reason, related to the first, was less dumb: a degree from Georgetown or Northwestern would allow me to practice anywhere. Those law schools had been built on the bright side of the moon. That was important to me because I was involved with a girl who didn't live in New Mexico. A brand-name law degree would help me find a job far from home. (Reader, I didn't marry her.)

Third, the year in Ireland had been the best of my life and the prospect of regular travel or even European residence seemed a basic requirement of happiness. So far as I could see, the vague specialty of "international law" offered the only way to combine those aspirations with a legal career. Georgetown was famous for international law. Northwestern's faculty included the author of a textbook in the field.

Fourth—although I'm sure I didn't write this down and wouldn't have admitted it to myself—a part of me wanted to tell the law review pooh-bahs, "Not good enough, eh? Watch this!"

The fifth reason for transferring had nothing to do with law or a legal career. When you're a student, you can have affairs with cities. You can live with them for a year or two without pressure to make a long-term commitment. That's not so easy to do with marriage, mortgage, and kids. And Chicago's a great city, except for the politics and winter weather. My best reason for transferring to Northwestern was to have a geographical fling.

THE FIRST DISILLUSIONMENT came on my first day at Northwestern, in late August. I arrived before the other second-years in order to participate in the new student orientation and to put together a course schedule. The new first-years were taking only prescribed courses, while the returning second-years had registered in the spring. I was given a list of courses that remained open for registration. It was a dismally short list. Making matters worse, many of their times conflicted. If I took this one, I couldn't take any of those. I picked a highest priority and tried to work around it, but that left me short of the hours I needed to be on track for graduation. So I started over with the second-highest priority. It was like working a Sudoku puzzle (not that I had ever heard of Sudoku back then). I ended up with a schedule that contained only one or two of the classes I actually wanted to take.

So my Northwestern career began with the unhappy realization that I was a second-class student. Among the closed classes were the trial practice courses, which were prerequisites for "clinical" courses, for which a student gets course credit for performing actual (if simple) lawyer's tasks. In essence, then, transfer students were forbidden from taking clinical classes in their second year. We (there were a dozen or so of us) were made to feel like boarders rather than members of the family. The studied disrespect made me wonder a little why the school went to the trouble of inviting us in.

The unofficial reason, I suspected, was that an equivalent number of students had transferred or dropped out and the school wanted to make up the lost tuition.

The official reason was explained to me by the associate dean: transfer students consistently outperform students admitted directly into Northwestern's first-year class. As he explained to me, the LSAT is designed to predict how a student will fare at law school. The first year's transcript shows how the student really *did* fare. It's obvious, really, which will be the better predictor of student performance in the second and third years.

But that point, which seems so obvious once it's pointed out, leads to another: that there's nothing special about Northwestern's first year. The tuition I paid at UNM was about one-twentieth of that I paid at Northwestern, and yet academically I was better prepared than the average survivor of Northwestern's first year. Over time, I came to believe the transfers were discriminated against to make the point that spending one's entire law school career at Northwestern had important advantages. Since those advantages weren't apparent in the academic performance of students, they had to be artificially enhanced.

Still, the point of law school isn't the education. It's the degree. In the legal job market, a Northwestern degree is indisputably better than one from UNM.

A MAJORITY OF my fellow first-year students at UNM were female. The average age of the incoming students was around 30. We came from a wide variety of ethnic and economic backgrounds, with many Hispanic and Native American students.

NULS was different. Most of my new classmates blasted straight through from high school to college to law school—the second year of law school was their 18th grade. They were almost all Anglo, mostly from the Midwest. The male–female ratio was two-to-one.

The best UNM students were easily an intellectual match for the top Northwestern students, but UNM's first-year class had a much wider range of intellectual attainments. By that I don't mean just a wider range of IQs but also a much wider range of interests and experience. The median IQ at Northwestern was doubtless higher, but Northwestern's brains lined up like iron filings around a magnet. There were no rebels or free spirits or late-bloomers among them. I had delivered myself into a nest of "A" students.

It wasn't just the students who were different. UNM had numerous female professors. When I arrived, Northwestern had one. She'd been hired in a package deal with her husband when he was lured away from the University of Virginia, which gave her (unfairly, I have no doubt) a reputation among the students of someone who hadn't made her own way. That impression seemed confirmed by the job she was given: supervising the all-female corps of research and writing instructors, who most definitely weren't regular faculty members. (Law school faculties are as hierarchical as an Iditarod dog team.) Writing instructors are the scullery maids of the legal academy for a reason that strikes students as ironic: because they teach skills of tremendous practical value. Such work is, more or less by definition, of little academic interest.

Meanwhile, the professors' academic interests are, more or less by definition, of no value to students who want to learn how to practice the profession.

The writing instructors were treated as full members of the faculty in only one way, so far as I could tell: the faculty photo spread in the school's recruitment brochure featured their feminine faces prominently, revealing that the administration was sufficiently sensitive about the gender imbalance to try to disguise it.

At UNM, where the professors were accessible to students and teaching was emphasized, scholarship was downplayed almost to the point of extinction. This made it a very comfortable place for the faculty, contributing to an atmosphere of in-group smugness that still clings to the place. At Northwestern, by contrast, the administration's anxiety to remain ranked in the top ten translated into enormous pressure on the professors to publish. A 1995 study showed that Northwestern boasted the sixth-most-productive law faculty in the nation. The study was almost indecently revealing of the law professor's concept of scholarship: it defined "productive" in terms of the number of law review pages filled.

But the number of law review pages covered by the words of one's professors makes no difference to the student's educational experience. If anything, there's a negative relationship between faculty scholarship and student education, because time spent on the one is time lost to the other. In law, unlike most academic fields, there's no natural relationship between scholarship and teaching. Law professors never make discoveries. They rarely collect data through experiment or observation. What's called legal scholarship is mostly just heavily footnoted argumentation—very long op-ed pieces on esoteric topics. Most legal instruction, by contrast, never gets past the basics, which isn't a negative thing. I took one class in tax law, another in wills and trusts, and a third in real-estate law because I thought I needed that much background. (Real estate was a waste of time.) My teachers may have been great scholars in their fields, but if they brought their brilliantly subtle insight into the classroom it was wasted on me. All I wanted to learn was the stuff that readers of their scholarly articles would have considered too obvious to bear mentioning.

PRIOR TO ITS big expansion, NULS had three main lecture halls for its 600 students. The biggest was called Lincoln Hall, named after the Illinois President who, at least according to legend, lectured at Northwestern's vo-tech predecessor, the Union College of Law. Lincoln Hall was a large, rectangular auditorium, very dark despite tall windows high up on the walls. Instead of ordinary theater seats it was fitted with long rows of individual wooden booths. Each booth had a high back and partial sides and a wide desktop, all of it stained a dark brown.

All the desktops were deeply etched by student graffiti; the wood was soft enough to give to a determined ballpoint. The booths rose in tiers from the narrow rectangle where the professor stood at a lectern. Two people could easily fit inside each booth, but they did so only for special events when space was tight. During ordinary classes the students sat evenly spaced about five feet apart, each isolated within the dark brown frame of his or her booth. It was a very strange setup for a lecture hall, supposedly modeled on the House of Commons in Westminster (to go with the faux-Oxbridge exterior, I suppose).

Directly above Lincoln Hall was the smaller lecture hall known—and I never got used to this—as Booth Hall. It was named after a long-ago Dean Booth, but I can't imagine any university naming adjoining theaters Kennedy Hall and Oswald Hall, even if "Oswald" happened to be the name of the university's most generous benefactor. Booth Hall was also equipped with booths, like Lincoln Hall, though it was perhaps half the size.

Five minutes into a Civil Procedure II class in Booth Hall, Professor Harry Reese looked down at his grade book and called out, "Mr. Jacobsen!" Reese was a slim, straight-backed man, probably about 60 then, who invariably wore solid black ties with his black suits. When I admitted my identity, he drew my attention to the Supreme Court's *Dairy Queen* case, a famous puzzler featured prominently in our textbook, and asked me to identify all of the various causes of action alleged by the plaintiffs, which was easy since the case listed them. He wrote their names on the blackboard and then asked me to classify them as legal (that is, derived ultimately from the common law developed in the courts of the King's Bench, which entitle a party to money damages and trial by jury) or equitable (derived ultimately from the maxims of medieval ecclesiastical courts; no money damages, no jury). I had to admit I had no clue how to classify them.

But I was wrong. I did know. Or, rather, I knew how to arrive at the right answer. Professor Reese didn't have to tell me. Instead he asked me more questions, easier ones, ones I could answer. Building on my responses he asked more questions, until by the end of 45 minutes I had correctly categorized all of the various causes of action. I remember giggling with nerves throughout the hour, and remember even more distinctly how my inane giggling increased my nervousness, but I was deeply impressed with Reese's skill.

That was the famous Socratic method, and Reese was the first and only professor I met with the pedagogical chops to use it. Maybe you don't, strictly speaking, need to possess the intellect of Socrates to be proficient in the Socratic method, but you do have to be intelligent and articulate; be able to listen closely to what the student is saying; be able to intuit what the student isn't saying; be patient; and be genuinely interested in the student's intellectual development. In my experience, very few law professors get past the first requirement.

That doesn't mean other professors didn't engage in what they probably told themselves was Socratic dialogue with their students. I'm pretty sure that's what my "clear as mud" Contracts teacher back at UNM thought he was doing. In the hands of every professor other than Harry Reese, though, all that I ever observed was really the reverse of the Socratic method. It deserves a reversed name: the Citarcos method. Reese started with my "I don't know" and led me to knowledge. In the backwards Citarcos method, the exchange begins with the student reciting what he or she knows about a case and ends with a series of abject "I don't knows" to the professor's bullying questions.

So far as I'm concerned, the Citarcos method is a professor's confession of psychopathology. It's a way to reveal one's need to bully and belittle those who make themselves vulnerable by seeking to learn. In my day, Northwestern had several professors suffering from the ailment. One of them taught first-year classes consisting of 100 students—half the incoming class, called a "section"—and required all students to be ready to be called on every class meeting. If they weren't prepared, they were supposed to come to the front of class and sign a register of shame in front of everybody. Students who didn't make that public confession were liable to be called upon without warning, which inevitably meant a pounding series of questions that never led anywhere but to pleas of ignorance. This particular professor taught only first-year students, which I figured was because his predatory style depended on the students being too intimidated—or depressed—to respond in kind.

I've heard a few half-hearted defenses of this teaching style, which have this in common: they're bullshit. Supposedly, being abused in front of your classmates toughens you up for what judges will do to you. But it's not true. Most judges don't abuse lawyers. They're far more likely to tune you out if they've already made up their minds. Some even swivel in their chairs, turning their backs to the lawyers. Besides, when judges ask tough questions, they're asking about cases the attorney has been immersed in for months or years, not a half-understood appellate opinion read the night before.

Another defense is that being bullied and belittled by law professors teaches a student to think on his or her feet, but the opposite is true: it produces panic, followed by self-loathing, followed by a heightened fear of its repetition, which after graduation is finally replaced by contempt for the professor.

Another defense is that it trains you in public speaking. That's like throwing you in the deep end of the pool to teach you how to pole vault.

This is not to say that the Citarcos method is without purpose. The traditional way of looking at it is as a form of hazing, the difference being that law students aren't hazed by upperclassmen, but by their professors. But I think a little more than that is going on. The bullying has, at bottom, a psychological rather than pedagogical purpose. Andrew Garcia expressed it vividly when he described the way he trained newbies: after first getting in their faces he "gave them back their self-respect a little at a time."[4] Garcia was a Marine Corps drill sergeant. The Parris Island technique of disassembling and reassembling a recruit's personality goes a long way toward explaining the traditional mode of law school instruction. It replaces the newcomer's prior identity by making membership in the new group the central fact of the student's self-conception. It tells the student: You're no longer the person you used to be. Now you're a lawyer. That makes you different from others in ways they can't fully appreciate unless they're lawyers, too, and have gone through the same initiation rites.

That's a powerful message. It makes the student feel a part of something big and important. It also has everything to do with the dissolving sense of self experienced by so many first-year students. That isn't just the consequence of the professorial bullying but its *purpose,* even if most of the professors themselves don't fully understand what they're doing to their students. (Most of them, I think, just see themselves as doing to others what was previously done to them.)

In my day, the most abusive aspects of the Citarcos method were becoming rare even at culturally conservative Northwestern. But the less frankly abusive aspects of the method lived on. Students were still subject to questioning throughout an entire class period, but now you might be told in advance what day you would be called upon, so you could prepare. One teacher moved steadily up and down the rows of our assigned seats, so day by day you could see your time approaching. It was like being a blade of grass waiting to be mown. This teacher was from New Zealand (I never learned how he wound up in Chicago), and while he put students on the hot seat for the entire class period, he wasn't nasty. Better yet, he didn't let the student's helpless bleating remain the last word on the subject. For instance, when called upon to define "subrogation," I couldn't do any better than parrot a phrase from the textbook: it means standing in another's shoes. He said that while he generally appreciated concreteness, in this instance he would prefer a little more abstraction—and then explained the concept in a way that allowed me to understand it. (It means standing in another's shoes.)

PROFESSOR INSIDER TRADING taught a course in Corporations. Well, "taught" is a bit of an exaggeration. We soon learned it was unnecessary to read the cases in the textbook, which was fine with us because they were tediously long-winded. Professor IT wouldn't even talk about the cases in class. He would condemn their reasoning as "insipid" and address his remarks to his own favorite ideas. There were exactly three of those, which in his worldview covered all situations pertaining to the governance of corporations. One was the Coase Theorum, which (in the version he taught us) meant that if there was any economic value in the regulation of business, private parties would have instituted it already, and so therefore all governmental regulation is without economic value and for that reason illegitimate. Another was that the only purpose of a corporation is to make money, which meant that expending corporate assets to pursue any goal but profit maximization was indefensible. The third idea, and by far his favorite, was that insider trading, a felony offense, is the ideal way to reward Scarce Managerial Talent.

I broke my usual rule of silence once by pointing out that a corporate insider who bought stock on the open market based on inside information would be buying his stock from shareholders of the very corporation he was supposed to be managing for the shareholders' benefit. Why should shareholders trust their money to a person prepared to rook them out of the profits of their investment that way? He pointed out that the seller was obviously willing to sell at the price he accepted for the shares. From an economic point of view, the identity of the buyer made no difference to him.

The final exam in Corporations was easy. We just had to repeat in writing the same three ideas Professor IT had repeated orally in every class. But during the winter break, Professor IT quit Northwestern, moving to a still-more-prestigious law school. He was, it would seem, considered an exceptionally good catch on the academic meat market. The new semester began in January and we hadn't yet received our grades for Corporations. February rolled by—still no grades. As I recall, it was April before we got grades for the fall semester, though maybe my memory exaggerates.

I received a B-plus. So did everybody else from the course that I talked to—not a scientific sampling, but still an odd coincidence. Now, B-plus is a fine grade. It's the sort of grade that will please many students and satisfy most of the rest. In each class there might be a few strivers who feel disappointed not to get an A, but even the most hypercompetitive would find it hard to get too worked up about a grade just one-half notch below. If I were a professor assigning grades at random, without bothering to read the students' final exams, I might very well choose universal B-plus as the grade least likely to cause problems for myself. Similarly, if I were a dean obliged to assign grades because a former professor refused to turn them in, I might consider B-plus the most politic way to go. Of course, it would be absurd to imagine anything of the kind could happen at a top-ten law school. None of us had information to suggest it, even remotely—no one told us anything at all. The malicious rumor-mongering of students knows no bounds.

Professor IT rose to great prestige at his new position. *The Wall Street Journal* began to quote him occasionally, usually with reference to some insider trading scandal. He testified before Congress and made tons of money consulting. Just a few years ago, with a great burst of self-congratulatory publicity, Northwestern triumphantly hired him back, greatly enhancing the school's prestige.

CHAPTER 4

The Continental System

"AN AMERICAN LAW student?" the law professor asked. "We don't get many of those. You're like a white Arab, as the saying goes."

A few moments later, being polite, he asked where in the States I came from. I told him *Neu Mexiko,* adding, "From the desert." I still remember the quizzical look he gave me as he repeated, *"aus der Wüste, eh?"* trying to figure out if I was joking. *Ja und nein, Herr Doktor Professor.* That string of titles might sound parodic translated directly into English, but it's the respectful way to address a professor, especially if you want something from him. I wanted a letter to the Fulbright Commission confirming that I was attending his lectures, and he obliged.

I applied for a Fulbright Scholarship for some of the same reasons I moved to Chicago. I was still young enough to spend a year someplace entirely new without complicating my life, but was beginning to understand I wouldn't be for long. I also hoped to re-create the excitement of my year in Dublin, the best year of my life. Also, it was unlike anything my classmates were doing, which was appealing in itself.

Most of what I know about English grammar I learned studying German. It wasn't that I spoke English ungrammatically, but that I didn't understand what it meant to speak it grammatically. For instance, I had always (or so far back as I could cast my memory) known when to turn "she" into "her," but I knew it by ear, the way an untrained musician learns new tunes. And while I'd long been familiar with the terms "direct object" and "indirect object," and could even recite the examples of them I'd learned by rote—"he threw the ball (D.O.) to him (I.O.)"—it took just a few weeks of internalizing the German case system to understand that English has its cases, too. Why hadn't anyone ever told me?

Once you understand the four grammatical cases of German, the characteristic long, winding sentences can be appreciated for their virtuosity, which is not so much an attribute of the writer as of the language itself. A German reader doesn't get lost in a 100-word sentence because the word forms convey their cases, and the cases explain how each clause relates to those surrounding it. Capitalizing nouns provides another visual clue. Unlike chronically ambiguous English, it's almost impossible not to know whether a German word is being used as a noun or verb.

And then there were the words themselves. I'd learned words such as "ambiguous" and "sympathy" as arbitrary collections of sound. There's no way a native English-speaking child can look at such words and figure out their meaning. The comparable German terms, by contrast, are *zweideutig* (two + meaning) and *mitleid* (with + sorrow). It would be difficult for a native German-speaking child to *fail* to get a sense of their meaning simply by looking at them. I found the language charmingly concrete, from *Fernsehen* (far + see) for television to *Scheide* for both sheath and vagina.

But then, as all the classics scholars among my readers are exclaiming, the English words I just listed have exactly the same literal meanings. The catch is they don't possess those literal meanings in their own language, but in Latin or Ancient Greek. Scratch the surface deeply enough and English words, or rather the words of which English is composed, often prove to be no less concrete than their German equivalents. But most of us native English-speakers learn our words by their definitions rather than their etymologies. English-speaking children experience their language as arbitrary in a way German children don't.

Also, German children don't study spelling or hold spelling bees. With very few exceptions, German words are spelled precisely as pronounced. There are no silent letters, and no letter combinations whose pronunciation change as arbitrarily as, say, the English "gh." Studying German made me realize how much we suffer from the sorry effects of what we're taught to regard as the great achievements of Samuel Johnson and Noah Webster, whose dictionaries fixed English spellings before they had time to finish evolving. Thanks to their heroic literary efforts, we're stuck at a larval stage of orthography.

Just as learning German taught me about English, being a white Arab in a German law school taught me about American law and legal education.

In Germany, law is an undergraduate subject. That's a little misleading, because German academic high schools are so much more demanding than their American counterparts. At a young age—around the age American pupils leave elementary school—German kids are tested for academic ability and then streamed into one of three different high school systems. It's not just a matter of honors or advanced placement or remedial or special education courses within a high school, but of entirely separate educational institutions. Almost all university students are graduates of the academically most demanding of the high schools, called *Gymnasium* (which most definitely doesn't mean gymnasium—the German language didn't entirely escape the blight of Hellenophilia). In practical effect, college admissions are largely settled when German kids are about 11 years old.

German universities don't charge tuition. I could always count on an amazed and scandalized reaction by revealing the cost of an elite American education. But I also noticed that the children most likely to be streamed into the *Gymnasium* are those who grow up with educated parents in enriched environments, with lots of books and sophisticated conversation in fluent German. Parents who can afford it, naturally, hire tutors to give their children that extra little push. In these and other subtle and not-so-subtle ways, the three-tiered German secondary school system reinforces class divisions. A Turkish immigrant pays taxes to support the children of the aristocracy and professional classes at universities the immigrant's own children have little prospect of attending. But the system also educates *Gymnasium* students to a level easily comparable to that of third-year students at an American university, and perhaps even beyond that.

So describing law as an undergraduate discipline doesn't mean the courses are attended by people who coasted through four years of high school doing the minimum their teachers required and looking forward to the prom. Nonetheless, it's just another course of study, like biology or literature, which made me wonder for the first time why American universities classify it as graduate school. There's no other American graduate degree without a parallel undergraduate major. Such "pre-law" courses as political science don't count, because a person could avoid them all—I did—and do just fine in law school, whereas an incoming medical student would be lost without a foundation in biology and chemistry. I think the only reason Americans conceive of legal studies as a graduate course of study is because law schools were originally independent trade schools. They were administratively engulfed by universities without ever being integrated into them.

American law schools, it must be said, provide an unpleasant environment for their students in comparison to most undergraduate degree programs. The teachers pile on a great deal more homework than the typical undergraduate professor. But there's little about the law that's conceptually difficult. The law is, in practical effect, an elaborate system of classification. It requires a great deal of mental effort to master the vast grid, but the effort involved requires memorization and the dexterous retrieval of memory, not original thought. "Legal analysis" is a matter of figuring out the best category in which to slot a legal problem. Legal analysis is different from sorting mail only in that the legal slots exist mentally rather than in the physical world, and there are many more of them than a letter carrier would find practical.

There's no reason why law can't be an undergraduate course in the United States. It could begin with the third year of college, with the law major taking two legal classes a term to cover eight foundational courses. A required fifth year could be devoted to the intensive study of specialized topics. A student who completed that program of study would be as well prepared as a typical JD but two years younger—and not so deeply in debt. That last item explains why there's no chance of such a sensible reform being introduced. American law schools are profit centers for their universities. A single law professor can instruct 100 students with no equipment but a podium and blackboard, although Internet access and a projector are useful extras. Law schools don't even have to pay graduate students to serve as teaching assistants, because no grades are assigned before the final exams and a single professor can take care of those. (B-pluses all around!) If the course of study were shortened and integrated into undergraduate school, the university would lose many tens of thousands of dollars in fees per student. The professors would feel they'd lost prestige, too.

The fact that law is an undergraduate course of study in Germany has another effect: the courses are *normal*. That was pretty amazing to me. The courses I took were lectures, not rituals of humiliation. Students could raise their hands and ask questions, but generally they just listened and took notes. Female students frequently knitted during the lectures—to have a girlfriend studying law must mean a steady stream of scarves, mittens, and sweaters. They would drop their work into their laps whenever they heard something they wanted to write down. Then, when they picked it up again, you'd see their lips moving silently as they counted the loops to reorient themselves.

The study of law was stressful for the German students, but it was *naturally* stressful. The stress was inherent in the course of study, not something imposed on students. They worried about learning the material, about the comprehensive state exams at the end of the second and fourth years (in effect, the bar exam is built into the German legal education), about the uncertain job prospects caused by too many students pursuing legal degrees, about career choices, and so on. They didn't additionally suffer from the *artificial* stress induced by teacher bullying and withholding. The German professors saw their job as imparting knowledge to the students—imagine that! At the end of the lectures, the students would perfunctorily shuffle their feet in applause, the way orchestra members salute the conductor without setting down their instruments.

The German law school I attended was at Bonn. The university's full name was Rheinische Friedrich-Wilhelms-Universität Bonn. The first part of the name, Rhinelandish, just tells you it's located right on the river. The next part, Friedrich-Wilhelms, tells you he was the Prussian Kaiser who ordained it into being. I never heard anyone use either of the first two parts of the name. It was just "the Uni" if you were in Bonn or the equivalent of "Bonn University" if you weren't. Bonn, the birthplace of Beethoven and burial place of Schumann, was then the capital of the country known in America as West Germany, but it didn't feel like a capital city. It was never intended to be more than a temporary capital, biding the nation's time until Berlin could once again be the capital of an undivided Germany. The Germans consciously avoided the marble-monument pomp of most capitals. I don't recall a single bronze equestrian statue. In its self-conscious provisionalism, Bonn was the very opposite of Washington, Brasilia, St. Petersburg, or Canberra. Government offices were concentrated in nondescript office towers south of town.

It was a very pleasant city, a perfect size for getting around by bicycle. There were tree-lined walks all along the river, which had been rationalized into something more like a canal as it flowed through town, nearly straight and busy with barge traffic. At twilight the swallows would come zooming between the trees, skimming just five or six feet over the ground. Of course they never fly into people, but at times it took a conscious effort not to throw up my hands to protect my face.

The main building of the university was just a couple of hundred yards from the river. It was a palace—literally a palace, the former residence of the ruling prince, hurriedly vacated when Napoleon's troops marched into the Rhineland. It remained unoccupied until 1818, when the Prussians came marching from the opposite direction and turned it into a university with the mission of training a managerial elite to run the new territory along Prussian lines. It was a long yellow baroque building located along one end of a long tree-lined avenue, at the opposite end of which, perhaps half a mile away, was a smaller and even prettier baroque palace set amid the university's botanical garden. It's difficult to conceive of a lovelier pair of university buildings. Unfortunately the law school was located a couple of blocks off to the side, one of those poured-concrete buildings that somehow manage to look aggressively modern and depressingly run down at the same time.

I attended some of the first lectures for incoming students. The lecture hall was standing-room only, and the professor used exactly the same example I heard in my first days at UNM Law School: If I invite a friend over for dinner, and he accepts, do we have a contract? Can I sue him if he doesn't show up? Why not? (The hypothetical—lawyers use "hypothetical" as a noun—had a little more piquancy in Germany, where social engagements are never made, or broken, lightly.)

I knew I'd have only a year in Germany. Spending it in classes for recent high school graduates who'd never before studied at a university, much less studied law, seemed an unproductive waste of time. On the other hand, attending more advanced classes, which built on the foundation of those introductory courses, was a different kind of waste of time, because I lacked the background, and the familiarity with the statutes, necessary to appreciate the more subtle legal points. Every class was either too elementary or too advanced. I never did find a good entry point.

I wound up attending a wide variety of lectures, including some in other subjects at the main university. I also attended trials, which for an American are remarkable mainly for the role played by the three judges. Lawyers were present but silent. The witness sat facing the three judges, who asked the questions. Usually the most senior judge, seated in the middle, led the questioning, with the second-most-senior occasionally pitching in and the junior judge mainly just taking notes. In one trial I watched in municipal court, the witness didn't have some information immediately to hand. The lead judge looked at his calendar and said, "Can you bring that next Wednesday at 2:30?" The witness could, and court adjourned until then. The trials were effectively a series of conferences conducted over a period of time.

What Americans call the Anglo-American legal system is really just the English legal system, which the English imposed upon their former colonies. There are lots and lots of former English colonies, so it could more aptly be termed the Anglo-Colonial legal system. It's a system of grand, sometimes hysterical drama, with trials building toward climactic impassioned arguments to the jury followed by the nearly unbearable suspense of waiting for the jury to return a verdict. The German legal system, by contrast, was calmly and rationally boring.

The year in Germany taught me far more about the American legal system than about the German one. It did that by making me see through German eyes features of the American system that, at both UNM and Northwestern, were so taken for granted they weren't even taught.

For instance, a German student once asked me at what point during law school American students decided whether to become judges. The question at first made no sense to me, as my puzzlement must have made no sense to the student with whom I was chatting. Because German judges usually hear cases in panels of three, while American trial judges work alone, there are many more judges per capita in Germany than in the United States. In Germany, becoming a judge is a career path. Promising students undergo years of training, then work their way up the career ladder. It's a rational, orderly way to choose judges.

The smaller number of American judges might suggest they would be better—the crème de la crème—but in practice it means the opposite, because competition for the jobs ensures that those with the power to fill them use that power to benefit themselves. That's why the American judiciary remains today the last part of the government still staffed by Andrew Jackson's spoils system. For ordinary government workers, the spoils system was eliminated by civil service reforms. We no longer hire paper-pushing government clerks based on their service to the party or usefulness to political bosses, but that's how we still choose our judges.

On another occasion a student asked about the practicum. How long did the practical training of lawyers last in America? That question, too, was somewhat embarrassing.

In Germany, students who complete four years of legal study become eligible to take the state exam, essentially the equivalent of our bar exam. (In practice, many students spend an entire fifth year getting ready for it, paying a tutor to guide them in the necessary intense study.) Once they pass that exam, the young lawyer begins a formal internship. It lasts three years. During that time the baby lawyers work their way through a variety of legal offices, typically on a three-month rotation. Rotations might include a corporate legal department, a prosecutor's office, a public defender's office, an administrative agency, a private law firm, and an insurance company. By the time they're licensed, German lawyers have a pretty good idea of how the legal world works.

Internships served by newly minted American lawyers, by contrast, don't exist.

Then there was the time I described the typical course of study at an American law school to a graduate student named Andreas. We were standing in Bonn's beautiful Cathedral Square, at one end of the wonderfully labyrinthine pedestrian shopping district, not far from the

Beethoven memorial. I mentioned that almost all law students take a course in Evidence. "Evidence?" Andreas asked, surprised. "What's to study about evidence? Either it's relevant or it's not."

Even as I had become generally familiar with the procedure of German courts, it somehow had never quite lodged in my mind that there were no rules of evidence. Lawyers never objected to questions, since the questions were asked by judges. Besides, what purpose would be served by limiting the judges' access to information pertinent to their decision?

The American Rules of Evidence include a definition of "relevance." The definition is one sentence long, consisting of 36 words. It says what everyone knows: information that it would be a waste of time to learn is irrelevant. Perhaps as much as 15 minutes of class time could profitably be devoted to the study of relevance. The rest of the semester-long Evidence class is devoted to all of the other evidentiary rules, almost all of which are much longer than 36 words. Their point is to *prevent* the decision-maker—the jury—from having access to all relevant information. That's the most fundamental point about the law of evidence to which I'd devoted a semester of study, and yet somehow it was a point I had never quite grasped.

Andreas got me thinking about the peculiarity of a system for resolving disputes that depends so heavily on the filtering of pertinent facts. I thought I could discern two reasons for it. First, in the Anglo-Colonial system the questions are asked by lawyers, not judges. That builds in an obvious bias against the truth. Whichever side would be hurt by the truth will try to keep it under wraps, or at least confuse the matter sufficiently to avoid the consequences that, by law, should attend upon its disclosure. Unless restrained, therefore, some of the lawyers asking questions at a trial will predictably steer the judge's or jurors' attention away from the important point. One purpose of the Rules of Evidence is to control the lawyers who would otherwise sabotage the whole purpose of having a trial in the first place.

That word "jurors" supplies the second reason. In the Anglo-Colonial system, lawyers are trying to sway nonlawyers, the jurors. Nonlawyers can't be counted upon to look at things the way lawyers are trained to look at them. Deliberating jurors are also the only trial participants who act independently of the judge. The parties, the lawyers, the witnesses, the spectators, the bailiff, the deputies or marshals—all are subject to the summary justice of the courtroom. But once the jurors shuffle out of the courtroom into the jury room to begin their deliberations, they are entirely free of the judge's control. The judge has told them to follow his or her instructions, but if the jurors decline to do so the judge has few options other than to start the whole trial all over again ("declare a mistrial")—and often not even that.

Much of the American legal history of the past century has consisted of judges inventing new ways to restrict the autonomy of jurors. One of their most conspicuous successes is the creation of highly technical rules of evidence that permit the judge to keep information from the jurors' ears. If we think of the jury room as the verdict factory, we can see that the judge has no control over the sausage eventually produced, but tight control over the ingredients that go into it. Today in the United States it's no exaggeration to say that in some trials, the lawyers and judge spend more time arguing about what evidence the jury will hear than the jurors spend actually hearing it.

AT SOME POINT I figured I shouldn't let academics interfere with my pursuit of an education. Sitting inside lecture halls came to seem like the waste of an educational opportunity. Part of my education consisted of visiting East Berlin. A train trip northeastward from Bavaria took us through mountain villages unbombed during World War II. Because East Germany was quite poor relative to the West, the villages we glimpsed through the train windows presented a time-warp glimpse of pre-1939 Germany, an astonishingly beautiful place.

The Fulbright Commission had summoned all that year's scholars to Berlin for a conference. The main thing I remember from it was a concert put on by the music students. One soprano with a thrillingly beautiful voice sang and acted out Bach's comic *Coffee Cantata*. She remains the only person I've ever met socially whose name is a *New York Times* crossword answer. The clue was "Soprano Fleming." But then, with a name consisting of 60 percent vowels, Renee is a crossword natural. At the same concert, a double bass player refuted all those who doubted that his could be a solo instrument. He stayed put in Berlin: Michael Wolf is now professor at its University of the Arts.

Another musician performing at that Berlin concert was a flute player I had met in the fall, even before I arrived in Germany. I had a four-hour layover at Heathrow Airport, London, beginning around 7:00 on a Sunday morning, and so did this flute player. She carried a bag of dried red chile, which, being from New Mexico, I was uniquely positioned to recognize. That was enough to start us talking. That's how I traveled 5,000 miles to meet someone who went to my junior high school. In addition to the chile Carla had some English money with her, with which she bought me a cup of tea. She had a Fulbright to study in Würzburg, a lovely small city in Hesse, which, conveniently enough, was a straight-shot three-hour train ride from Bonn. Better yet, the train followed the gorgeous Rhine and Main valleys.

I'd seen the Berlin Wall before, but Carla hadn't. It was impressive, in its spirit-crushing way, ten or so feet tall and topped with a revolving cylinder to prevent anyone from getting a handhold on the top. The 50 or so feet immediately east of the wall was cleared of vegetation and meticulously smoothed, with German shepherd dogs on patrol. After the wall came down it was revealed that many of these dogs, and perhaps all of them, weren't actually trained to kill. But they were scary-looking, especially as they ran back and forth before the guard towers on which uniformed men with binoculars and machine guns impassively stared at the Westerners gathered on grandstands to stare at them.

On our side, the wall was covered with graffiti, often political and witty. There were also crosses marking where escapees were shot by East German guards.

Underground, where the old subway crossed beneath the wall, you'd see soldiers with machine guns isolated on deserted, dark subway platforms at which the train didn't stop, or even slow down. It was a strangely disturbing and surreal sight. They were stationed there, apparently, to ensure that no one tried to escape by clinging to the hurtling subway cars.

Back in the land of daylight, we rode a tourist bus to East Berlin, passing bomb damage still unrepaired after 40 years. East German soldiers in gray uniforms *goose-stepped* before a war memorial. On our way back, the guards ran a mirror on wheels beneath the bus, checking the undercarriage for riders. They also assigned us all numbers and required us to stand in sequence, though I couldn't tell whether there was any reason for that other than to demonstrate that they could do it.

East Germany—the German Democratic Republic—was a police state without Jews, which was pretty much what Hitler had in mind. The progress from Prussian authoritarianism to Nazism to Communism had been sadly incremental. In German history, West Germany was the revolutionary state.

In the movie *The Lives of Others,* the Stasi captain, demoted to steaming open letters, hears over the radio that the wall has been breached. He instantly gets up from his work and leaves. After a moment's hesitation, everyone else in his department follows his lead. It's a perfect cinematic moment. The captain understood that without the wall—without the apparatus of oppression—the East German state had instantly ceased to exist.

∞

PART TWO

Neither Fish Nor Fowl

*The rituals marking the transition
from law student to lawyer.*

CHAPTER 5

Raw Recruiting

B EGINNING ONE MONDAY in the fall semester, NULS students started showing up to class in lawyer clothes. As with prom outfits, the female of the species generally carried it off better than the male. Which is to say, the girls looked like women in their suits, the boys like boys in theirs.

For men, dressing like a lawyer has always been easy: you just dress as conservatively as you can without looking positively anachronistic. Dark suits, white shirts, either a red or a blue tie. Done. In the U.S. Supreme Court, where everything is just a bit more extreme so you don't forget you're in the Supreme Court, the chief clerk and the assistant solicitor generals—the band of Department of Justice lawyers representing the federal government—go right over the edge into anachronism, dressing in morning suits, tails and all. Once at a seminar on practice in the Supreme Court I asked a panelist, a member of the Solicitor General's office, what his female colleagues wore. He said they have more flexibility in choice of dress but generally wore "the female equivalent of a morning suit." Another panelist—a woman in private practice—pointed out his error: "The female equivalent of a morning suit is a wedding dress."

In general it's always true that women lawyers have more flexibility in their dress, but that's just another way of saying they have more choices to make, which adds another point of stress. Women of the mid-1980s dressed like little men, wearing dark gray or navy skirts and matching jackets with white blouses and, often, frilly little ties in front. That quasi–Brooks Brothers look, de-emphasizing the differences between the sexes, sometimes struck me as a tad counterproductive, making me think of little boys dressed up to attend a wedding. Which is pretty much what most of the male students looked like anyway, with the reds of their ties picking up the pimples on their faces.

Describing the boys' suits as ill-fitting would capture the impression they gave, sitting in the brown booths of Lincoln Hall in their dark power suits, but it wouldn't be quite accurate. Most of my classmates came from money. Their suits were tailored, or at least purchased with the unctuous assistance of discreetly expert salesmen. They fit just fine. I think it was more that the wearers hadn't gotten used to the feeling of a tie cinched up to their throats. The movements of their heads revealed their discomfort in a way that was both unmistakable and just a shade too subtle to be described in a single adjective.

The costume-party efflorescence signaled the beginning of recruiting season. For a set period of time during the fall semester, I think six weeks, recruiters flocked to Northwestern from big law firms and corporations to interview students for summer jobs—"clerkships," in the lingo. (The Supreme Court clerk I mentioned earlier is an actual clerk, the person in charge of a court's paperwork. A law firm's summer clerk isn't a clerk at all but a law student spending a summer on the law firm's payroll. Yet a third type of clerk is described in chapter 6. There's no reason why three such distinct positions should all have the same title, except the usual reason for everything in the legal biz: that's how it's always been, like striped trousers and tails in the Supreme Court.)

At the big law firms, one or two junior partners become designated as recruiters and get sent on a circuit of prestigious law schools to interview students back-to-back-to-back. The students submitted their résumés ahead of time, and at Northwestern, at least, the recruiters couldn't refuse to see them. That didn't stop the recruiters from discriminating, of course, but just ensured the discrimination took the form of wasting the student's time for 20 minutes. The rejection letter—what Northwestern students called a bullet—followed.

The students could choose the law firms with which they wished to interview, but we had remarkably little information on which to base our decisions. If you didn't have Daddy the senior partner to give you expert advice, the application process was pretty random. The firms each filled out information sheets that told us how many lawyers they had, where their offices were located, and what fields they specialized in, but they all specialized in the same fields. The firms weren't asked to provide the type of information that would actually have helped us decide where to apply, such as: Are you a sweatshop? Do you outrageously abuse your associates? In addition to making them work endless hours, do you also require them to do brain-numbingly dull tasks? Do you lie to them about their expected compensation and prospects of partnership? Is the atmosphere of your firm characterized by rumor, complaint, furtiveness, backstabbing, and frequent defections as entire departments break off to join other firms? Is your managing partner a megalomaniac? a vindictive liar? a spectacularly incompetent businessman who thinks he's a financial wizard? What percentage of your senior partners are out-and-out psychopaths?

One recruiter broke the nondiscrimination rules by being exceptionally honest with me. He said, right off the bat, "We never make offers to transfer students from schools we don't recruit at, and we don't recruit at the University of New Mexico, so I'm afraid we won't be able to extend an offer to you." That was against the rules, but I didn't much mind because I didn't exactly have my heart set on his firm. I don't even remember what it was, except that it was based in Los Angeles. I'd submitted my résumé to it more or less randomly, and once I'd had time to recover I appreciated that he didn't go through the motions with me, and told him so. He said, "But I have 20 minutes set aside for you, so if there's anything I can tell you about the firm or practicing in L.A., I'd be happy to chat with you."

So for five or ten minutes I asked him questions, and he answered them cheerfully and apparently forthrightly, and as I got up to leave he shook my hand and said, "Let's keep up the relationship, Joel."

For a second I felt like I was really in Hollywood. Sadly, though, somehow we've never done lunch.

From the law student's point of view, there were two objects to be gained by going through the weird dress-up game of recruitment. The longer-term goal was to get a summer job, which with luck would translate into a permanent job after graduation, as we'll see in the next chapter.

The immediate goal was to get a fly-back.

A fly-back was when the firm flew you to their main office. The firm would buy you a plane ticket to Los Angeles, or New York, or wherever, put you up in a luxury hotel for a couple of nights, and schedule a whole day of activities for you. The activities almost invariably consisted of some sort of sales pitch about the firm itself, a tour of its offices, lunch in a fancy restaurant with some junior associates, and a long, wearying string of interviews with partners. Then, when you were good and bleary-eyed from repeating yourself, constantly distracted by the inability to remember whether you'd previously said the same thing to this particular person—or was it the last person?—you might have a fancy dinner with a table full of strangers followed by a taxi ride back to the luxury hotel.

It was dreadful.

One Phoenix firm put me up in the Arizona Biltmore, the first time I'd ever slept in a hotel room larger than the average two-bedroom apartment. I remember sitting in front of the floor-to-ceiling window, eating my room-service breakfast with the strangest feeling that I was living someone else's life, as if in some horror story my brain had been transplanted into an accident victim's body. That sense of unreality—which wasn't altogether unpleasant, given the sunshine (a welcome break from November in Chicago) and the tasty food—was much more memorable than the firm, whose name I no longer recall.

It might have been at that firm, but maybe at another one, where a partner noticed from my résumé that I'd reviewed movies and asked me who I preferred, Gene Siskel or Roger Ebert. They were the reviewers for the *Chicago Tribune* and *Sun-Times* respectively, who were then doing a weekly half-hour TV show together. I said I tended to agree more often with Siskel. He immediately said, "I prefer Ebert." So much for my job prospects at that firm.

In later years I had enough experience on the other side of the recruitment game to know that as soon as I left each interview, the partner would dictate a short memo giving his or her impression of me and recommending for or against extending an offer to me, before turning back to the serious business of billing clients.

The luxurious meals and absurd hotel rooms felt a bit ridiculous for anyone used to the student life. Money was spent freely, but as bribes the expenditures were almost insultingly petty. The firms wanted to influence my career decision—my entire future life—by spending a couple hundred dollars more than necessary. What did it imply about the firms that they thought a room at the Biltmore would make the difference? What did it imply about my fellow students that it evidently *worked*?

As my close personal friend from L.A. had explained, the prestigious firms recruited only at the prestigious schools. That made the students at those schools feel special, but over time I came to realize it equally made the firms feel special. Fly-backs were a way for law students and law firms to confirm each other's desirability. I started the process with the idea that I was the buyer, looking to obtain something of value for myself, but it quickly became apparent that the law firms thought of themselves in similar terms. From their point of view, I was the seller. The thing I had to offer wasn't myself; it was my status as a high-achieving student at a highly ranked law school.

For many students at Northwestern, the really big deal was to accrue the maximum number of fly-backs. That was a status thing, too. The more places you jetted off to, the more you proved how amazingly desirable you were. Some people went on 25 or 30 fly-backs, visiting many firms they would never consider working for, in cities they considered backwaters, making a point of ordering the most expensive item on every menu. And they made sure everyone back in Chicago knew it. I couldn't keep myself from feeling a little bit of the envy they worked so hard to engender in us.

I'm sure the professors hated recruitment season. Students would miss many classes as they jetted off around the country, and those who showed up for class in their suits with their overnight bags probably weren't concentrating entirely on the material. Looking at the Northwestern website today I see that recruitment season has been moved from the middle of the fall semester to the middle of August, before the semester begins, which is doubtless better from the professors' point of view but would seem to create certain problems for students who wish to maintain a life away from law school. The website also promises all sorts of career counseling services that, if they were available during my day, were well concealed. Maybe today's well-counseled students don't experience recruitment as an essentially random series of events. But I did.

The firms that participated in this kind of recruitment were, naturally, the big firms, and a few others that wanted to be like the big boys. Although I didn't realize it at the time, they represented only the thin upper crust of the greasy meat pie that is the practice of law. In time I came to understand that Northwestern has traditionally been the supplier to Chicago's corporate law firms—the LaSalle Street firms, as they're called, referring to a street in the Loop where they were once concentrated. That explained much of Northwestern's curriculum, such as its rather eccentric custom of devoting entire semesters to each article of the Uniform Commercial Code, a massive statute that governs a wide variety of business transactions. No one really needs to spend a semester on each of those articles unless he or she is going to specialize in those areas of business law, which is to say Northwestern assumed its students would specialize in them.

Northwestern didn't give its students an accurate picture of the legal marketplace—because it, too, was a buyer in this market. In its promotional materials it brags about the average starting salaries of its graduates. (For my entire career I've been well below the average starting salary of each year's NULS graduates.) The school's prestige is enhanced by placing graduates at prestigious firms with their sky-high starting salaries, setting up a feedback loop of prestige that helps to attract high-achieving students, making the school more prestigious. Moreover, students pulling down the biggest bucks have the potential to become the biggest donors. Besides, if students weren't streamed into the prestigious firms—if they weren't led to accept that working at a prestigious firm is the goal to which the best law students naturally aspire—they might start to question whether they really need to go to a prestigious law school.

For the top-tier law schools, providing unbiased information about legal careers would be the equivalent of deliberately introducing rust into the undercarriage of a vintage Cadillac.

CHAPTER 6

Initiation by Lotus-Eating

M OST BIG LAW firms accomplish most of their lawyer hiring through summer clerkship programs. The summer clerk isn't a clerk at all but a law student between years of study, spending the summer as a temporary employee at a law firm or corporation. The more dignified name used at some firms is "summer associate," but that's subtly denigrating of the real associates, the junior attorneys, who fill far more demanding positions. For law students and law firms, summer months are a period of mutual audition, at the end of which the firms extend job offers to some of their clerks but not others. Some of the clerks accept the offers, but not others.

It's been a long time since I was a summer clerk, and I began to wonder whether things had changed dramatically since my day. So I got on the Internet to look at law firms' descriptions of their summer clerkship programs. Picking a firm at random, I discovered things hadn't changed at all:

> The [prestigious law firm] summer program is more than just work. Our firm is a lot of fun, as is the surrounding area—especially in the summer. The summer program includes a calendar full of social and recreational activities where clerks can meet and interact with our employees and their families.

Past summer events have included a group outing to a major league baseball game, golfing, a firm picnic, bowling, a pool tournament, cookouts on our loading dock and a number of happy hour excursions.

I've edited out the local references from this extract because my point isn't to single out the particular firm, but the opposite: its description of its summer clerkship program puts it comfortably in the mainstream of firms fishing in the stream where the students of the prestigious law schools swim.

The firm illustrates its summer program with a photograph of two young men, presumably summer clerks, at a baseball game, looking like they've been enjoying a beer per inning and have just sat down after the seventh inning stretch. That's an entirely accurate image of summer clerkship programs in general. Like a certain type of would-be seducer, law firms encourage their clerks to go on "happy hour excursions."

Oddly, none of the description of summer clerkship programs I've ever run across describes one of its traditional purposes, which is to provide entertainment for the support staff. Law firms are strictly hierarchical, and one of the lower courses of the pyramid consists of the support staff. "Support staff" includes a wide variety of positions, but by far the largest category is secretaries. Traditionally, secretaries were young and female while summer clerks were young and male. Those young aspiring professional men didn't have anything particularly pressing to occupy their time, and it was summer. Perhaps some of the support staff harbored fantasies of a desirable marriage, but in my day it seemed they mainly viewed the male summer clerks as delightful toys.

Perhaps there will come a tipping point—perhaps we've reached it already—when the growing preponderance of female law students and hence of law clerks, and the slightly higher incidence of male secretaries, will change the social dynamic of clerkship summers. Even at institutions as conservative as law firms, cultures gradually change.

In 1983 that lawyers at one of the biggest of Atlanta law firms, King & Spalding, proposed a wet T-shirt contest for the female summer clerks. As James B. Stewart reported in the *Wall Street Journal*, "cooler heads prevailed. The lawyers had to content themselves with a more old-fashioned, and not quite so revealing, bathing-suit competition."[1] Those days, it's safe to say, are gone, thanks in large part to King & Spalding itself, which took a sex-discrimination employment lawsuit (though not one directly related to organized boob-ogling) all the way to the Supreme Court—and lost. There's nothing quite like a nationally publicized lawsuit against a law firm to capture the attention of fellow lawyers. These days, a greater level of discretion is utilized when the old vultures roosting high in the pyramid's rafters find themselves stirred to the sexual exploitation of female job-seekers.

But while sex is, after drinks, the defining feature of many a summer clerkship, it's not one that gets advertised on the firm websites or even (if I remember correctly) on those fill-in-the-blank firm résumés that I reviewed by the truckload at Northwestern. The summer clerks are theoretically supposed to work. They're supposed to dress up as lawyers, show up in the morning, accompany lawyers to depositions or trials as spectators, and perform legal tasks assigned to them. The tasks consist of research and writing, and the characteristic work product is the memo to a partner.

The one project I remember distinctly had to do with the tort of "wrongful birth"—a phrase that requires a great deal of repetition before it sounds normal. The firm had been hired (in lawyer-speak, "retained") by a medical malpractice insurer to represent a surgeon who performed a tubal ligation. According to the plaintiff, the surgeon located only one fallopian tube and assumed the patient didn't have a second one. He then compounded that dubious—and, as it turned out, incorrect—assumption by not informing the patient he'd had occasion to make it, with the result that she stopped using birth control, with the result you'd expect. I was given the assignment of finding out how other states dealt with claims of wrongful birth, and particularly how they calculated monetary damages. Was the negligent surgeon financially responsible for raising the child to adulthood, or for the costs of the pregnancy and a second sterilization procedure, or for something in between those extremes? I read as many of the cases from around the country as I could find and summarized them in a lengthy memo. I'm sure the assigning lawyers double-checked my work before relying on it in their court filings, but I'm also sure the work I did was useful to them.

Most law clerk assignments aren't as big or interesting as that, but they typically follow that pattern. A firm's lawyers will evaluate the memos. Did the student understand the issue and analyze it correctly? Was the student's research thorough—did he or she "touch bottom"? (That's a swimming metaphor, not a sexual harassment one.) Can he or she write well? The lawyers will evaluate the student directly, by talking about the case. Is the clerk intelligent and articulate? Is he or she someone you could stand having around day after day, week after week, for the rest of your career? And then there's the matter of work ethic. Is he or she someone who will bill a lot of hours for the firm, pulling in money for the partners to divvy up among themselves?

Meanwhile, the student is evaluating the firm, which lays on the dissembling charm. That's where the ball games come in, and the happy hours, and the picnics, and the bowling, and the happy hours, and the parties at partners' houses, and impromptu lunch crews checking out all the restaurants within walking distance of the office, and the happy hours. None of those things is normal law-firm behavior. They don't occur any of the rest of the year. As I later discovered, the lawyers at my firm referred to summer as the social season.

Once during my clerkship summer I was invited to dinner, along with one of the other male clerks, at the home of one of the senior partners. This partner and his wife invited all the clerks in groups of two or three, and this week it happened to be our turn. The partner had a daughter who was about 17 and unbelievably, movie-star beautiful. It was hard not to stare, but I disciplined myself to gaze at her lovely face only when she was speaking or I was speaking to her. For her part she had no problem ignoring me, because she was instantly taken by my fellow clerk, Andy. She spent dinner with her eyes fixed on Andy's handsome face, and as the meal progressed he kept his eyes more and more fixed on his plate. I've never again felt such a combination of envy and sympathy as I felt for Andy that evening. The envy I don't need to explain, but the sympathy was a little more complicated. In the first place, I liked Andy, who was smart and witty—the partner's daughter had correctly sized him up. But in the second place, she was so amazingly beautiful. It would have been impossible *not* to respond even as it was equally impossible, for quite different reasons, to respond. Such are the complications of a summer clerk's life.

I later worked at that firm for four years and was never once invited back to that partner's home for dinner. I'm pretty sure that wasn't a reflection on how I'd behaved that night at dinner, since as far as I knew none of the other associates was ever invited, either. The partner and his wife just had no particular desire to socialize with young lawyers from the firm. I'm confident that they (unlike their daughter) had no desire to socialize with summer clerks, either. Dinner that night was strictly business. The business was accomplished with hospitality, splendid cooking, and delightful, if complicated, scenery. But it was the business of recruiting for the firm.

The impression I gained of my firm during my summer clerkship wasn't false, but it also was far from complete. As I was to discover, the concept of not-false is central to the practice of law. With rare exceptions, lawyers are scrupulously careful never to say in court or write in their pleadings any proposition that can be proved false. It doesn't have to be correct, just not-false. The test is whether there's an argument to be made. If so, the lawyer is expected to make it—to spin the facts in the way most favorable to the client. Summer clerkship programs do something similar. The impression they create of what it's like to work full-time at the firm is a not-false one.

The associates were open and honest with me, up to a point. That point was defined as disloyalty to the firm—sabotaging the recruitment program. They refrained from spelling out certain things. I didn't have the background necessary to understand the full import of what they told me, and still less to intuit what they weren't quite saying. I had no baseline, no "normal," to which I could compare my very agreeable summer experience.

Summer clerkships at the big firms amount to fly-backs writ large. The summer of undemanding work with alcohol and secretaries and social outings and paychecks grossly disproportionate to the work performed adds up to another bribe. Law firms shell out the money to influence the students' career decisions—which is to say, to alter their entire life trajectories. Law firms persuade summer clerks to build their lives around working at the firm by providing an experience that has almost nothing to do with work at the firm.

Let the clerk return to law school for that final year, study for and pass the bar exam (the big firms will pay him or her during the weeks of study), and join the firm as a regular associate. There will be no excursions to ball games or pool tournaments or picnics at the zoo until the following June, when the new crop of summer clerks shows up—and the associates are reminded of their duty to treat the social events as part of their jobs, as recruiting, rather than as social events. Loyalty to the firm will be stressed.

Once the graduate joins the firm as an associate, dalliances with the support staff are no longer summer flings but matters for the concerned attention of the executive committee. The lazy succession of research projects is replaced by the relentless grind of billable hours. And brand-new associates are expected to have absorbed from midair the secrets of managing clients.

The internships endured by recent graduates of medical schools are infinitely less pleasant than the summer clerkships of law students. But a medical internship gives the baby doc exposure to patients and a chance to see what life in the profession, at least at that particular institution, really means. Internships are followed by residencies that alert young doctors to what various practices will do to their lives. For doctors, there's no disgrace in making a sudden change of plan after the first residency; they just do another residency in another field. Doctors' career decisions are based on their extended experiences with reality. Many law students, by contrast, make career decisions based on pleasant summer-long fantasies.

CHAPTER 7

The Judge's Ghostwriter

L AW STUDENTS WHO graduate near the top of their class can apply for judicial "clerkships," which means working as a judge's legal assistant for a set term, usually one or two years, beginning in the fall after graduation. (Some federal judges now hire permanent clerks, but I'm not talking about them in this chapter.) Because I graduated mid-year, I didn't fit into any clerkship schedules. The positions come open in August or September, not January. So I was never a clerk, which I rather regret. I think I would have enjoyed it.

A judicial clerkship is a traditional transition period between law school and the cold world of legal practice. Being a clerk is prestigious, though the level of prestige varies according to that of the judge for which one clerks. The clerk receives a handsome salary, and the prestige of the position—not to mention the recommendation letters—will make him or her alluring to those making hiring decisions for years into the future.

Justice Oliver Wendell Holmes, who served on the Court into his nineties, habitually hired recent graduates of Harvard Law School to work as his "secretaries." They all came from Harvard because Holmes did, and because he developed relationships with a succession of professors who channeled promising young men to him. Holmes insisted that his secretaries be unmarried; one who defied the marriage ban was Alger Hiss, later to become one of the most famous Americans of the Cold War, although not for his clerkship. Each young man worked as secretary for one year. After that the fortunate young man would forever be known as Holmes's protégé, making him a seller in the legal market who offered something highly desirable—a type of prestige that firms couldn't obtain from anywhere else.

In Holmes's day, before the construction of the current mausoleum-shaped Supreme Court building (a pet project of William Howard Taft, the only man to serve as both President and Chief Justice), all of the justices worked from their homes. The young law school graduates relieved Holmes of the less-interesting routines of his job, prompting him when he became forgetful, seeing that he got his afternoon nap, and listening to his charming reminiscences.[1]

Over time the other justices became envious of Holmes, or saw the secretary's usefulness as a labor-saving device. By the mid-1920s they were all acquiring secretaries of their own, although at some point the accepted term became "clerk." Since then, Congress has indulged the justices by expanding the Court's budget to add ordinary secretaries—no fewer than three for the Chief Justice—in addition to four clerks for every justice.

The clerks are no longer secretaries but the "Junior Supreme Court," in William O. Douglas's half-mocking phrase.[2] They perform most of the tasks of a judge: they review trial records and briefs, perform legal research, and draft opinions. Many of the words published in the Supreme Court's official compilation of opinions were written by clerks, although no one on the outside can know the exact percentage.

Perhaps most important, the clerks have enormous influence over the cases the Court chooses to hear. Those outside the profession are generally surprised to discover that the Supreme Court acquired complete discretion over its docket in 1988. Since then, the justices have halved their workload, which is pretty much what everyone should have expected. (The opinions have become much longer, another unmistakable sign of indiscipline: it's easy to dump a clerk's sprawling research memo into an opinion.) In *Bush v. Gore,* the controversial decision that resolved the 2000 presidential election, the five justices in the majority wrote of their "unsought responsibility."[3] But that was eyewash. The justices have no responsibilities at all, only desires.

Since 1988, it's been impossible "to appeal all the way to the Supreme Court." You can get your case heard in the Supreme Court only by begging. The begging takes the form of something called a "petition for writ of certiorari"—the name, which conveys nothing at all to the uninitiated, being a typical piece of costume-party obscurantism. A cert petition ("cert" is pronounced exactly like the breath mint) is nothing but a formal request to the Court to hear one's case. Between seven and eight thousand petitions are filed each year, although that number is misleading. The great majority are filed by prisoners, who don't have to pay filing fees. Not all of the prisoners' petitions are frivolous, but enough are that the Court just about never hears any of them. About 2,000 of the petitions are filed by parties flush enough to pay the outrageous filing fee and comply with the Court's ludicrous printing requirements—the petitions must be bound as little paperback books with color-coded covers. Almost all of the 70 to 80 opinions issued by the Court in a given year pertain to one of these 2,000 or so "paid petitions."

The task of wading through the slush pile of petitions for certiorari is delegated to the justices' clerks. They read the petitions and then write memoranda to prepare "their" justices for the weekly conference during which members of the Court gather in secrecy to vote for or against hearing the cases. So far as is publicly known, it takes the affirmative votes of four justices to grant a petition for certiorari. But the justices, always conscious of their mystique, won't officially confirm that.[4]

In theory, the clerks don't decide which cases the Court will hear, but in practice they decide which cases the Court *won't* hear. They make the rough cut, and if your case is one of those roughly cut, the distinction won't seem important to you. Not that you'll ever learn at what stage your case was deemed unworthy—the justices never reveal that secret, either.

The role of clerks takes on added importance in the case of a justice's infirmity. We know of at least two justices—Stephen Field and Joseph McKenna—who became senile while serving on the Supreme Court, probably as a consequence of Alzheimer's disease (although that diagnosis wasn't yet available in their day and wouldn't have been publicized if it were). Salmon P. Chase and Nathan Greer were debilitated by strokes, Charles E. Whittaker suffered from clinical depression, and William H. Rehnquist abused prescription drugs, to the point that his speech was slurred on the bench. William O. Douglas suffered a devastating stroke, the effects of which made it clear to all—except to Douglas himself—that he should resign. Douglas hated the thought of his replacement being named by then-President Gerald Ford, who while serving in Congress once led an effort to impeach him. So the old justice, his body decaying and his mind mostly gone, clung to office, his secretary spraying Lysol behind his wheelchair to mask the smell produced by his incontinence.[5]

Thurgood Marshall, after a lifetime of heroic service, refused to allow his ideological nemesis Ronald Reagan to appoint his successor. As he neared his eightieth birthday, Marshall supposedly told his clerks, "If I die while that man's President, just prop me up and keep on voting."[6] According to some, they more or less did so, except he wasn't quite dead yet. Opinions continued to flow from his office, but none (we're told, perhaps with more maliciousness than truth) was written by the man many consider the greatest American lawyer of the 20th century.[7]

Stories about Marshall's decline were given a public airing by a story in the conservative *National Review,* the cover of which depicted a cartoon Marshall asleep in his judge's chair. The article claimed that justices William Brennan and Harry Blackmun, too, were almost completely dependent on their clerks. By no coincidence, those same three justices were labeled "liberal extremists" by the magazine.[8] It seems certain that the article's source was the group of politically conservative clerks called "the cabal" in Edward Lazarus's account of his own clerkship of the same year.[9] If so, the article must be seen as an artifact of the Court's internal strife that would not have seen the light of day but for the conservative clerks' sense of grievance against Marshall and Brennan, monuments to 1950s liberalism, and Blackmun, author of *Roe v. Wade*. But that doesn't necessarily mean the stories were untrue. If we don't hear similar stories about other justices, it may mean only that a similar corps of ideologically committed law clerks hasn't emerged to tell tales against them in public.

Perhaps all of the justices spend their afternoons watching soap operas on TV, as the *National Review* claimed Marshall did. How would we know? If justices Field and McKenna were on the bench today and suffering from Alzheimer's disease, they could continue serving indefinitely and no one outside the Court would know the difference, so long as they kept quiet during oral argument or asked only questions prepared in advance by their clerks, the way Strom Thurmond continued acting as a senator long after his mind was mostly gone. The flow of opinions from the senile justices' chambers could continue unabated, drafted by a committee of four clerks and two secretaries. For all we know of the Court's inner workings, this may already be an accurate description of the way some of the justices operate.

A danger greater even than Alzheimer's is excessive comfort. The abolition of the right to appeal to the Supreme Court has made the Court an exceedingly comfortable rest home for elderly lawyers. If a justice wants to slack off, the desire can easily be accommodated by reducing the number of opinions and allowing the Junior Court to draft them. The late Chief Justice William Rehnquist was said to work a five-hour day, plus lunch.[10] All the justices take about four months of vacation a year, often jetting off to exotic locales to "teach," all expenses paid. There's no reason for a justice ever to retire, since retirement would be only marginally more restful than work while eliminating the occasional opportunity to exercise decisive political power. As the average age of the justices creeps ever closer to 100, one less-obvious side effect is that the nomination of a new justice, being increasingly rare, becomes a proportionately more significant political event. This dynamic has contributed much to the ferocity of recent confirmation battles.

Given the importance of clerks, and the subtle and not-so-subtle ways they have altered the institution of the Court itself, you might expect the justices to recruit top-notch, experienced lawyers. But you'd be wrong. The justices today pick clerks the way Oliver Wendell Holmes did a century ago. They hire recent graduates of Harvard and Yale who have never practiced law.

In 1998, *USA Today* reporter Tony Mauro wrote a package of stories about Supreme Court clerks that, among other things, revealed that justices Rehnquist, Scalia, Kennedy, Souter, and for that matter, the late liberal icon Brennan, had never hired a single black law clerk.[11] Justice Scalia retaliated, two years later, by writing a letter to Mauro's publisher describing his work as "Mauronic"[12]—wordplay lame enough to suggest that Scalia's writing, when done by Scalia himself, is a step or two down the scale of intellectual sophistication from the work done by his clerks and printed in the official reports under his name.

In the wake of Mauro's articles, leaders of the National Bar Association, an organization of African-American lawyers formed at a time when the American Bar Association didn't admit blacks into its ranks, asked to meet with Chief Justice Rehnquist to discuss the paucity of black clerks. Rehnquist refused, asserting that such a meeting wouldn't "serve any useful purpose," by which he apparently meant useful to himself.[13] (Try to imagine a President or Speaker of the House responding in a similar manner to a similar request.) The chief no doubt hoped the controversy would die down. But half a year later, prodded by individual members of Congress, he was obliged to acknowledge "the underrepresentation of minorities" on the justices' personal staffs, which he attributed to "the demographic makeup" of the pool of law school graduates from which the Court recruits.[14]

In directing attention away from the clerks' lily-whiteness to that of the pool from which they were drawn, Rehnquist only emphasized the irrationality of the clerk selection process. Of the 394 clerks hired by Supreme Court justices from 1971 through 1997, 40 percent came from Harvard and Yale. Two-thirds came from a total of five law schools (those two plus Chicago, Stanford, and Columbia). Fully 85 percent were graduates of one of just ten law schools corresponding slavishly to *U.S. News and World Report*'s top ten. (The second tier consisted of Virginia, Michigan, Berkeley, Northwestern, and Penn.)[15] Rehnquist explained that he chose as clerks only "those who have very strong academic backgrounds."[16] Only students who served on law review need apply. Service on law review, as we've seen, is traditionally based strictly on class ranking.[17] Rehnquist's defense to the charge of lily-whiteness, in sum, was that the Court was helpless to hire anyone but recent top-ranked graduates of the top ten law schools, who tend to look like one another (and, for that matter, like the professors who graded and recommended them).

We can agree that anyone at the top of the Harvard Law School graduating class is smart. So the one positive thing you can say about the Supreme Court's clerk selection process is that it recruits smart people. But no one seriously believes that graduating first from Harvard Law makes you any smarter than graduating second, or for that matter fiftieth. Factors other than sheer brains explain differences in class ranking. Sometimes it's as simple as selecting classes based on a given professor's reputation as an easy grader. Personality factors are also important. The sociologist Karen D. Arnold conducted a groundbreaking study of high school valedictorians, cataloguing the characteristics that set them apart from their classmates. The same characteristics doubtless help high-achieving students win the next decade's paper chase, too. Arnold found, "Over and over again, star students told us they rose to the top partly because they were intelligent, partly because they were schoolwise, and mostly because they worked hard, persisted, and drove to achieve . . . The top students readily identified themselves as 'school smart.' Academic talent, to them, meant the ability to excel at academic learning and school tasks like note taking, memorization, and testing." The valedictorians had a talent for school the way other students had a talent for music or athletics, and they put school at the center of their lives.[18]

Mauro's *USA Today* articles attracted attention to the racial and ethnic uniformity of the Supreme Court's clerks. Easy to overlook is their even greater intellectual uniformity. The clerks tend to be unadventurous, hardworking, and conventional. They are, in Meg Greenfield's Washington taxonomy, Grown-Up Good Children, who live to please.[19] None of the clerks has ever practiced law. At most they've eaten lotuses as summer clerks. But few have much life experience, either, because you don't climb to the top of a hierarchy as competitive as Harvard Law School without the advantage of obsession. Future Supreme Court law clerks spend their law school years reading and memorizing to the near-exclusion of everything else. Having enough money that you don't have to work is essential to a would-be clerk. Just as in Holmes's day, not having a spouse, let alone children, is almost a requirement. (Next best is to be a neglectful spouse and absent parent.) A social life or interest in the arts would only be a distraction.

These are the people to whom Supreme Court justices delegate substantial chunks of their authority—smart, obsessive conformists with an extraordinarily narrow range of interests.

Why do the justices cling to such an irrational, even absurd, personnel system? Perhaps because they're as convention-bound as the clerks whose company they keep. Rehnquist, Stevens, Breyer, and Roberts were Supreme Court clerks themselves, suggesting a laboratory experiment being taken over by the white rats.

The justices *could* hire experienced lawyers who have proved their ability in the actual practice of the profession. Some justices did, before World War II. Today the Court has no trouble attracting experienced professionals to its Supreme Court Fellows program, which offers only the promise of a year filled with administrative tasks of infinitely less interest than the clerks' work. Many first-rate American lawyers would leap at the opportunity to clerk at the Supreme Court, and most legal employers would be happy to grant them a year's leave of absence because they would return from Washington with client-attracting (and judge-intimidating) prestige.

The task of picking cases for the highest court in the land would no longer be entrusted to inexperienced Grown-Up Good Children. First drafts of opinions would be prepared by people with some concept of what the opinion will mean in the real world. But could an experienced and legally sophisticated clerk be counted on to listen adoringly to an elderly justice's reminiscences?

FOR A NEWLY minted lawyer, nothing is greater than being a clerk of the Supreme Court. It is a distinction the clerk will wear like a badge through-out his or (much less frequently) her entire professional career. A former Supreme Court clerk can teach at any law school and get hired at any big law firm, so long as he manages to avoid getting disbarred or arrested. Actual skill in either teaching or practicing law is (as they say in want ads) desirable but not required. The clerk, in short, will spend the rest of his life as a seller of prestige, and buyers will always be willing to line up.

If your ambition is to become a Supreme Court clerk, you would be well advised to go to a law school ranked in the top 5 percent for tuition, though one of three public universities will do in a pinch: Michigan, Virginia, and California-Berkeley. Once you're there, you need to get straight A's, become an editor of the law review, and also assiduously cultivate the professor who has a tradition of "feeding" students to a federal appeals court judge who in turn has a reputation for "feeding" clerks to the Supreme Court. Many years of goal-directed ass-kissing are required, and even then the odds are heavily against you, since there are never more than 36 clerks in a year. But if you win the lottery, the payoff is huge.

On the downside, it means that you reach the peak of your legal career before you begin it. Everything else is downhill for the ex–Supreme Court clerk, unless he goes on to win the next lottery and becomes a justice himself.

The next best thing to being a Supreme Court clerk is to clerk for a federal appeals court judge. Appeals court clerks do the same things as Supreme Court clerks, except for weeding out cert petitions, which means they spend proportionately more energy actually deciding cases. (It would be interesting to know what percentage of the Supreme Court's resources is devoted to the cases the court *doesn't* hear. It wouldn't surprise me to learn that it's more than 50 percent.) Also, at each of the federal appeals courts the clerks are backed up by a vast corps of staff attorneys, who actually do much of the work the judges take credit for. Seventh Circuit judge Richard Posner informed a *New Yorker* profiler that he devoted only about half time to the job.[20]

Appeals courts are relatively anonymous compared to the Supreme Court, and the atmosphere seems to be a tad less stuffily self-important. Dahlia Lithwick, the great legal reporter from *Slate,* has revealed that appellate clerks have been known to play the game of Opinion Bingo, in which "[p]oints are earned for working a randomly selected word from Webster's into any published opinion."[21] The winner gets free pizza and beer.

In 2000, Ninth Circuit judge Ferdinand F. Fernandez put his name to an opinion describing difficulties as "sempiternal" and an argument as "aduncous" before announcing the court's unwillingness to "rely on some resident numen or wait for Fulgora to light our way."[22] Some clerk gorged on pizza the night the opinion was issued.

If you can't land a position with a court as distinguished as the Ninth Circuit, you might still hope for a position with a district court judge. Alternatively you could try a state supreme court or, failing that, a state intermediate appeals court. The work is the same, but the prestige fades quickly.

CHAPTER 8

Crossing the Bar

I SPENT ONE MORE semester at Northwestern after my Fulbright year in Germany, making me that unusual thing, a fourth-year law student. One of the highlights of my final semester was the opportunity to play the role of a witness in a friend's trial practice class. Specifically, I played the role of a recently disbarred attorney. This was in the wake of the Operation Greylord scandal, which exposed widespread, systemized corruption in Chicago's courts. Numerous judges went to jail for taking bribes. One previously acquitted murderer was retried and convicted—something usually forbidden by the Constitution's double-jeopardy clause. The courts concluded reasonably enough that this particular mobster hadn't actually been in jeopardy at his first trial, thanks to his $10,000 investment in his trial judge.[1]

The mock trial took place on a Saturday in a courtroom inside the Daley Center, the one with the Picasso statue. A group of high school students served as jurors for extra credit in their civics class. A real judge presided. I testified on direct examination about the payoffs I'd made to judges. It felt strange to sitting in the witness box beside the judge, describing the bribing of judges. When my friend tried to "impeach" me—attack my credibility—by getting me to admit that I was a crook and a criminal, I slipped in remarks like "to help my clients" and "that's just what you have to do in Chicago." My friend was pretty irritated with my refusal to "just answer the questions," but he later told me that the high school students thought I was the most credible of all the witnesses. Hey, it's Chicago.

When the semester was almost over, the powers that be informed me that I was ineligible for "the Order of the Coif." That's not the award for the top graduate of beautician's school, as the name implies, but an honor society for law students graduating in the top 10 percent of their class. (I'm sure there's an explanation for the name, but discovering what it is runs the risk of spoiling its delightful absurdity.) I was informed that, in order to be eligible, I would have needed to take two more hours of classes. Adding two hours would have been easy to do if the eligibility rules had been made public, or indeed had previously existed. But by the time the news was delivered to me it was far too late to add another two-hour seminar. Similarly, although I had the grades to receive my degree cum laude, I was ineligible for honors because I spent only three semesters in residence in Chicago.

The news was upsetting, because I'd already begun to think about teaching law for a living. Being the only person I knew who had attended three different law schools—and very different law schools, at that—I thought I had some unique insight into the best ways to convey complex information to law students. But to become a professor, I knew, it was important to amass gewgaws like Coif and honors.

I experienced the last-second news of my ineligibility as a pair of parting shots against the transfer student, neatly bookending an experience that began with the Sudoku puzzle of trying to assemble a schedule from the few classes still open to me. So far as the NULS was concerned, I was still a boarder, not a member of the family.

The real issue, I've always suspected, was that I paid tuition for only three semesters of study. That meant I got a Northwestern diploma at half-price, so it seemed fair to the administrators that I got a cut-rate degree.

I see from the website that the law school now charges a flat fee to all students, regardless of the number of semesters they actually attend the school. I'd like to think of that as the Jacobsen rule, but I imagine I wasn't the only one to figure out how to give myself a discount.

I'd received 17 hours of academic credit for my year in Germany, during which I paid no tuition but rather received a stipend from the Fulbright Commission. It was easy to arrange to receive credit for that year because the law school registrar was a wonderful woman. Her motto was "Unlike most bureaucracies, we're more flexible at the bottom," which was true—and something to be proud of.

Shortly after I had returned to my parents' home in December 1985, though, I received a call from Chicago. It was from the registrar. It had to do with the Ethics class I'd taken in my last semester, which was required for graduation. The professor, Stephen Lubet, was consistently entertaining and thought-provoking, though I remember the hooting reaction he got from the students when he tried to tell us that lawyers are more important to society than doctors, because who wants to live, however healthily, in a world without justice? The students pointed out that doctors actually produce health.

Only a handful of students from that class typed their final exams. I was one of them. We did our pounding in a little-used classroom on the third floor. The exam wasn't proctored. Our instructions were to leave the exams, face down, on the desk at the front of the class, and someone from the Registrar's office was to pick them up. But, I was told over the phone, no one did. Our exams were thrown away by the cleaning crew.

I instantly had visions of flying back to Chicago to re-take the Ethics exam, and the registrar told me that was indeed an option. But, if I preferred, I could change my grading option to pass/fail and receive a "pass," and that would be the end of it. I gratefully accepted that option.

A month or so later I received a letter from the professor who ran the Order of the Coif program—a recently arrived female, harbinger of a changing era—pointing out that since I'd made the choice to take the Ethics class on a pass/fail basis, I was even farther from qualifying for the exalted status of Top Beautician, making my protests all the more ridiculous.

THE "BAR" IS a physical object, the railing that divides an American courtroom into two sections. The front is for lawyers. Nonlawyers are allowed past it when they're parties to a legal action or appearing as witnesses. Unless you have some such definite role to play, if you're not a member of the bar you have to stay behind the bar.

In the old days, which weren't so very long ago, a lawyer joined the bar of a particular court by appearing before the local judge upon a sponsoring lawyer's "motion." (A legal motion is just a request, by anybody for anything, addressed to a judge. It can be spoken or written. No one knows why lawyers call them "motions," but that's the *only* term they ever use.) The sponsor would attest to the candidate's legal knowledge and moral character. The judge would conduct an impromptu *viva voce* examination from the bench, more or less perfunctory or searching depending on his personality, his knowledge of the candidate, or his regard for the sponsoring attorney. If the candidate answered the judge's questions satisfactorily, he was admitted to the bar of that court with hearty congratulations and drinks later on.

The system almost certainly worked far better than the current impersonal system, precisely because it *wasn't* impersonal. The real testing was done by the sponsoring lawyer, who had accepted the aspirant as an apprentice, allowing him to "read the law" in his office. The sponsor put his reputation on the line by moving for the candidate's admission.

Local bars weren't necessarily close-knit, but the members knew each other intimately—a significant distinction. Most judges were required to "ride the circuit" from county to county within their districts, traveling many thousands of miles annually to conduct court in far-flung corners of the new republic. The lawyers, naturally, followed the judge. Henry Clay Whitney has left a vivid portrait of riding the state judicial circuit in central Illinois with the young Abraham Lincoln.[2] Twice a year the local judge—in Lincoln and Whitney's time, the rotund future Supreme Court justice David Davis—and a passel of lawyers would travel from town to town together. In this way, the courts came to the communities where judicial services were needed instead of summoning citizens to travel to them in the imperious manner of modern courts.

Because the judge, lawyers, and any out-of-town witnesses all descended upon small county seats together, lodging was chronically at a premium. After holding court together all day, the whole group might end up eating together at a boarding house and then retiring to sleep together, frequently two to a bed and with multiple beds in the same room, a chamber pot in the corner, and the outhouse out back. Today such intimacy is nearly inconceivable (and would be overloaded with sexual undertones), but the alternative to a shared bed was an uninsulated floor in a house without central heating—and choosing that alternative would give one a reputation for excessive fastidiousness, which would instantly become a subject for endless chafing over shared meals and during downtime at the courthouse. So when imagining what it meant to belong to the bar in Illinois in the 19th century, we should think of the long, tall Lincoln in bed with the nearly spherical Davis, each tugging on his side of the quilt.

Originally the federal circuits operated along the same lines but over an even wider geographical range, and Supreme Court justices staffed them, presiding over trials. The sheer unpleasantness of so much travel by horse-drawn conveyance on the muddy lanes of the early United States, in the malarial heat of the South and Arctic cold of New England, had the useful side effect of encouraging justices to retire before reaching the extreme old age characteristic of the modern, cushy Court.[3] All that bracing circuit riding was abolished for Supreme Court justices in the 19th century, and judges of the federal appeals courts were relieved of the duty by 1912. While "circuit" remains part of the name of the 13 federal appellate courts, only vestiges of old-time circuit riding remain. For instance, a panel of the Tenth Circuit Court of Appeals traveled to Santa Fe to hear one of my cases on the beautiful summer day when the Georgia O'Keeffe Museum had its grand opening. In this way, once-onerous circuit-riding duties have become a perk of judicial office, a way to get the federal government to pay for the judges' vacations.

The forced intimacy of the old circuit-riding days meant that an established lawyer wouldn't sponsor an aspirant lightly. Agreeing to take on an apprentice was a responsible task, moving for his admission to the bar was momentous, and the mentor would always feel—and be held—responsible for the protégé.

That kind of literal bar examination—an examination at the bar itself—isn't remotely possible with the modern practice of law, and those of us who appreciate having a bed to ourselves, private bathrooms, and little complimentary bottles of shampoo aren't sorry about it. What we have instead is the modern three-day bar examination, taken in a big room in the company of lots and lots of stressed-out strangers.

The precise format of the bar exam varies from state to state and over time. But almost all states use the Multistate Bar Examination, one of those standardized multiple-choice exams, like the SAT and ACT, where you use a number-2 pencil to fill in the oval on a separate sheet. The exam consists of legal problems and asks the applicant to commit professional malpractice by making an off-the-cuff analysis, taking no more than a minute or two to study and think about a problem that inevitably has many dimensions. The correct answer to every question on the Multistate is "Let me do some research and get back to you," but that's never an option.

Not only is the applicant required to spout off irresponsibly, but he or she is often not given the option to choose the correct answer. The four options typically include two obviously wrong answers and two that are arguably right, but often both of the latter are a little too simplistic to be altogether correct, or a little off-topic. So the applicant has to choose between an answer that's about 75 percent correct and one that's about 65 percent correct. That's a more significant conceptual problem than it might at first seem, because the object of a lawyer's advocacy isn't to be right but to make the best available argument on behalf of the client. For three years we're trained to see all the possible alternative ways of analyzing a problem, and then we're tested on our ability to see only one. The Multistate tests the applicant's ability to function more like a judge than an advocate, but uses that to grade the applicant's capability as an advocate.

On the plus side, the Multistate exam can be graded by machine.

The Multistate I took lasted one day—three hours in the morning, three in the afternoon. As its name implies, it's intended to be valid in all the states and territories, testing broad legal concepts rather than the particular law of the jurisdiction where the applicant wants to practice law. Obviously some knowledge of local law is also desirable, so we were tested on that separately. Nowadays many states have a problem-solving component to their bar exam, but in my day we had only essays. I wrote 15 of them over a day and a half. I think we got 40 minutes for each.

Most law students graduate in May or June, and the bar exam traditionally follows in July, with another administration in February. The July bar exam always attracts a big crowd. But because I finished law school in December, I took the February bar exam instead, which is always a much less crowded affair. Generally the core group of people taking the February bar are those who flunked the July test. Their numbers are topped off with established lawyers just moving into the state, with a sprinkling of weird cases like me on top.

I spent the six weeks leading up to the bar exam taking a "bar review" course, which isn't a guide to the nightspots. Enrollees received a stack of notebook-sized paperbacks outlining the law in numerous subject areas to study. Videotapes of lectures given the previous summer were projected on a screen at the law school. I attended the screenings religiously, just as I had always made a point of attending class in law school on the theory that hearing the material was easier than rereading it. I also figured, rather vaguely, that the brain stores memories of reading and hearing in different places, so getting reinforcement in a different medium provided a backup file in case the first one failed. Hearing the concept explained in different words also gave me two angles on it—a stereoscopic view, with at least the illusion of depth.

The 15 essays were just like law school exams. The applicant had to read a little story raising the maximum number of potential legal issues, figure out what sort of answer it was fishing for, and then write or type that answer, all in 40 minutes. There was no advance warning about what topics would be on the exam, although everyone said it was an absolute certainty that there would be at least one question on community property, the Spanish-inherited system of marital property division found in the four border states and a few others. Community property wasn't anything I'd studied at Northwestern, and studying it without a teacher was strangely unnerving because I received no feedback. If it seemed straightforward and simple, didn't that imply I was missing its subtleties?

The one essay I distinctly remember from the bar exam did, as it happens, involve community property. It presented a little story of a complicated family tree and asked who was entitled to what in the distribution of the great-grandfather's estate. Stuffed to the gills with community property law, I began confidently. Then, after typing two paragraphs, I perceived something I had initially overlooked. So the third paragraph of my answer began: "No, that's wrong," and began again. I could have kicked myself for having wasted so much time. And then I perceived yet another twist, which meant I'd been right the first time. It felt like a disaster: I had analyzed the problem three different ways, which was as good as announcing that I didn't know which way was right. Later when I graded bar exams I came to understand that mine was the best possible answer, because I had seen such a succession of issues. But I stressed about it for the two months that elapsed before receiving word that I'd passed.

Because fewer people took the February exam than the July exam, it was offered only in Santa Fe, the state capital. We were put in the library of the College of Santa Fe, and we typists were in the same large room with the scribblers, which must have been maddening to them. That didn't mean we were free of our own distractions. The library wasn't closed to students, or if it was closed, no one enforced the rule against students wandering about. At one point a young man began searching for a book on the shelf directly behind me. There were only a couple feet of space between the shelf and my chair, and he inserted himself into it. That made the caveman part of my brain start sending signals ("there's a guy sneaking up behind us") that were doubtless adaptive for most of the previous million years of my ancestors' existences but that my frontal lobes found very distracting. It really wasn't an ideal setup.

When I graded exams later, I learned how wasted my angst had been. New Mexico passes about 85 percent of test-takers, and the bottom 15 percent made themselves conspicuous to the graders. One blue-book I opened had nothing written in it but a pathetic little apology: "I'm sorry to have wasted everyone's time." The Board of Bar Examiners told us volunteer graders to give the applicant a point if he or she wrote, "This is a tort question" (although only if it was, at least arguably, a tort question). The bar exam isn't designed to identify the people who would make capable lawyers. It identifies those who would be positively hazardous to the public.

But the bar exam serves another purpose, too. It discourages economic competition. By and large, only lawyers licensed in a particular state can appear on behalf of clients in the courts of that state, which is another way of saying that New Mexico lawyers have a monopoly on the practice of law in New Mexico. So if, say, a large insurance company has to defend a lawsuit in New Mexico, it has to hire a New Mexico lawyer to represent it. Sometimes the New Mexico lawyer is "local counsel"—a beard. Local counsel get paid for doing nothing but signing pleadings prepared by out-of-town lawyers and then seeing they get filed in the right court. Providing that service can be worth thousands of dollars.

Obviously the big insurance companies and other out-of-staters would eliminate the middlemen if they could. To prevent that, New Mexico (unlike some other states) doesn't allow experienced lawyers to "waive in" to the bar. Even if you've practiced for 30 years without a single malpractice complaint or "bar bitch" (disciplinary complaint) filed against you, you still can't practice in our state unless you're prepared to lose three days to the bar exam and undergo the stress of preparation before and worry afterward, not to mention risk the potential humiliation of failure. And did we mention that the fee is $800? Think carefully whether you really want to do it. Perhaps it would be easier just to hire one of us to be your local counsel.

PART THREE

Baby Lawyer

That's the term lawyers use to describe someone just out of law school. It's not insulting, exactly. Just belittling.

CHAPTER 9

Roll dem Bones

THE GERMAN LAW graduate, who spends three years rotating through the stations of the practicum, learns something of what the actual practice of law is like. She gets some idea of the variety of practices and—equally important to her future happiness—the different atmospheres in different workplaces. Career decisions are made after playing the field. American law graduates get married on blind dates.

Law schools today emphasize trial practice and "clinical" courses, meaning courses in which the student gets credit for prosecuting or defending petty misdemeanors under the eye of an instructor, helping low-income clients draft their wills, springing violent offenders from prison, or performing similar public services. (Somewhat ironically, from my point of view, Northwestern advertises itself as a leader in clinical courses, although as a transfer student I was effectively forbidden to participate in any of them. The limited number of slots were filled long before I showed up.) But while such courses are a welcome acknowledgment that law schools are primarily vocational institutions, they're far too limited to give the student any idea of the variety of practices available in the wider world.

Students whose parents are lawyers, or who have a mentor who isn't trying to recruit them, might be able to sketch a rough map of the legal landscape, but their view is unlikely to be much more encompassing than that of a Dutch cartographer standing on a dike. The most sophisticated and knowledgeable lawyer will have no clue what lawyers working in far distant fields do. A patent lawyer will have no clue how a bankruptcy practitioner fills his days, and neither has the foggiest about habeas corpus.

Moreover, students fortunate enough to have a source of factual information acquire with it a set of hand-me-down attitudes, usually without any means of distinguishing between the two. In some fields, such as torts and criminal law, attorneys tend to look on their adversaries as members of a different species, the way Cro-Magnons must have regarded Neanderthals. A student might think she's getting the inside dope when all she's really learning is that the lawyers who enter certain fields have surrendered some significant portion of their humanity.

Law schools can tell the student what areas of the law are interesting to study, but not which ones are interesting to practice. For example, I studied antitrust law with Professor James Rahl and found it fascinating, leading me to think I might enjoy practicing it, a fate I was spared by the Reagan administration's ideological opposition to antitrust enforcement. Not only did the administration cease bringing enforcement actions, but it appointed judges who dismissed any lawsuit that smacked of business regulation, so even private antitrust suits became nearly impossible to maintain. That spared me the fate of digging tunnels through mountains of business records. Professor Rahl was a great teacher, but if he ever explained just how tedious "paper cases" are to litigate, I must have missed the class.

It's not just that law school doesn't teach what it's like to practice in various areas. Even more important, from the student's point of view, it can't begin to explain the differences between employers. The differences are nearly impossible for the student or recent graduate to perceive. All law firms seem the same when you interview. Their offices are all laid out according to the same basic plan, except that some are bigger, and some firms spend money on expensive interior decorators who work hard to make the law firm look like every other law firm except more obviously worked over by an expensive interior decorator. When interviewing students, lawyers all say exactly the same things about a balance between work and life and a collegial atmosphere and high level of professionalism and commitment to the community, and on and on. But 20 law firms will differ from one another as dramatically as 20 families. And, you know, some families are dysfunctional. Some law firms are bad places to work, and many are a good deal worse than that.

A friend of mine was hired as a secretary at a law firm for $35,000. When her first paycheck arrived, it was for a sum that worked out to an annual salary of $30,000. When she inquired, the managing partner told her that she would be paid $30,000 during her three-month probationary period, after which she would start to receive the promised salary. Three months came and went and her salary wasn't adjusted. The managing partner said he'd never promised her $35,000, and was she calling him a liar? (Why, yes.)

A lawyer friend took a job with a different firm. The starting salary was quite low but he was assured that the firm had a tradition of generous Christmas bonuses, often equaling the associate's entire yearly salary though they weren't, strictly speaking, guaranteed. Christmas came and, alas, the firm's profits had taken a hit and there would be no bonus that year. By talking with those who had previously left the firm he learned that there had never been any bonuses in any year, ever. It was just a ruse to get associates to work for a year at a below-market salary.

In every legal community there are lawyers with reputations. "Everybody knows" that if you can't avoid a phone conversation with one of these lawyers, you need to send out an immediate letter documenting the conversation. Often it will cross in the mail with a letter from him, misrepresenting everything that was said. From time to time these lawyers take on associates to teach them the ropes. You always wonder whether the associates have any idea what they're learning.

A firm can be a snake pit while its lawyers observe the profession's rules of ethics scrupulously. Another friend went to work for a firm that had grown rapidly during the past several decades. One of the founding partners was still around and, with the air of an old master passing on the wisdom of the tribe, shared with my friend a "war story" (as lawyers call their anecdotes about the practice). Once, many years before, he had represented an insurance company against a woman who'd been catastrophically injured. Among other injuries for which she was seeking compensation were psychological problems requiring long-term treatment. The senior partner, telling his tale with self-congratulatory relish, explained how he made a low-ball settlement offer of just a couple thousand dollars, which the woman's attorney indignantly refused. The case was easily worth $100,000, as the senior partner well knew. He then arranged to depose the woman—that is, question her under oath with a court reporter taking down every word, just as at a trial, except in a private office with no judge or jury present. He scheduled the deposition to begin at 10:30 A.M. He had a particular reason for choosing that time. For 90 minutes he questioned the injured woman about her psychological condition, asking superficially appropriate questions but loading his voice with all the considerable hostility and scorn he was capable of assuming. His every question insinuated that if she wasn't outright faking, she was a contemptible weakling. Repeatedly he brought her to tears. Then came lunch. When the senior partner returned to the conference room at 1:00, only the woman's attorney was there, looking grim. He said she would now accept the low-ball settlement offer rather than prolong the ordeal. And that's how he settled a $100,000 case for $2,000! Let that be a lesson to you, young'un!

My friend did, in fact, learn from the master—he quit as soon as he could line up another job. But plenty of other associates have stayed over the years, and that firm still enjoys a reputation for what I'm sure its partners would call "aggressiveness"—needless unpleasantness that may intimidate a few but inspires others to dig in their heels.

Unless they have a relative or friend in the practice, new lawyers have no way of knowing what "everybody knows" about the firms that offer them employment. The greatest value of a practicum would be the opportunity to hear the gossip. Instead, the traditional method by which young lawyers make their way in the American legal profession is trial and error. Law graduates sort themselves out on the once bitten, twice shy principle.

IN 1983 JAMES B. STEWART published *The Partners: Inside America's Most Powerful Law Firms,* which explained with devastating clarity the pyramidal structure of the big law firms of the day. The main difference today is that the biggest firms are much bigger. As Stewart explained, a group of, say, 100 partners sits at the top of the pyramid, with 300 or more associates below them. The associates are paid a flat salary. The partners draw a much larger salary and also share profits. All of the associates are brought on board with the promise that if they work hard enough, they can become partners after seven or so years. But out of a cohort of 30 law school graduates hired in a given year, no more than one or two ever actually "make" partner. The rest are fired if they don't leave quietly. The partners let the associates know that their chance to make partner depends on how many hours they bill to clients, making "billable hours" a competition among the associates.

The billable hour is the defining feature of an associate's life at a big firm. A person who works a 40-hour week, with two weeks' vacation and the equivalent of another two weeks in holidays (the United States recognizes ten federal holidays a year), will put in 1,920 hours at the job during the course of a year. Of course, it's not possible for any lawyer to bill every hour of the day to a client—there are firm meetings to attend, continuing education credits that must be accrued to keep one's license, bills to prepare, job-seekers to interview, extramarital affairs to conduct, and so on. All told, a lawyer who works a relatively normal workday at constant peak efficiency, without ever getting sick or going to the gym or having to take time off to deal with an injury or emergency, can hope to bill a maximum of about 1,800 hours per year.

Many of the biggest firms demand far in excess of 2,000 hours per year, sometimes as much as 2,400 hours—16 months of work per calendar year. There are only two ways for the associates to make quotas like that: (a) work insanely hard, and (b) defraud their clients, for instance by "double-billing" (charging two clients for the same hours) or simply inflating the number of hours worked. There are many stories of lawyers billing more than 24 hours of their time in a single day.

Most of the big law firms require their associates to do both (a) and (b). Naturally, only the first is talked about openly, although "bragged" is perhaps the better term. There are strong echoes of Marine Corps macho in the way big-firm lawyers talk about their days as associates. (One old-timer said to me, "After awhile, they start to believe they really worked that much.") Those few associates who successfully climb over the corpses of their colleagues to the upper courses of the pyramid naturally feel they've earned the rewards of their superior merit, and since they had to go through it they can't see any reason for exempting the next generation of associates from the abuse.

I remember once reading about a secretary's lawsuit against her employer, a big New York law firm. As I recall, she was seeking redress for the injury she received when an associate threw a telephone at her. What I found even more remarkable than the phone-chucking was the time of day the incident occurred: 11:00 P.M.

One might question how much value a new associate, just out of law school, can provide to a client in need of legal services—particularly when the new associate is so punch-drunk that flinging telephones becomes an option. One might also question whether multiplying an hour of inexperience by 2,400 can actually produce a significant fraction of a million dollars in value for *anyone*. The answer is: of course it can. It produces great value for the partners.

The new associates are paid outrageously high starting salaries because they're expected to bring in at least three times as much revenue. One-third stays with them. Another third goes to pay "overhead" (which includes not just rent and secretarial services but funding for the partners' retirement plans, their insurance, the leases on their luxury cars, expenses for their continuing education seminars in Aruba or Vail, and so on). The final third is free money for the partners. *That's* why the dangled partnership is such a lure for so many associates. They keep telling themselves: I only have to make partner and I'll be set for life!

The pyramidal structure also offers the partners something less tangible than money but nearly as valuable. As Louis Auchincloss has memorably dramatized, the years-long process of winnowing the associates down to the chosen one or two gives the partners plenty of opportunity to ensure that only People Like Us make it into the club. Graduating from Yale Law might have gotten you a position as an associate at a high-prestige firm, but to make partner you need to be a true Yalie. For years, the best advice to an upwardly mobile young associate fresh out of law school was choose your parents for their networking skills; prep at Andover, Exeter, or Hotchkiss; and get selected for one of the better eating clubs at Princeton. Things have loosened up some, but that remains useful advice for the wannabe big-firm partner.

What does the client obtain in return for paying millions of dollars in legal fees to such firms? In theory, the client gets the legal services of the great wizards of the profession. Few clients are in a position to know whether their lawyers are actually any good at their jobs. And no firm, no matter how expensive, can guarantee success. What the law firms can offer, though, is the next-best-thing to a guarantee: prestige. It used to be said that nobody ever got fired for buying IBM. Big Blue was such a safe choice that even if the computer system failed catastrophically, the corporate officer in charge of making the purchase would be safe from blame. The big law firms promote themselves as the legal world's IBMs. They're very conscious about their image: the suits, the décor, the letterhead, the much-publicized starting salaries for associates (we hire only the best!)—everything is directed toward the goal of projecting prestige. Prestige shields the corporate counsel from blame if the big firm loses the case. From the counsel's point of view, it's easily worth millions of dollars of the company's funds to buy that peace of mind.

The big firms' aura of omni-competence isn't entirely an illusion. The partners at the biggest firms are frequently very good at what they do, even if not necessarily any better than thousands of others working in less pretentious digs. Even more important, however, the big firms can crush opponents with their weight. They're sumo wrestlers. As I was writing this chapter, a news story appeared about 2,500-lawyer Jones Day. (For ages it was Jones, Day, Reavis & Pogue, but a few years back, branding consultants started a fad among the big firms to lose the commas and chop off all but the first two names.) A small website devoted to high-end real estate transactions included links to the websites of the buyers' and sellers' employers. Jones Day sued, claiming the weblinks infringed its trademark. The legal theory sounds laughable to me, but the judge in Jones Day's hometown of Cleveland evidently was able to keep a straight face, denying a motion to dismiss. The owner of the website told a reporter he spent $100,000 in legal fees before caving, complaining, "They had no shot at winning, but they were going to bleed us dry." [1]

The biggest law firms have more than 3,000 lawyers. The richest have annual gross revenue of more than $2 billion, according to *American Lawyer*. They can throw infinite resources at any legal problem, making them the bullies on the block. They can Do What It Takes. As a corporation, wouldn't you rather have them on your side than your opponent's?

IN THE LEGAL WORLD, the big firms are prestigious for two primary reasons. First, they've always been prestigious. Second, the big firms pay well. If you practice law with the goal of receiving a big paycheck every two weeks, there can be no better place to practice.

Associates' starting salaries are public information, since the big firms use them as fishing lures. But it was only in the 1980s that *American Lawyer* began publishing annual charts revealing estimated profits per lawyer at the 100 biggest firms. The firms initially responded with great harumphing indignation—that's never been done! But soon they realized the annual *Am Law* 100 was a new arena in which to compete in public for the attention of prospective clients. Gross revenue and profits per partner are objective measures of prestige. Besides, letting everyone in the profession know you're bringing home a cool million per year is emotionally even more satisfying than bringing it home.

Today, just as when Stewart wrote *The Partners,* the secret of the big firms' financial success is the pyramidal structure. According to *National Law Journal,* in 2008 Skadden Arps (which sounds like one of the Orkney Isles, or a particularly nasty croup you might catch there if you don't get out of the rain) had 1,994 lawyers but only 440 equity partners to share the profits, a ratio of 4.5 to 1. Gross revenue per lawyer topped $1 million. Latham & Watkins had 2,074 lawyers and 305 equity partners, for a ratio of 6.8 to 1 and gross revenue per lawyer of $915,000. White & Case had 2,074 lawyers, 305 equity partners (6.8 to 1), and $705,000 per lawyer. And so on through hundreds of successively smaller big firms.[2] (In New Mexico and other less populated states the "big" firms have fewer than 100 lawyers, but lots of big-firm attitude.) The ratios of lawyers to equity partners tell you that the big firms chew up their associates and spit them out, while the revenue per lawyer gives some hint of how much money the partners skim off the associates' work. Paying an associate $140,000 to bring in half a million is an excellent deal for the equity partners.

Why do young lawyers join these firms? Don't they understand that the promise of future partnership is a cynical ruse, and that their lives are going to be made miserable by relentless exploitation, as they're required to work around the clock for no higher purpose than to extract the maximum amount of money out of the client?

Sure, they know that. The sophisticated associates understand they have no realistic chance of making partner, but that's okay because they have no aspiration to it. They join the big firms with the intention to stay only a few years—just long enough to buy a nice townhouse and a nice car and to pay down their student loans. The first two items seem significant to someone finally finishing school at age 25, but the last is particularly important. Without a big trust fund, it's more or less impossible to graduate from law school debt-free. If you work your butt off at a big firm for, say, three years, you can pay down your student loans, maybe even pay them off. Then you can quit, getting your life under control again. For these sophisticated associates, work at the big firms is a kind of indentured servitude. Just as poor immigrants of the 17th century contracted to work a set number of years in America in return for paid passage across the ocean, some associates endure life (or whatever the correct term is) at a 3,000-lawyer firm for a certain number of years in order to afford law school. For them, big firms provide a metaphorical passage across the water from the continent of nonlawyers.

But many other law graduates fall into the prestige trap. They believe they'll be the exception to the rule. They really expect to make partner. They succeed in fooling themselves because they're so dazzled by the big firms' prestige.

There have been numerous social science studies of law students, who collectively make a fascinating subject. One 2004 study found that students who received high grades in their first semester (as I did) "evidenced significant shifts towards high-stress, money-oriented legal career preferences, and significant shifts away from more service-oriented career preferences." Translated, this means they internally reoriented themselves toward the pursuit of "image-based values"—prestige.[3]

There are a number of mutually reinforcing reasons for that, I think. The hierarchies within hierarchies encourage the top-ranked students at the top-ranked schools to think of themselves as the best, which in turn makes them aspire to the best jobs available. The big firms recruit from only the top ranks of the law schools, offering admission into an exclusive club. In addition, those who do well in law school generally have a long history of receiving approval for their academic accomplishments. For many, that's been their main source of feelings of self-worth. They're competitive. Landing the most prestigious / highest-paid (they mean the same) job on offer is one more competition won.

And then, perhaps—like me—they drifted into law school with no very clear career goal in mind, providing no counter-pull against the tug of conventional career expectations. Or, as expressed by the authors of a 2007 study, "the motivation-dampening effects of law school" replace students' internal motivation with an external set of yardsticks by which to measure success.[4] Those with the weakest internal motivations naturally find it hardest to resist. When students accept external measures of success—those "image-based values"—predictable things happen, many of them involving alcohol, divorce, clinical depression, and suicide, all of which lawyers experience two or three times as frequently as nonlawyers.

As I mentioned, I accepted the first summer clerkship offer I received. I received an offer of employment from the firm while I was living in Germany. By that time I was involved with Carla (that fateful cup of tea at Heathrow!), which made starting my career in my hometown seem like a far better idea than it had seemed when I transferred to Northwestern. I knew that by New Mexico standards there could be no more prestigious place to start a career, and no higher starting salary on offer. The decision to accept didn't feel random, but that's only because there was never a single moment quite as dramatic as the dice hitting the table.

∞

CHAPTER 10

The Prestige Trap

I HAVE MANY FRIENDS at my old firm and don't want to hurt their feelings. And the whole point of this chapter is to describe experiences that are typical of big-firm life, as seen from a new associate's perspective, rather than what was unique about the particular place I ended up. For both those reasons I'm using a pseudonym. In New Mexico the custom is to refer to firms by only one name, like Cher. Jones, Day, Reavis & Pogue, for instance, would be "the Jones firm," although "the Pogues" is a much cooler name.

For no reason beyond the pleasant associations of too much Guinness and belligerently off-key singing, I'll call my first full-time legal employer "the Pogue firm." One of the things I quickly discovered, although it took me some time to acquire the perspective to perceive it, is that big firms have some of the qualities of total institutions. That's a term coined by the sociologist Erving Goffman, referring specifically to asylums (which is where seriously mentally ill people were kept before more enlightened policy put them on the street). Subsequent researchers have expanded the concept to describe many other, less sinister environments, such as cruise ships, which program every moment of their passengers' lives, making every key decision for them, though always very nicely and with complimentary food. Gangs share many of the features of total institutions, although they generally occupy no physical structure at all.

Law firms share some of those qualities, too. They become part of their lawyers' identities, competing with their marriages. Even before I began work, during the period I was studying for the bar, I was told, as if it were a positive thing, that the wife of one of the firm's star litigators sometimes brought dinner to the office so they could enjoy family time together in the break room. That shook me a little. (Years later Carla was talking to the wife of this litigator, an intelligent and friendly woman, who described problems she was having with their teenage son: "He needed a father when he was growing up, and let's face it, he didn't have one." They divorced soon after.)

In the broader legal community we were known collectively as "Pogue lawyers." We sometimes described ourselves that way. "Loyalty to the firm" was talked up as a cardinal virtue. We had monthly firm dinners, annual firm photographs, even firm retreats to various resorts. (I made the Phoenix one but missed San Diego due to a conflict with the birth of our first child.) We dressed alike. The dress code wasn't enforced because it didn't need to be. The male lawyers hung their suit coats on the hooks behind their office doors in the morning and walked around with collars buttoned to the neck and conservative ties. (Funny ties were permitted at Christmas, and loud ties were welcomed as occasional sources of comical comment.) All of the offices were squares of exactly the same size (which I liked for its egalitarian symbolism, although the more powerful partners had the corners and the best mountain views), and we all had identical Danish modern desks and credenzas. The potted plants were all rented from the same supplier, who had exclusive charge of the watering.

We saw ourselves atop the hierarchy of New Mexico law firms, the best in the state. While two or three other firms probably thought the same of themselves, there wasn't much doubt that the three or four of us were the closest the state had to "full-service" firms, with lawyers on staff capable of handling with skill almost any type of legal problem. (The one area we never touched was criminal law.) We were also at the top of the heap with regard to the starting salaries paid our associates. That doesn't mean our senior lawyers were the richest in the state—not by a long shot. The really big money was to be made on the other side, doing plaintiff's work, suing doctors and manufacturers. We were the ones who defended the doctors and manufacturers. That meant we didn't make the big score, but the money was steady.

Just as law schools are ranked in strict hierarchy by *U.S. News and World Report,* and law firms are ranked in strict hierarchy by the *Am Law* 100 list, the law firms themselves are strictly hierarchical. In the biggest of the big firms, some partners are more equal than others. Even among equity partners status will be carefully calibrated, with "name partners" (those whose names are on the door), senior partners, and junior partners. There will be a CEO (called the managing director at the Pogue firm), followed in rank by the members of the executive committee and the heads of departments or practice groups. The behemoth firms now have "non-equity partners" (f/k/a permanent associates), lawyers who remain permanently on salary rather than competing with associates for the chance to make partner. They are definitely second-class. Beneath the junior partners in the pyramid are the senior associates, the survivors of previous culls who teeter on the brink of a partnership decision. Then there are the run-of-the-mill associates, usually ranked (for purposes of salary and bonus) by years out of law school, and then the baby lawyers. Below them are the staff attorneys (you'll hear more about them in chapter 12), followed by the nonlawyers. Tops among the nonlawyers are the administrators, and below them is the support staff itself, in strict hierarchy: librarians, IT, accountants, paralegals, secretaries, and at the bottom the only truly indispensable people: the runners, the mail-room guys, and others who keep the place functioning on a day-to-day basis. At each level of the hierarchy, salaries faithfully reflect status.

Cases are usually staffed by a team of lawyers, typically including a senior partner, sometimes a junior partner, a senior associate, and a junior associate. All their names will appear on every court document, always listed in that order. At trial, one lawyer will be first-chair, the others assisting. On appeal, the associate will write the brief but the partner will argue it before the appellate court, whose members will seat themselves according to seniority, with the chief in the center and the most senior judge to his or her right. Always, wherever you look in the legal world, hierarchy is replicated like fractals.

A quarter-century ago the Harvard professor Duncan Kennedy wrote a famous paper titled "Legal Education and the Reproduction of Hierarchy" (it exists in various versions with slightly different titles). Everybody took Kennedy's challenge to hierarchy seriously because he was a Harvard Law professor, reinforcing the hierarchy with cross-braces of irony.

As a baby lawyer, I was given dreadful cases "for the experience." These were, I think, accepted by the firm as favors to the clients. For instance, one of the partners, whom I'll call Arrowsmith, did real-estate work for a client who built and managed large apartment buildings (before declaring bankruptcy and fleeing town). In my first months of practice I was given the task of evicting tenants from one of the client's properties. It wasn't a slum by any means, but neither was it a luxury condominium, and most tenants didn't show up for the eviction hearings. As soon as they received the notice to quit, they skipped. When they didn't appear, little more was involved than telling the judge what dollar figures to enter in the judgments. We might easily do 20 or 30 evictions in an hour.

The hearings were conducted in our small claims court, officially known as Metropolitan Court but universally known as Metro Court, according to the old joke, because it was run like a subway. At the time the court was housed in a six-story structure next to the jail. Although the building was relatively new, it was falling apart. The elevators were completely inadequate for the traffic. Prisoners in orange jumpsuits and leg shackles shuffled with their deputies into already crowded cars.

The lobby, with its cashier's windows for paying fines, was frequently as crowded as a subway station at rush hour. To avoid the long, chaotic lines through security, I took the view that as a lawyer wearing the uniform of my profession—a suit, with briefcase in hand—I didn't need to stop, and the security guards never disagreed. Nowadays they would taser me. (In the early 2000s the court built itself a new and much grander courthouse, the construction facilitated by kickbacks to the president pro tem of the state senate, a lawyer who's now in prison.)

Unfortunately, not all the evictions were uncontested. From time to time tenants would show up. One man brought in Polaroid pictures of the washers in the laundry room, saying that he withheld rent to force the landlord to replace broken machines. He said he had even more photographs at home. The judge told him he could stop by the courthouse sometime to show him those photographs. It is unethical for a judge to have ex parte contact with a party—communications in the absence of the other party. I said I would be happy to be present whenever the judge viewed the photographs. The judge looked at me sharply and said, "That won't be necessary." He found in our favor, so I guess he was just humoring the tenant. But it was a lesson that Metro Court isn't a real court.

On another occasion a young man and his wife showed up and explained that he had been hospitalized with a condition that had impaired his hearing, and they didn't have insurance, and they had to leave the children with relatives in Española with a little money to pay for groceries, and they were armed with every sort of documentation to prove it. But they hadn't paid their rent, and I didn't have the authority to forgive the debt. Or myself.

One day my supervisor, the head of the commercial litigation department, told me Arrowsmith was complaining about the way I'd screwed up the evictions, enraging the client. I had no idea what it was all about. It turned out that my contact person at the apartment complex, some sort of assistant manager, had failed to pass along information to me, with the result that some nonpaying tenants weren't evicted. When confronted by his boss, he lied, claiming to have done all the paperwork and delivered it to me. Arrowsmith accepted the little weasel's story without first talking to me. Instead she went straight to my supervisor. Although I didn't see it in this light at the time, the episode was a lesson about the one-way flow of loyalty between firm and associate. Arrowsmith's only interest was with maintaining her value to the firm by ensuring the flow of fees from her client. She had no interest in the new associate doing her dirty work to keep her client happy. As Casper Gutman said in *The Maltese Falcon,* "If you lose an associate it's possible to get another."

The first real trial I did was on behalf of a small-time developer of a shopping center who had entered into a lease with a tenant, making all the tenant improvements requested. At the last second, though, the tenant decided not to go through with the deal. We sued to recover the cost of the tenant improvements and rent until a new tenant was located. The tenant countersued, contending that our client had broken the lease first in some way or another. We tried the case to a judge without a jury. I thought the very short trial, just a few hours long, went well. All the evidence I offered was admitted, and all my objections were upheld. Later I was to learn that those were warning signs: it meant the judge had already decided against me and was trying to keep me from having any issues to appeal. When the judge eventually issued his ruling a month or two later, he declared that there had been no contract at all, even though both parties had sued each other for breaking it.

The ruling was both dishonest and ridiculous.[1] When I was complaining about it to one of the partners, she asked who my judge was. I told her and she said, "Oh, well, he always rules against Pogue lawyers the first time they appear in his court." And when I told her who my opposing counsel had been, she said, "You never had a chance. He always rules for the good ol' boys."

What was illuminating about that conversation wasn't what it revealed about the judge—I already had a pretty good idea about him—but the casualness with which judicial dishonesty was accepted in the New Mexico legal culture. I've long thought the state's motto should be "Because that's the way we've always done it."

I'm sure that by sticking it to the young snots from the big firms this baby boomer judge made himself feel like some kind of anti-Establishment rebel, even as his position, which gave him the power he used to reinforce the old-boy network, made him the Establishment personified. But then, when you're a judge, it's easy to have it both ways, so long as you confine your social circle to people who want something from you. They can be counted on to pretend not to notice.

While I did those little cases "for the experience," most of my time was spent being second- or third-chair on much bigger cases. I was assigned to what was called the commercial litigation department, which is to say business litigation. Most of the cases involved companies suing other companies for many millions of dollars. The powers-that-be considered me particularly well suited for that kind of work because it required a great deal of research and writing. It was largely what lawyers sometimes call a "motions practice" (one of those phrases that has several distinct meanings). Motions flew back and forth between the parties, but the cases always settled before trial. The "litigation" in "commercial litigation" didn't mean trying cases, but engaging in a type of highly formalized negotiation. It resembled car shopping more than it did *Perry Mason*.

If our client was the defendant, our job was to reduce the risk by narrowing down the issues and, if possible, to expose the plaintiff to commensurate risk by filing a countersuit. If our client was the plaintiff, roles were reversed. Most of the time it didn't matter on which side of the "vs." our client's name was listed. The litigation involved months of skirmishing about discovery (more on that anon) capped with motions to dismiss and for summary judgment—that is, judgment without trial. Often the motions would be granted in part and denied in part, narrowing the scope of the dispute to a few core issues.

Once both sides perceived the same core issues, a settlement could usually be reached.

Because these were disputes between companies about money, there was relatively little emotion involved. The lawyers generally didn't identify all that closely with their clients—we could just as easily have represented the other side. It wasn't good versus evil, which meant that evil never triumphed. In fact, it was rare for *anyone* to triumph. Everybody compromised. We would work the case, then enter settlement negotiations, and the case would go away.

There are real advantages to working in a morally neutral field of law. There's little to get upset about, other than obnoxious opposing counsel and bad judges—the irreducible minimum of irritants in every lawyer's life. There was never anything to brood about. But it also meant there was little to care about.

From time to time I had the opportunity to work on cases involving reporters for the evening paper, the now-defunct *Albuquerque Tribune,* and a TV news program. I loved the first-amendment work, which gave me lots to care about, and the reporters were terrific clients. Best of all, the parent companies perceived every case as a matter of principle and were prepared to spend what it took to win. In the media business, you can't become a patsy or you'll never stop paying out. One case settled for the plaintiff's out-of-pocket costs, which were trivial. The attorney failed to ask for a confidentiality clause in the settlement agreement. The morning paper, the *Albuquerque Journal,* was always eager to report on the TV stations and a reporter asked me how much the case was settled for. The next day the paper quoted me. The figure was around $8,000, a risibly small amount after two or three years of litigation, including an appeal. That sent out a message to others. The libel suits dried up, which was great for the clients but meant I had to devote more of my time to the contentless business litigation.

I took two weeks off for my honeymoon and was told (gently—it wasn't a dressing-down) that I needed to do a better job of clearing off my desk before going away so long, and should also make a point of checking in regularly with the office. I wasn't permitted to be off the leash.

A minimum of 150 billable hours was registered every month, and I tried to stay comfortably above the minimum. I worked many evenings and on about half of the weekends. In some ways, working on the weekend was pleasant. I could wear jeans, and there was a sense of camaraderie with the other associates in their jeans. The only distractions were our chatting, but since the other associates were all good company the distractions were welcome. We also socialized some away from the office, going out for lunch or for drinks in the evening.

I was working with a group of people I liked. I was paid well. In my first years of practice I got to handle some of my own cases, and while they were all unpleasant and one was a disaster, I was learning the ropes. Most of my time was spent on complex litigation work that was, in a legal sense, relatively sophisticated. I was beginning to acquire some confidence in my abilities. What was there to complain about?

And yet the sensation I first experienced in the Arizona Biltmore kept recurring. I felt as though I was living someone else's life. People pulled back from the brink of death sometimes describe out-of-body experiences. This was the opposite—an inside-the-body experience, in which I found myself filling up a body that somehow wasn't me. And it was becoming a chronic condition, not a déjà vu–like episode. I kept trying to talk myself into being happy: where are you going to find a better job? But when my best friends from college visited me at the office, I felt like the world's biggest phony in my necktie. I was clumsy and tongue-tied around the people who really knew me.

By the fall of 1989 I was involved in a logjam of significant suits, working for different partners, all of whom wanted me to make their case my highest priority. Many months I billed more than 200 hours.

At home, Carla was pregnant. In the first trimester she'd suffered dreadfully from morning sickness—all-day sickness, really—but now we were approaching term. For months I'd been slipping out of the office at odd hours during the day to attend appointments with the obstetrician. In the last weeks of the pregnancy the doctor announced he would be leaving on his first vacation in years, but not to worry, as another experienced OB would be on call.

The other OB was a horror. He was an old guy who shuffled in and out, mumbling. He never talked to either of us. We arrived at the hospital around 11:00 P.M. At first the labor proceeded quickly, but then everything stopped because the baby was turned "sunny side up." It wasn't until 10:30 the following morning, after four agonizing hours of pushing, that the OB mentioned, in his mumbly offhand way, that he could easily turn the baby's head with a suction, "but then it wouldn't be a natural childbirth."

No one had said anything about a natural childbirth until that very moment. I have no idea where the old bastard got the idea that we had gone to this ultramodern hospital to have a natural childbirth. He had let Carla suffer for hours based on an inexplicable assumption. He turned the baby's head and Alexander was born almost immediately, coming out as blue as the Microsoft welcome screen with the cord around his neck.

When I first held him, an hour or two later, I was dressed in a sterile gown, a sterile paper cap covering my hair. I gave him his first bath in the pediatric intensive care unit. He was fine, though. Much more than fine. Carla was a wreck.

I took a week off from work. A week! To this day I'm ashamed to admit how thoroughly the firm had come to dominate my identity. I felt the obligation to bill, and tallied well over the requisite 150 hours during the first month of Alex's life—one of the truly unforgivable acts of my life.

I finished the year with 2,100 hours, which works out to 14 months of work in the calendar year. The revenue I brought into the firm was roughly four times my salary. And the firm denied me a year-end bonus.

I didn't get the bonus received by all the other associates because I'd angered one of the partners by attending a court hearing in another partner's case rather than spending time on his case. I found out about his anger only at second hand, because he never once intimated the least unhappiness to me. His message, although indirectly delivered, came through loud and clear: he was on top and I wasn't.

The withheld bonus broke the spell of loyalty to the firm, for which today I'm grateful. I had never noticed how tightly enclosed I was in a booth of tinted glass until the glass shattered, when suddenly I could see that there was no shortage of better jobs out there. My problem, I finally realized, was that I had so passively accepted the firm's definition of what a "better" job would be—it would be exactly like a job at the Pogue firm, only more so. Northwestern, conveyor belt to La Salle Street, had primed me to accept that "best" and "most prestigious" were synonyms. Now I could let myself realize that another job would be better precisely to the extent that it was unlike working at a prestigious firm.

CHAPTER 11

Impersonating a Lawyer

A LL YOUNG LAWYERS are haunted by the feeling that they're only impersonating a lawyer and someone is going to find out. The first time I found myself saying to a judge, "I move the admission of Exhibit 1," I felt ridiculous, as if I were reciting a line from a B movie, as indeed I was.

At least law school and the movies had taught me the line. Unfortunately, neither had showed me how to "manage clients"—the slightly supercilious term lawyers use to describe the complex dance steps necessary to keep clients happy while reducing their expectations to the reasonable and dissuading them from foolishness. Clients don't always want to be managed. Once I was given the task of advising mid-level bank officials about options for repossessing equipment after the borrower's default. I began, in what I thought was a jocular manner, by saying, "Well, we have three legal options and one illegal one." I explained the three. Then one of the officials said, perfectly seriously, "Tell us the other alternative."

I'd already been in the practice for a couple of years before I finally received some concrete practical advice about communicating with clients. A wise partner told me that I should always make a point of underestimating the chance of success. That way, if you fail, the client understands you did the best you could against daunting odds. And if you win, you look like a genius.

It was frequently difficult to avoid the feeling that everyone else was in the know while I was only faking it. I remember feeling that way during my clerkship summer as I sat in on a deposition involving a table full of lawyers. Before getting started, the plaintiff's lawyer said, "The usual stipulations, counsel?" and everyone murmured assent. I had no idea what that meant, but figured that was only because I was a student with lots to learn. Twenty-five years have passed and I still have no idea.

Lawyers use jargon all the time, but like any slang it's not that difficult to learn once you become attuned to it. Some of what sounds like jargon to nonlawyers isn't, really. It's just a shorthand way of describing things with long or awkward names, the way English majors refer to Joyce's first novel as *Portrait* rather than *A Portrait of the Artist as a Young Man*. Cases, for example, are usually known by one party's name. Sometimes when lawyers are chatting, someone will say something like, "And then there's *Jenkins*. Boy, talk about a trap for the unwary!" Listening, you might experience a momentary comprehension lag. Obviously, you're expected to know what *Jenkins* was all about, which makes it probable that you do, even if you can't bring it to mind. So you might listen for a bit to see whether context gives you a clue, but if it doesn't, it's already too late to admit you've been smiling and nodding while drawing a complete blank. Besides, part of being a lawyer is knowing the law, which makes it embarrassing to admit you don't. (I've since learned how to request the missing information without admitting ignorance. I say, "What's *Jenkins* again? I can never remember case names." And sometimes I really do remember the case, once I'm reminded.)

I learned a lesson about faking it the first time I argued a case in the New Mexico Supreme Court. I was extremely nervous. A lot of it was just anxiety about the unknown. For example, I knew the Supreme Court building had no parking garage, or even parking lot, and parking was always at a premium in central Santa Fe. So where do I park? Inside the courtroom, at which table am I supposed to sit? Do I speak into a microphone or do I have to project into a reverberating hall? Will the justices interrupt with a barrage of questions, requiring quickness on my feet? Or will they let me talk uninterruptedly, providing an opportunity for Daniel Webster oratory? What if they ask *this?* How was I to answer *that?* The particular case involved a failed bank taken over by the federal government with numerous claimants, and you didn't have to take very many steps in any direction to find yourself in a wilderness of banking law, or insurance law, or federal statutes with 127 subparts, or bankruptcy law, or ... What am I supposed to do if they ask a question and I don't know the answer?

Worse than that, what if they ask me a question to which I know the answer but forget it because I'm so nervous? That last thought *really* made me nervous.

It was in this revved-up state that I found my way into the Supreme Court courtroom. My opposing counsel wasn't much older than myself, which indicates that our partners didn't think there was much money riding on the case—otherwise they would have done the argument themselves. He was first to the podium. As he spoke I was seated at counsel's table a little behind him and to his side, and I could see his hands visibly shaking. Big shakes. Drop-the-pencil shakes. He was croaking as if his mouth was dry and the words were sticking to his tongue. And suddenly I felt a whole lot calmer.

The calming effect wasn't *schadenfreude.* It didn't make me happy to discover he was even more nervous than I was. He was a nice guy and a far better lawyer than the justices had any reason to suspect from his performance. I felt sorry for him, not in the superior sense of pity but with strong fellow-feeling: he was just like me. *That* was the comforting realization.

Years later I came across a passage in Ulysses S. Grant's memoirs that describes a similar, if far more serious and vivid, moment of insight. In one of his first Civil War commands he was sent out to find Confederate colonel Thomas Harris, said to be encamped with his troops 25 miles distant. The march, through rural Missouri, was eerie.

They rode past deserted house after deserted house, not encountering a soul. Then, in the afternoon, they spied two horsemen in the distance. "As soon as they saw us they decamped as fast as their horses could carry them." Grant and his troops set up tents overnight and in the morning approached the showdown:

> Harris had been encamped in a creek bottom for the sake of being near water. The hills on either side of the creek extend to a considerable height, possibly more than a hundred feet. As we approached the brow of the hill from which it was expected we could see Harris' camp, and possibly find his men ready formed to meet us, my heart kept getting higher and higher until it felt to me as though it was in my throat. I would have given anything then to have been back in Illinois, but I had not the moral courage to halt and consider what to do; I kept right on. When we reached a point from which the valley below was in full view I halted. The place where Harris had been encamped a few days before was still there and the marks of a recent encampment were plainly visible, but the troops were gone. My heart resumed its place. It occurred to me at once that Harris had been as much afraid of me as I had been of him. This was a view of the question I had never taken before; but it was one I never forgot afterwards. From that event to the close of the war, I never experienced trepidation upon confronting an enemy, though I always felt more or less anxiety. I never forgot that he had as much reason to fear my forces as I had his. The lesson was valuable.

My situation wasn't remotely the same, of course, and not only because nothing particularly serious was in the balance. My opposing counsel didn't fear *me,* but the court, or rather the unfamiliar experience before the court that awaited him. And yet the reassurance I experienced was almost exactly the same. It was the reassurance of suddenly seeing the situation from the opponent's point of view. It turned out not to be true that everybody other than me knew exactly what to do.

That was the moment I stopped worrying about being exposed as an impostor.

CHAPTER 12

Discovering Discovery

O N MY VERY first day of work at my new firm, I was sent out to oversee a "document production." Anyone who knew what that phrase meant would have been sick with disappointment. I was mildly intrigued. The partner who gave me the assignment apologized for springing it on me without warning but said that the associate regularly assigned to the case was doing depositions out of state and they were up against a crunch caused by a court deadline. He explained that my task was simple: I just needed to review the files before turning them over to the other side. "Just pull out the documents that are privileged or otherwise nondiscoverable. Err on the side of withholding. We can always turn them over later, but we can't pull them back; you know what I mean?" Um, sort of.

He drove me over to a half-finished office building on the other side of downtown. The fourth floor was an empty shell, a concrete-floored rectangle around the smaller rectangle of the toilets and elevator shaft. No interior walls had been installed yet. You could see from one end to the other, but there wasn't much point in looking as the space was the same from any angle.

At one end of the rectangle was our team, three female paralegals, one of whom I half-recognized from my summer stint a year and a half before. They sat on folding chairs amid a pile of 50 or so banker's boxes. The partner introduced us and left us on our own.

At the other end of the building was the other team, a group of young people, some of them younger than I was, clustered around a much smaller group of boxes. They acknowledged me with appraising stares. They were all dressed in student-type clothing, so I wasn't sure whether any of them were lawyers.

Disconcertingly, our paralegals were deferential. They were well schooled in the old-school formality of Pogue firm hierarchy and treated me as someone higher up in the ranks—as a lawyer. But each of them knew infinitely more about what we were doing than I did. From time to time one of them would bring a document over for my opinion. Each time I had the anxious feeling that she was teasing me, stringing me along, testing to see just how pompous I would turn out to be. But nothing in any of their faces suggested malicious intent. I dealt with their questions by thinking out loud with them, hoping that I might hit on buzzwords that would tell them how to proceed.

I also vaguely wondered whether I was supposed to be a supervisor. If so, what were they doing that needed to be supervised? The firm was extremely clear about status, but I hadn't had occasion before to notice that responsibility wasn't always so clearly defined. By personality I'm not a supervising type. But was I expected to assume a different personality?

Our client was the successor in interest to a failed financial institution that, in the spirit of the mortgage guaranty agencies Fannie Mae and Freddie Mac, I'll call Connie Game. This was the era of the first Bush administration, and we were in the midst of the first Bush banking crisis, the one that eliminated the savings and loan industry. Connie Game had grown quickly from nothing to a giant, its name in big illuminated letters on a couple of prominent buildings around town. Then it went bust, embarrassing a lot of politically connected people who had become somehow connected to it. It was a state-regulated institution, but its affairs entwined it with numerous federal banks, federal regulatory agencies, insurance companies, and creditors, all of which mobbed the company's carcass like seagulls and crabs attracted to a beached whale.

Naturally enough, the investors, who had been happy with the dividends as the stock rose, wanted their principal back now that the stock was delisted. The document production in the unfinished office building I was nominally overseeing had to do with one of the investor suits.

The paralegals had Bates-stamped every piece of paper in those 50 or so boxes as well as in the boxes that had already migrated to the other side. (If you don't know what Bates stamping is, consider yourself lucky. It means stamping a unique six-digit number on each page, using a little hand-held self-inking stamp with six revolving 0–9 wheels that automatically advance with each impression made.) My task was to look through every piece of paper in those 50 or so boxes and mark with paper clips and Post-it notes the privileged and "undiscoverable" ones. When I was done with a box, I would push it over to one of the paralegals, who would remove the flagged page or pages and carefully note the Bates stamp numbers memorializing the removal with a pre-printed piece of colored paper. After the flagged pages were removed, the boxes would be delivered to the surly team on the other side, who would look through them and decide what documents to copy in order to support their claims against Connie Game's management.

I understood in a theoretical way all of the recognized evidentiary privileges—they were on the bar exam—but I'd never tried to apply the abstract definitions to documents that hadn't been prepared by a law professor for the sole purpose of testing my knowledge. And, come to think of it, what did "undiscoverable" mean, anyway? I should have asked the partner on the way over, but he was so friendly and chatty and breezy that I was lulled into the impression that I had only to listen to learn what to do. Besides, I didn't know enough to know what questions to ask.

I spent several days in that unfinished office building, going through financial files, never becoming entirely clear on what to look for but remembering the partner's advice to err on the side of withholding. I evolved a fairly expansive definition of "undiscoverable." For instance, I repeatedly came across minutes of "board meetings" conducted by telephone, in which the board unanimously approved large loans to one of their number. All of the directors, it seemed, borrowed huge sums of cash from Connie Game. According to the minutes, there was never any discussion of the advisability of these loans, or of collateral, or repayment schedules. It was almost as if no one had any intention of ever repaying them.

Maybe that's the way all banks operate, but I thought I detected the cordite smell of a smoking gun. Actually, a whole lot of smoking guns. A smoking arsenal. I flagged those documents because I was spooked by the thought of becoming the new associate who, in his first week of work, condemned the client to defeat in a multimillion-dollar lawsuit because he didn't understand a concept as simple and self-explanatory as "undiscoverable." ("Can you believe it? He turned over the minutes of board meetings that documented the directors in the very act of violating their fiduciary responsibilities!") Before long I was pulling out anything that confirmed what a sleazy business Connie Game had run. If the partner determined the documents were discoverable, after all, he could turn them over. Let it be on his head.

Which, I suppose, was the same attitude the paralegals were showing when they asked my legal advice. They weren't under the delusion that I had any idea what I was doing. But when they came across a decision that had to be made, and that potentially could have unpleasant consequences for the client, they made sure it would have no unpleasant consequences for themselves. They insulated themselves from blame by deferring to a person who secretly wondered if they were making fun of him by asking his advice. Working on the lower courses of a hierarchical pyramid has its advantages, too.

My involvement in the Connie Game case ended quickly, when the older associate assigned to the case returned to town. That was my introduction to discovery. Discovery was to be most of my professional life for my first four years in the profession.

A couple of years later I was on the other side of a big document production. It was a natural resources case involving lots of wells and many leases and something like a 30-year business relationship. We had requested the production of documents in various relatively narrow categories specified by our forensic accountant. My assignment was to locate and copy the documents he needed. I went to the office of the opposing party and was ushered into a conference room filled with dozens upon dozens of boxes and stacks of individual files. That's a common strategy, deliberately over-responding to a request for production by distributing the needles among many haystacks. I could have asked for copies of everything, but that would have cost a fantastic amount of money at a dollar a page or whatever the maximum permitted by the judge might be. So I sat down to paw through the boxes, reflecting that if I possessed the ability to identify which documents a forensic accountant would consider important I'd be a forensic accountant myself. I'm quite sure the days I spent in that conference room were entirely wasted, except in the sense that I made sure our client was billed for every hour of futility, including those I spent stewing about the fiasco—I mean, brainstorming about alternative strategies for completing the document production—back at the motel room.

DOCUMENT PRODUCTIONS HAVE been revolutionized by the computer and the rise of "e-discovery." Now they're even more boring. Before, we only had to worry about paper cuts, dust allergies, and the occasional spider. Now associates have to worry about carpal tunnel syndrome and repetitive stress injuries. In 2009, Covington & Burling, whose name always makes me think of railroads but is actually a firm of some 700 lawyers with offices on three continents, was sued by a former employee who'd been passed over for a permanent position. The plaintiff, Yolanda Young, an African-American lawyer, had been given a right-to-sue letter by the Equal Employment Opportunity Commission.

Ms. Young had worked at Covington as something called a "staff attorney." The firm acknowledged that she hadn't been offered permanent employment as an associate but explained that was inherent in the very nature of being a staff attorney, whose position in the hierarchy is below that of associates. When staff attorneys are hired, the firm told the EEOC, they are clearly informed "that a staff attorney's primary job function consists almost entirely of online document review."[1]

Those are words to put an icy grip on any lawyer's heart. They mean 60 hours a week of staring at electronic files, disclosed email messages, and scanned copies of paper documents, all of them pertaining to something in which you have absolutely no interest. That's modern discovery. And, as Ms. Young discovered, it provides very little job security. Supposedly, Covington fired a bunch of staff attorneys, then hired some of them back. The implication seems to be that they returned. Why would a smart person with a law degree do that to him- or herself?

A hint is provided by Ms. Young's complaint, which reports that her 2006 year-end bonus was only $5,000, down $4,000 from the previous year. Her annual salary at the time she was fired was $130,000. That was in 2007, when the median household income in the United States was $50,233. According to the Census Bureau, earning more than $100,000 that year put a person in the top quintile of American earners. So while Ms. Young's salary didn't make her rich, she was getting close.[2]

Adjusted for inflation and cost of living (Ms. Young worked in D.C.), Ms. Young's salary was nearly 25 percent more than I earned in my second year at the Pogue firm. But at least I got out of the office now and then.

IT WASN'T THAT long ago that civil lawsuits were decided by trial. That's now rare. Most civil suits are settled before trial. On the Web, the most commonly cited figure is that 97 percent of all civil cases settle. The precision of that figure strikes me as suspect, but it corresponds with my experience. For four years I worked on big business litigation cases and not one of them went to trial. Businesspeople manage risks, but trials are unmanageably risky. It would be unbusinesslike to try a case that can be settled on reasonable terms.

Lawyer directories now recognize a specialty in "bet-the-company litigation," a term that tells you just how great the risk can be. A sensible businessperson will pay a great deal of money to avoid it.

Discovery is the phase of litigation during which the parties figure out how much a case is "worth"—the appropriate settlement figure. It's a period of pretrial jousting that allows the parties to sound out the other side, calculating their odds of prevailing at trial and estimating the consequences of losing. By multiplying the estimated odds of victory against the projected dollar range of a verdict, the lawyers can come up with a ballpark figure for a settlement. Discovery, in practical terms, is a highly stylized form of negotiation. It's kabuki negotiation, in which the lawyers put on masks and make stereotyped gestures.

Document productions are only one form of discovery. Because they're so incredibly tedious, they're generally relegated to associates or, as Ms. Young discovered, the new lowest level of attorneys, the staffers. Yet because documents are potentially so important—a single indiscreet memo callously calculating the cost–benefit ratio of modifying a product to kill fewer children can destroy the opponent—the associate must maintain concentration through all the tedium. It's a deadly combination.

Another much-used form of discovery is written "interrogatories"—written questions that the opposing party must answer under oath in writing. In the old days—the 1970s—lawyers used to cream each other with thousands of interrogatories. Judges tried to stop the abuse by limiting the number of interrogatories to a set number, upon which lawyers began sending out the set number of interrogatories, each with dozens of lettered subparts. So the Federal Rules now limit parties to "no more than 25 written interrogatories, including all discrete subparts," inviting lawyers to send out lengthy interrogatories that aren't explicitly subdivided. ("It may be a subpart, your honor, but it's not discrete, and that's the critical point under the rule.")

Although interrogatories are nominally addressed to the opposing party, they're invariably both written and answered by associates. Young lawyers spend a ridiculous amount of time drafting them, attempting to achieve loophole-free prose. That's not easy—in fact, it's not even possible, but impossibility hasn't stopped generations of associates from billing millennia in the attempt. Once interrogatories are sent out, an associate on the other side receives the assignment of drafting answers that provide the minimum amount of pertinent information consistent with a superficial show of candor. That's not so easy, either. You might not really misinterpret the question or discern any ambiguities, but you have to devote some thought to figuring out a way by which you might plausibly *pretend* to have done so. Interrogatories are, in short, an opportunity for associates to bill many hours devoted to the task of avoiding the exchange of information.

By far the most important form of discovery is the "deposition," a term that has nothing to do with rivers silting or kings getting assassinated. Probably the term originally referred to the "deposit" of transcripts with the court, a practice that has long since been eliminated. (What court would want them?) The term is still in use for no other reason than that it's been in use for a long time, which for lawyers is reason enough.

Depositions are the taking of witness testimony. In format, they're almost identical to the courtroom examination of witnesses during trial, except that depositions take place in private. Depositions usually occur in the offices of lawyers or court reporters, or in hotel conference rooms. The witness is sworn to tell the truth, and a court reporter transcribes every word. But there's no judge or jury. Depositions are *almost* identical in format to court room examinations, but the difference is huge. Inside the courtroom, lawyers' questions must be relevant to the legal issues raised by the case. That's to avoid wasting the jurors' and, especially, the judge's time. But once the judge and jurors are out of the picture, that consideration is removed. Accordingly, a lawyer conducting a deposition is permitted to ask irrelevant questions, and good lawyers won't hesitate to do so—who knows what might come up? Depositions can, and frequently do, last for days.

Depositions are trials without courtroom, judge, or jury—and without verdict. They're trials without end, or rather with only the arbitrary end imposed by a "discovery deadline" established by the judge.

Another function of discovery is to give the parties something to file motions about. If one party thinks the responses it received to its document requests, interrogatories, or deposition questions were excessively evasive, it files a motion to compel discovery. If the party thinks the other side's requests, et cetera, are too broad, it files a motion for protective order. Regardless of how the matter is presented, judges are strongly inclined to "split the baby"—rather more like Shlomo in Joseph Heller's *God Knows,* who was really ready to cut the baby with a sword, than the King Solomon of legendary wisdom. So usually the parties have to go through a supplementary or substitute round of discovery in response to the judge's orders, which opens up the possibility for a second round of motions.

In this way, discovery means that instead of going to court to resolve the parties' dispute at trial, as in the old days, lawyers go to court to resolve their *own* disputes in a series of pretrial hearings. Discovery has grown into a way to deal with a big legal dispute by surrounding it with lots of little ones, all of which must be addressed first. It's like sending out dozens of tugboats to guide an ocean liner into port, then requiring the liner to wait in the bay as all the tugs are docked.

Modern discovery dates only from 1938, when the Federal Rules of Civil Procedure were sprung on an unsuspecting nation. All the states have since adopted their own variations on the federal rules, typically by order of the state's supreme court, the governing body of each state's legal profession. The members of each court naturally see litigation from a lawyer's perspective, given that they're lawyers themselves. The rules they approve inevitably benefit the profession.

In 1938, every town had its own movie palace, where projectionists expertly turned a succession of individual reels of film into something the audience experienced as a continuous show. The trials of 1938 were similar, in a way. Although comprised of numerous distinct components, a trial was a single entity: it started, then went on for a certain length of time, and then it was over. The federal rules effectively divide a trial into its separate components, so that, for instance, witness testimony is no longer taken in crisp succession as witness follows witness to the stand, but is instead taken in random order over the course of months as private depositions. Instead of making closing arguments to the jury, lawyers make arguments in the form of motions to dismiss and for summary judgment, sometimes many of them in a single case, all of them addressed to the judge alone. The discovery revolution requires each reel of the trial to be projected separately, vastly increasing the number of hours attorneys can bill their clients.

On the rare occasions when a business lawsuit is actually tried to a jury, the witnesses are expected to repeat what they said in their earlier depositions. A civil trial is a recapitulation of discovery in front of a jury. The lawyers will have the deposition transcripts handy, either in bound hard-copy form or loaded onto a laptop, in either medium meticulously indexed by some paralegal. Often cross-examination is deliberately designed to get the witness to say something different from what he or she said at deposition—the difference doesn't need to be much—so the lawyer can pounce (well, lawyers think of it as pouncing, though it wouldn't remind anyone else of a hungry jaguar, or even a playful kitten): "Do you recall being deposed in this matter on such-and-such a date? Do you recall being asked this question? Do you recall what your answer was at that time?" Then, on redirect examination, the first lawyer will go over the same material, giving the witness the opportunity to explain why the supposed discrepancy means nothing. It doesn't take long until the jurors are kept awake only by the urge to scream.

PART FOUR

Practice Makes...?

Variations on a theme.

CHAPTER 13

A Taxonomy of Bad Judges

THE JUDGE WHO presided over my first trial was bad. He was dishonest and malicious in the way he defended the good ol' boy network against snotty upstarts, but he wasn't uniquely bad. He wasn't even out of the ordinary. As in everything else he's ever done with his life, he was mediocre—just a run-of-the-mill, everyday sort of bad judge. The classic form of his type of badness is called "hometowning"—a judge favoring a local lawyer or client by sticking it to the outsider. But, as I learned, geography is only one source of the hometowning impulse.

The hometowning judge is common as dirt, and he's only one variety of bad judge. There are many others. It's entirely predictable that young lawyers will encounter every variety, but law schools don't prepare their students for any of them.

THE LUSH

IT WAS WIDELY known that you could always find one of our since-deceased federal judges at a certain downtown bar every lunch hour. This judge was also said to have acquired the habit of sniffing frequently even in the absence of other symptoms of a cold or hay fever. That last remained mere malicious rumor about him. But it was proved beyond a reasonable doubt about the presiding judge of the state district court when he pled guilty to cocaine possession. The papers reported that he was one of four state district judges widely rumored to use cocaine. The perplexing thing for most lawyers in town is that when we compared our lists of candidates, we inevitably came up with the names of the same *five* judges.

The rate of alcoholism and substance abuse in lawyers as a group is roughly twice that of the population as a whole, and I've long suspected that social isolation pushes the numbers even higher among judges. It must be disconcerting the first time a new judge enters a gathering of lawyers and they all fall silent. Old pals will start calling him "judge" even in the most casual conversation, as if that had become his name.

Alcoholic judges are *normal.* In every sizeable city in the country, there's at least one judge in whose courtroom the lawyers make a point of scheduling important witnesses for the morning, before the judge starts drinking his lunch.

THE CLICHÉ MASTER

IT'S A DISILLUSIONING moment in every baby lawyer's life when he or she realizes that the judge assigned to a case is ... intellectually torpid. Probably there are relatively few judges with IQs more than one standard deviation below 100, though I'm confident there are some. The mental deficiencies of judges usually reveals itselves in ways that wouldn't qualify them for special education.

For instance, I was once called "disingenuous" in a published opinion from the Tenth Circuit Court of Appeals in Denver. "Disingenuous," a word that doesn't exist in ordinary conversation, is a way to call someone a liar without directly commenting on his or her motives. It's a classic lawyer's insult, much loved by judges (members of the Tenth Circuit, a small court, have used it more than 190 times, according to the legal database Westlaw), because no lawyer will willingly admit to being its opposite, ingenuous.

The argument I made to the Tenth Circuit wasn't disingenuous in the least. It was straightforward and logically irrefutable. The state court had required the prosecution to prove four things, while federal constitutional law required proof of only the first three. I pointed out that proving four things is, axiomatically, more demanding than proving three things, so the criminal would hardly complain. The judge seemed to believe I was saying that item #4 could substitute for one of the first three. Charitably, perhaps his clerk was playing Opinion Bingo, and "disingenuous" just happened to be the random word chosen. But I suspect the judge genuinely misunderstood my argument, not because it was difficult but because he didn't have a readymade response to it. I think that when the judge read my brief, he mentally lined up its arguments with the responses he already knew, and then in his opinion provided those responses without further regard to what I had actually written. By translating thought into cliché in that way, he successfully avoided having to engage in any mental effort at all.

THE LAZYBONES

ONCE WHEN I asked a prosecutor why a judge had dismissed a case on the morning of trial for a transparently inadequate reason, she told me it had been the morning of the first really gorgeous day of spring. The judge was known to be an avid golfer. Need she say more?

I worked on another case in which the trial judge dismissed a murder prosecution because he thought police had been mean to the person who was the source of the only fingerprints found on the rifle that sent a bullet through the brain of a sleeping man. The judge had no legal basis to dismiss the case, but for whatever reason he had become emotionally committed to the defense cause. I got the dismissal reversed on appeal. The case returned to the trial court, but when the prosecutor asked the judge to recuse himself, the judge refused, claiming loftily that he could be impartial. When the prosecutor told me about the judge's refusal to step aside, I started to commiserate. But he cut me off. "It's not a problem," he said. "I'll just tell him it's going to be a two-week trial. That's too much work for him."

I thought he was joking, but the stratagem worked. The judge withdrew from the case as soon as he learned he would be expected to devote that much time to it.

Judges can control their own workload, and some of them do.

THE BULLY

FEDERAL DISTRICT JUDGE Samuel Kent of Galveston pled guilty to a federal crime—obstructing justice, fittingly enough—in 2009. But he had spent years before that deserving to be removed from the bench. The *Houston Chronicle*'s legal blogger Mary Flood once referred to Judge Kent's "national reputation for training his biting wit on lawyers." For a judge to train "biting wit" on lawyers who appear in front of him is very similar to a prison guard exercising his knack for hilarious practical jokes on the job, with this difference: the guard has power only over the prisoner, while the judge holds the lawyer's clients hostage.

A judge can be "bitingly witty" at the expense of lawyers for one reason and one reason only: because he possesses the power to hurt the lawyers and their clients for years or decades to come, if the lawyer should respond with anything but "heh heh." Judge Kent's national reputation wasn't for "biting wit" but for sadistically abusing his power. In his plea for a lenient sentence, ex-Judge Kent revealed he was under psychiatric treatment. I don't know what the diagnosis was—whatever his lawyer thought would be most useful at sentencing, I imagine—but it's obvious he suffered from a serious mental illness. It's sometimes called Black Robe disease, or the Napoleon complex. Kent, it is said, liked to think he was always the smartest lawyer in the room. Lawyers who practiced in his court learned that they could flatter him by pretending to share his self-appraisal, becoming calculating toadies like Lord Copper's aides in Evelyn Waugh's *Scoop*. Kent perceived their playacting as the real thing, as an acknowledgment of his intellectual superiority. In that way, the lawyers' contemptuous manipulations fed the delusional judge's megalomania.

The majority of judges maintain a grip on reality. But I'm sorry to say the only thing unique about Kent's story is that he got so badly out of control that he was prosecuted for a felony.

THE RETIREE

A PRACTICING LAWYER will regularly come across judges who have retired without vacating their seats. I've found myself actually *hoping* that a particular judge didn't read a particular opinion before he signed it. It was either that or he had forgotten what little law he ever knew, because it read like a first draft from a clerk just out of law school.

Being a judge becomes such an important part of some judges' identities that they can't stand the thought of giving it up. It's what makes them special. Hanging up the robe would tumble them back to the insecure place from which they began their ascent.

But while retired-in-place judges are reluctant to give up the fawning of lawyers—they adore being adored—they've been doing the work so long that nothing is new. The technical side of cases is just boring. So they have their clerks and the staff attorneys decide the cases and write the opinions.

The necessary shove can only come from the judge's colleagues on the bench, but naturally they're reluctant to do to another what they would hate to have done to themselves.

THE FEDERAL MAGISTRATE

FEDERAL MAGISTRATES POPULATE a special category of judges retired in place. Their job title was originally "commissioner," but then it was upgraded to "magistrate." A few years ago it was upgraded again to "magistrate judge," apparently to fight the lingering impression that they're not real judges, though no one actually calls them "magistrate judge" except in formal court filings or when addressing them to their faces. The changing nomenclature reflects the amorphous nature of their jobs. Some of them—in my experience, roughly half—are conscientious, capable, and intelligent judges. But the other half are pretty much useless.

There's a good reason why federal magistrates tend to cluster around the two poles of great and no skill. It has to do both with the nature of the job and with the way they're selected for it. The real federal trial judges, the ones theoretically nominated by the President and approved by the Senate (though in practice they're nominated by the senators themselves, who out of self-interest won't vote into office any nominee opposed by the senators of the judge's state), choose their own magistrates, who then act as their assistants. The district judges enjoy what amounts to life tenure, but the magistrates are appointed for eight-year terms.

The magistrate's job is to do all the tasks that a district judge finds boring or undignified. That means magistrates mediate in discovery disputes, listening to civil lawyers whine about each other. They preside over petty misdemeanor cases from military bases, Indian reservations, and national forests and parks. They arraign the more serious federal defendants, which means reciting a script. And they get to make recommendations to their district judges about how to dispose of habeas corpus petitions by state and federal prisoners, a high percentage of which are handwritten and, once you decipher the handwriting, incoherent.

So a magistrate's caseload is full of the dull and the routine. That's a negative, but it also means the job isn't very demanding. On top of that, it pays handsomely, even outrageously. In New Mexico, magistrates get nearly half as much again as a member of the state supreme court. That makes it a financial step up from far more interesting judgeships in the state system, which makes it an attractive option for those sitting state judges who already qualify for their state pension but wouldn't mind qualifying for another, or who like money more than intellectual stimulation. Older lawyers in private practice who are emotionally done with lawyering similarly find a magistrate's position a comfortable way to transition into retirement.

The federal district judges, who skew old, appoint friends to magistrate positions. That means that magistrates are typically respectable older lights of the bar, who might be forgiven for having an unwarrantedly high opinion of their legal abilities. Sometimes that shades over into a belief that there's not much worth knowing about the practice of law that they don't already know.

In short, the chief characteristic of the retired-in-place magistrate judge is pompous self-regard in the service of a trivial and even somewhat demeaning position as a real judge's caddy. Not every magistrate meets this description, but those that do conform to type as rigorously as characters in an old French farce.

Unfortunately, the comical become dangerous when entrusted with even a little bit of power. A little bit is all magistrates get, but it's enough to make the bad ones dangerous. When confronted with legal concepts they don't understand—such as the fantastically convoluted procedural rules governing federal habeas corpus, the only body of legal procedure designed to *prevent* judges from ruling on the merits of cases—retired-in-place magistrates feel resentful about receiving instructions from the lawyers. Instruction suggests they need it, an implication that grows in offensiveness in proportion to its truth. Bad magistrates daily prove the adage that arrogance is just ignorance with an attitude.

The incompetence of magistrates is supposed to be corrected by district judges, who in theory review every magistrate's ruling. But the district judges are the magistrates' sponsors. They respond defensively to any suggestion that their protégés have no clue what they're doing. After all, if the magistrate's an idiot, what would that say about the judge who personally selected him or her?

The amazing thing is that despite all these lavish inducements to intellectual sloth, a good half of federal magistrates exert themselves to do a good job. Some even succeed.

THE DITHERER

DURING TRIALS, LAWYERS frequently "approach the bench"—walk up to the judge's desk—for what is variously called a bench conference or sidebar. Almost always the lawyers are arguing about whether the jury should be permitted to hear certain evidence.

Decisive judges will rule one time and remember their ruling, and get testy if a lawyer brings the matter up again, at least absent a significant change in circumstances. But not all judges are decisive. Some dither. Lawyer A says one thing, and the judge agrees. Then, at the next bench conference, lawyer B says the opposite thing, and the judge agrees. Then, at the next bench conference, lawyer A repeats her original argument, and the judge goes back to his or her initial ruling. Timing becomes crucial—whether the evidence is admitted or not depends on the last lawyer to reach the judge before the moment of its introduction.

A judge's sole job is to make decisions, and so ditherers can drive you frantic if you expect professional competence from them. On the other hand, if you approach the trial as an opportunity to sharpen your skills in judge management, the experience can be rewarding.

THE OLD FOOL

A WOMAN I worked with for many years told me a story from her law school days in the 1970s. She and her female colleagues were joining a profession that wasn't just male-dominated but very nearly all-male. As late as 1970, only 5 percent of the nation's lawyers were women. The local women's bar association organized a special seminar for UNM's female law students to discuss glass ceilings, sexism, gender stereotypes, and so on. Speaker after speaker emphasized that the students would be subjecting themselves to the power of a legal establishment whose leading members almost without exception were male. One talk had to do with dressing for success. A certain law student, whom we'll call Vivian, asked the speaker, "Is it useful to wear low-necked blouses, so when you approach the bench the judge can get an eyeful?"

I don't know how the seminar speaker answered the question, but I know how Vivian answered it for herself. I've seen her in court, swinging her hips, flipping her hair. Another female lawyer I know described watching Vivian in court with an older judge—a retired man, back on the bench "pro tem" to fill a temporary vacancy—who, according to my informant, "almost literally drooled. Whatever Vivian wanted, Vivian got. She kept flirting and he kept eating it up. He was *cackling*."

The two women who told me these stories both resented Vivian as a cynical throwback, someone who decided she was big-bosomed enough to make sexism her friend. "The thing is," one of them said, "she doesn't need it. She's plenty smart enough." But it worked for her. She made herself one of the most prominent female lawyers in the state by being the anti-feminist, taking care to ensure she *wasn't* accepted on the same terms as her male colleagues. She gave establishment males a way to prove their enlightened attitude toward women in the profession without the inconvenience of actually having to develop one.

It worked for Vivian's clients, and you can't argue with success. But what of the elderly male judges, sitting up there on their benches, peering down at the lawyers arrayed before him for bench conferences, and then peering a little farther down? Do they really believe that Vivian finds them attractive? Or do they derive sexual pleasure from the pathetic fantasy even while recognizing it as such, as with a porno webcam? Whatever the explanation, New Mexico's judges have repeatedly shown it's unquestionably true—there's no fool like an old fool.

THE CONTROL FREAK

IN 1998, A KANSAS CITY, Kansas, man named Earl E. O'Connor shot and killed his wife, Jean, then turned the gun on himself. O'Connor's friends portrayed his murder of his wife as an act of euthanasia, reporting that Jean, ten years his junior, was "seriously ill," although the *Kansas City Star* could describe the illness only rather vaguely as "painful neurological problems." The paper added that she also suffered from diabetes and "had had several bouts of pneumonia," which are certainly matters to be taken seriously but not normally considered grounds for a mercy killing. Much more to the point, it would seem, the paper also reported that Earl was being treated for depression.[1]

The reason Jean O'Connor's health was considered news is that her killer was a federal district judge. He had overseen the Kansas side of the long-running lawsuit to integrate the Kansas City schools, wielding nearly dictatorial power over the system responsible for educating a significant portion of Kansas's youth. I've always thought it must be strange for kids from the Kansas half of KC to know their childhood schools were overseen by a killer.

I was reminded of Jean O'Connor's death in August 2005, when a retired New Mexico judge, Gerald Cole, shot his younger wife to death and then committed suicide. Cole had once had a reputation as a fairly good civil court judge, but in later years his reputation dimmed. A former colleague told a reporter that "some lawyers complained that he could be controlling."[2] I've heard tales of the care with which he kept objects on his bench lined up just so, and the way he started court an hour earlier than any other judge, yanking the lawyers' leashes. A friend who lived just a few houses down from him said the judge spent a lot of time working on his meticulous lawn. Lawns aren't easy to keep meticulous in the high-desert sunshine of Albuquerque summers. For Judge Cole, it wasn't enough that the grass remained green through the hottest days. He kept the sod perfectly edged, as straight as the lines of the sidewalk and driveway it bordered. Everything in his life whispered a neurotic need for control, and his death screamed it. His wife, Nancy Mayland Cole, had filed a petition for divorce several weeks before he murdered her. She was attempting to free herself from him. That's why he killed her.

Back in Kansas City, a colleague described Judge O'Connor as someone who was always "in control."[3] A second colleague said he "had a gruff persona on the bench and put lawyers through their paces."[4]

Putting lawyers "through their paces" means requiring them to per-form, as you would have a horse perform before you put down good money for it. It's extraordinary that a person who wished to speak well of a recently deceased person would use that phrase.

The Tenth Circuit Court of Appeals has on its website a profile of O'Connor that doesn't even mention his wife or the fact that he shot her, although you might think committing a violent felony would be a significant part of any judge's life story. The profile does, however, call him "a judge's judge."[5] The same curious phrase was used by a former colleague talking about Judge Cole.[6] So while it's anybody's guess what "a judge's judge" actually means, it seems prudent to refrain from marrying one.

For some people, becoming a judge and wielding dictatorial power in the courtroom is a gratifying way to indulge their most debilitating personality flaw.

THE GENIUS

I USED TO THINK that the defining characteristic of the really, super-latively bad judge is that he's so stupid he thinks he's smart. He's so incapable of understanding what intelligence is that he doesn't realize he lacks it. But on closer inspection of a couple of specimens, I've come to think such judges secretly realize their intellectual incapacity but try to suppress that self-awareness. They expend great effort attempt-ing to prevent others from learning their "secret"—which, as with the classic closeted gay man of comedy, is no secret. Those self-evasions, rather than the relatively low IQ, are what make the superlatively bad judge so calamitously bad.

I use "he" advisedly, because in my experience the wannabe genius judge is always male. Perhaps that's coincidence, but I think not. He approaches each case as an opportunity to intellectually dominate oth-ers—something he's incapable of doing without the props of judicial office. Acquiring those props is why he wanted to become a judge in the first place. Such judges are sometimes described as "arrogant," but that's only part of it. Intellectual arrogance married to intellectual incapacity is the public acting-out of an interior psychodrama.

When a lawyer points out to such a judge that he's wrong, it produces symptoms of panic. If it were true that the judge was wrong, it would mean that his underlying insecurities are justified. That would be emotionally intolerable, and so therefore it cannot possibly be true that he's wrong. Rather, the person who tried to convince him of his error is a threat, or even an enemy, to be dealt with accordingly.

I once encountered an appellate judge known in his legal community for two things: he thought he was a genius; and he wasn't very bright. It was possible to view this judge as an object worthy of our compassion. But I didn't, because I had to appear in front of him.

This judge had a characteristic way of revealing his neuroses in his written opinions. Because he felt the psychological need to dominate intellectually by refuting the arguments of whichever lawyer struck him as a threat, but lacked the intellectual ability to refute them on their own terms, he would misrepresent either the lawyers' arguments or the facts of the case, or both. Rather than dealing with the case as it was presented to him, he would deal with straw men of his own invention, straw being a substance he could outthink a good two-thirds of the time.

Such a judge runs little risk of having his lies exposed, because most lawyers reading his opinions (and no one but lawyers ever read them) will know nothing about the case except what he himself chooses to reveal (or invent). The only lawyers in a position to expose his lies would fall into one of two camps: those who weren't going to risk their client's victory by complaining; and those whose complaints would sound like sour grapes—and would provoke massive retaliation.

In theory, the other judges serving on an appellate panel could refuse to sign off on dishonest opinions. But why would they want to? What would be in it for them? As Judge Richard Posner has pointed out, appellate judges benefit in multiple ways by raising no objections to their colleagues' opinions. Going along to get along is rewarded by increased leisure, while scruples only mean extra work.[7]

Perhaps even more important, passivity maintains cordial relations among colleagues. If Judge X points out that Judge Y has misrepresented the facts, Judge Y will retaliate by dissenting from Judge X's next opinion, forcing Judge X to write crabbing footnotes in rebuttal, and so on, until someone boycotts the annual holiday party and the feud becomes a real drag for everyone who works at the court. Judges have to decide which is more important: justice for strangers, or comfortable workplaces for themselves. Judges aren't ashamed to acknowledge making the trade-off, though they describe it with the euphemism "collegiality."

Professor Anthony d'Amato once published a paper called "The Ultimate Injustice: When a Court Misstates the Facts." I think there are plenty of reasons why judges lie (which is what the professor means by "misstates the facts"). Bribes are a powerful incentive, and so is ideology, and friendship with an individual lawyer or antipathy to another. But the single most common reason for judicial lying, I think, is the superlatively bad judge's need for intellectual dominance. After all, what better job could there be for the person who needs constant reassurance that he's not the intellectual mediocrity he secretly knows himself to be?

CHAPTER 14

Personality Tests

THE POGUE FIRM did a lot of medical malpractice defense. It was one of only two New Mexico firms hired by insurance companies to defend the most complex and/or potentially catastrophic cases. A few other firms handled less complex cases, but the big and potentially expensive cases always went to the same two firms. Because they got all of the most interesting cases, they could count on attracting the best legal talent, which reinforced their market dominance. At the Pogue firm, to earn the right to do med mal (as our tort department lawyers called it), young lawyers had to pay their dues, starting out on workers' compensation cases and working their way up through an entire hierarchy of tort cases.

I wasn't assigned to the tort department. Nonetheless, from time to time I was asked to "cover" depositions for fellow associates who were. One such deposition of a doctor was conducted by a young plaintiff's lawyer who showed up in jeans and an open-necked shirt. At the conclusion he drove away in one of those open Jeeps with plastic flaps for windows.

No lawyer at the Pogue firm drove a vehicle like that. I'm not sure if Buick was statistically the most common car, but our cars all tended toward the Buick genotype. Even those who wanted a little zip got it in safe and discreet ways, as with a super-reliable Toyota Supra or the old boxy BMWs, whose greatest attraction, as Tom Wolfe once observed, was that you had to *know* they were high-performance cars, since nothing about their appearance advertised it. The Beemers might have had the motor of a Lotus, but they hid it behind a Buicky mien.

The firm's dress code was courtroom wear whenever the courts were open or clients were expected. That meant conservative suits for men and women both, although the women were permitted to wear properly accessorized dresses, too. I never was without a tie during the weekday and felt uncomfortable about making myself comfortable by unbuttoning my collar until safely after 5:00 P.M.

Watching that plaintiff's lawyer in his comfortable clothes zipping away in his mud-spattered Jeep made me realize something a bit distressing about us (and I had reached the point of thinking of the firm as "us"): we were a bunch of people who didn't mind driving Buicks and dressing to match. (I drove an old Volvo without air conditioning or a stereo, which I foolishly gave up for a Ford Escort, an econo-Buick. It had a sound system and also the A/C that made it bearable to dress for New York in the New Mexico summer. The Escort promptly sent pieces of its water pump through the engine block as I was on my way to a deposition. If you ever saw a young man in a blue summer suit very gingerly climbing the chain-link fence at the top of an embankment near the freeway interchange, that was me. I bet the young man didn't look happy.)

In politics, the lawyers who represent injured people call their lobbying organization the Trial Lawyers Association, a name resented by the trial lawyers who oppose them. The Trial Lawyers are strong supporters of the Democratic Party. Insurance companies tend, reflexively, to support Republicans. In exchange, each party's platform supports programs that benefit its respective backer.

A Republican friend once told me, "Your party is owned by the Trial Lawyers and my party is owned by the insurance companies." That's about right. But the alignment is a matter of purchase, not of ideology.

I think the lawyers of the Pogue firm were overall probably a little more Republican than Democratic, but it was something like a 60/40 split. In my day we had two lawyers serving in the state legislature, one on each side of the aisle, and it was always fun to hear them talk politics together, as they did nearly every day. The firm's attitude toward its members' private lives was tolerant to the point of indifference, which can be thought either liberal or libertarian. The firm's culture wasn't conservative with respect to politics and social issues, but it was *very* conservative in other respects: in our dress, our cars, our standards of behavior, and our tolerance for risk. We were nongovernmental bureaucrats, belt-and-suspender types, clinging to the assurance of a biweekly paycheck, unwilling to make any career moves without at least one safety net and preferably two. We were the "People in Grey" of postwar Britain that The Kinks sang about, a breed brought to power by the Labour Party's soft socialism.

But some people despise that kind of bureaucratic pusillanimity. Margaret Thatcher, the champion of the entrepreneur, wanted to usher in an era of risk-taking and big fortunes made quickly. In America, the Republicans have long positioned themselves as the party of the small-businessperson who dreams of making it big. Lawyers with that kind of entrepreneurial spirit become plaintiffs' lawyers. They're almost always paid on contingency fees: no fee unless you win. Typically the fee is 33 percent of the client's recovery (plus costs) although sometimes it goes higher, and on rare occasions it goes lower. A lawyer working on a contingency-fee basis might spend two years on a big med mal case, going toe to toe with the inexhaustible resources of a Pogue-represented insurer, and at the end get "zeroed out"—no recovery for the client, no fee for the lawyer, two years of work for free. But the lawyer might also win the maximum permitted by legislative damage caps, providing a contingency fee sufficient to buy a ski condo outright with enough left over for a Jeep with windows.

Other tort defendants don't have the doctors' protection of damage caps. A lawyer suing one of them could hope to retire in luxury after a single victory.

The personal injury system strongly favors individual initiative over collective action. Ten people might be seriously injured by the same negligent conduct, but if only one sues, only that one receives compensation for the injury. If two of them sue, but only one is represented by a good or lucky attorney, only that one receives any money. The compensation isn't paid directly by the government but it comes courtesy of the government, since it wouldn't be paid without a court order, and so tort awards are a tax on the negligent as well as a payout to the injured. The tort system provides social legislation on an individual, case-by-case basis. The injured person first has to prove him- or herself a person of initiative and persistence before becoming worthy of the government's solicitude. The tort system is dog-eat-dog welfare. It's social Darwinist social remediation.

For the Trial Lawyers Association, the worst possible political development would be a system of comprehensive governmental regulation of manufacturers and meaningful oversight of professionals coupled with a reliable social safety net to pay medical costs and provide retraining for injured people. The staunchly Democratic Trial Lawyers may not know it, but they're among the most conservative forces in American society.

LAWYERS ARE OF two minds about what a lawyer's choice of field says about the lawyer's beliefs. On the one hand, lawyers are mere mouthpieces, representing their clients as best they can without necessarily believing anything their clients have told them. Much less do they necessarily believe in anything their clients stand for. Law students in trial practice classes, such as the friend I embittered with my convincing impression of a disbarred Chicago lawyer, are trained to represent both sides with equal facility and faux-conviction.

On the other hand, every lawyer knows that lawyers sort themselves into fields of practice. Entrepreneurial trial lawyers and peas-in-a-pod insurance defense lawyers offer the most vivid contrast. If they were put into a lineup, I don't think other lawyers would have much difficulty sorting them. A lawyer who goes to work in the wrong field will be miserable, often without quite understanding why.

Lawyers know that representing a certain client means nothing; they also know that it means a great deal. Both propositions are true, but they're true for different purposes, as illustrated by a highly contentious Wisconsin supreme court race of 2008. The incumbent, Louis Butler, was a former public defender while the challenger, Michael Gableman, was a former prosecutor. Gableman was quoted as telling a reporter, "You don't get a more stark contrast or clear contrast than that between a prosecutor and criminal defense attorney." He was acknowledging something that all criminal law practitioners accept: there's them, and then there's us.

In the *Wisconsin Bar Journal,* a weekly trade magazine, a lawyer-columnist was outraged by the remark, calling it a "twisted view of our adversary justice system and downright demagoguery." The columnist wrote that Butler had only been "doing his job" when he defended a child molester who, upon being freed, molested another child. Doing that job said nothing whatsoever about how he would rule as a member of the state supreme court. "Judges should be fair and impartial, not the police choice versus those who defend criminals."[1]

And yet it was inarguably true that Butler, once he got appointed to the state supreme court, repeatedly voted to free men who had committed violent acts against women and children. He didn't hesitate to change the law when necessary to reverse their convictions. For instance, he wrote an opinion altering the meaning of the state constitution to overturn the conviction of a man who beat a woman to death with a baseball bat, and he wrote an opinion overturning a 1981 murder conviction of a multiply convicted rapist because a new DNA test revealed the dead woman had sex with her fiancé during the last days of her life.[2] From my distant perspective, Butler seems like a classic type of seriously bad judge omitted from the last chapter: one who does favors to his former self, using his newfound judicial power to reverse the defeats he suffered as a practitioner.

The lawyer-columnist who was so outraged that the voters' choice should be presented in terms of "the police choice versus those who defend criminals" doubtless understood that the choice before the voters was really that stark, although a more accurate statement of its terms would have been "a judge who consistently votes in favor of criminals versus one who probably won't." I don't mean to imply the columnist's outrage was necessarily feigned. Effective lawyers have instant access to bottomless reservoirs of indignation, all of it always genuine, at least for the moment of its upwelling.

But even if his outrage was entirely genuine when he wrote that you can't judge a lawyer by his clients, he also believed that you can tell a great deal about a lawyer by the professional company he keeps. His self-description on the *Wisconsin Bar Journal* website pegs him as "a veteran criminal defense and constitutional law attorney . . . [and] a former ACLU legal director and public defender." Obviously he thought those facts about himself had some informative value, even as he thought it twisted and demagogic to publicize similar facts about now ex-Justice Butler.

CHAPTER 15

Situational Ethics

"LEGAL ETHICS" ISN'T an oxymoron, but it's amazingly difficult to violate the Model Rules of Professional Conduct, which were drafted by the American Bar Association and have been adopted in all but two states to govern the ethics of the profession. For instance, they establish as an iron-clad rule that lawyers shall not reveal information pertaining to a client's case and then immediately follow the iron-clad rule with "unless" and a list, which includes the following (with weasel words boldfaced and italicized by me):

(b) A lawyer *may* reveal information relating to the representation of a client *to the extent* the lawyer *reasonably believes* [note the two-headed weasel] necessary:

(1) to prevent *reasonably certain* [ditto] death or *substantial* bodily harm; ...

In March 2008, CBS News ran a story on Alton Logan, who served 26 years in prison for the murder of a McDonald's security guard. For that whole time, two lawyers had in their possession an affidavit—a sworn statement—signed by the real killer, attesting to his guilt. The lawyers didn't reveal that affidavit to anyone, knowing that Logan remained in jail as a consequence of their silence. Neither of the lawyers had anything against Logan. So what made them knowingly collude to keep an innocent man in prison? The answer is in that block quotation above.[1]

The affidavit, as well as an oral confession to the murder, was made by the attorneys' client, a convicted cop-killer named Andrew Wilson (who, as he confessed to his lawyers, "smiled and kind of giggled. He hugged himself, and said, 'Yeah, it was me.'"). Despite all the weasel words of the ABA's Rules of Professional Conduct, there are a handful of unambiguously unethical things a lawyer can do, and one of them is to reveal the confidences of a client merely to prevent a terrible injustice being perpetrated against a nonclient. Wilson's two lawyers had no choice in the matter, unless they wished to risk loss of the right to practice their profession. Seeking justice for Logan, a nonclient, at the cost of Wilson, a client, would have been grounds for disbarment. The only ethical thing was to allow an innocent man to serve hard time for a quarter-century.

The very meaning of the word "attorney" is one appointed to act on behalf of another. So long as Andrew Wilson chose not to reveal his guilt to authorities, his attorneys were extensions of his twisted, giggling ego. That's what it means to be a lawyer in an adversarial system: ethically speaking, you have no interests independent of your clients' interests, except to the extent you *may* choose to exert yourself to prevent *reasonably certain* death or *substantial* bodily harm. Until that point is reached, if your client is a murderous psychopath, your duty is to adopt the moral code of a murderous psychopath. That's what ethics is all about.

THE ETHICAL RULES prohibit a lawyer from representing a client while suffering from a "concurrent conflict of interest," which arises when

> there is a *significant risk* that the representation of one
> or more clients will be *materially* limited by the lawyer's

responsibilities to another client, a former client or a third person or by a personal interest of the lawyer. [Boldface and italics added as before.]

But many conflicts of interest are accepted as so completely normal within the profession that, I suspect, the committee responsible for drafting the ABA's Model Rules didn't even perceive them as conflicts of interest. For instance, beginning with his reelection in 1998, New Mexico's governor Gary Johnson became the nation's most prominent proponent of drug decriminalization. New Mexico's drug laws are severe, on paper. When I began work as a prosecutor, selling a single rock of cocaine was punished as severely as child abuse resulting in death. The penalty for killing a child has since been increased, but a second conviction for selling even a tiny amount of cocaine will still result in a sentence longer than that prescribed for second-degree murder. In practice, drug defendants in the northern part of the state never receive the maximum sentence while those in the southern and eastern parts always do, which adds imbalance to the disproportion.

In New Mexico, the state's criminal defense attorneys are a very active and influential lobbying group, far more politically powerful than the prosecutors. During the years the governor was jetting around the country arguing the libertarian case for drug decriminalization, criminal defense attorneys dominated legislative committees with jurisdiction over criminal laws. But the defense lawyers never made a push to rationalize the state's drug laws. Why not? Because drug dealers are people who have access to large amounts of ready cash. The threat of severe consequences provides them with an incentive to transfer that cash to their lawyers. Better yet, forfeiture laws allow the government to seize all proceeds from drug sales as well as property bought with such proceeds, with a single exception—money earmarked for attorneys' fees. That provides another incentive for dealers to make over their estates to their attorneys. You can give your money and fancy car to me, your last remaining friend, or you can let the cops have it. The biggest beneficiaries of draconian drug laws aren't the police or prosecutors but criminal defense lawyers.

A similar conflict of interest characterizes the professional lives of insurance defense lawyers, such as those at the Pogue firm, who benefit from the expanding tort liability they fight against. The Pogue firm eventually lost the wrongful birth case I worked on as a summer clerk. The state supreme court ruled that the surgeon who tied only one fallopian tube but supposedly failed to inform his patient of his failure to tie the other was responsible for the costs of raising the child to adulthood. That was a stinging defeat for the Pogue firm. But the long-term effect was to expand the range of cases for which doctors and their insurers would henceforth have need of the firm's services.

Similarly, I worked on one of the earliest "premises liability" cases in New Mexico, representing the landlord of a Circle K store whose clerk had been badly beaten by shoplifting thugs, suffering permanent injury. Was the owner of the building responsible for the injuries that criminals inflicted on an employee of its tenant? No, the courts eventually decided, because it had no control over the way Circle K ran its business. Circle K itself, though, was hit with an $11 million verdict. Just a few years earlier, the universally recognized rule everywhere in the country had been that no property owner could ever be held civilly liable for the criminal acts of others, since criminality was unforeseeable. Back then, judges allowed people to assume others would follow the law. By the late 1980s that assumption was getting pretty threadbare and courts around the country dumped it, opening up owners of apartment complexes, hotels, and retail stores to tort liability for crimes committed on their property. Every single one of those cases was a legal defeat for an insurance defense firm and a financial defeat for the insurance company that retained it. But each also represented another reason for landlords, hoteliers, and store owners to buy more insurance, and for insurance companies to pay top dollar for the best insurance defense firms. The losers were the big winners.

Whenever insurance companies talk about "tort reform," they're trying to institutionalize the conflict of interest by which they benefit at the cost of their customers. Their proposals never do anything to stop the recognition of new theories of tort liability. From the insurers' point of view, the more ways by which a client can be held liable, the better. Their only goal is to cap damage awards in order to make them actuarially predictable.

All lawyers face another, far more pervasive, conflict of interest: the imperative of getting along with judges. In smaller communities, lawyers might find a third, or half, or even all of their cases assigned to the same judge. Keeping the judge happy is a significant part of a small-town practice. Even in the most populous jurisdictions, appellate practitioners address the same small pool of judges over and over again. Most state supreme courts have just five or seven members. Offending one of them can be disastrous for the attorney, or rather for the attorney's clients.

I don't think many judges admit to themselves when they decide a case based on their personal feelings about the lawyers, but they don't have to. It's always easy to find a plausible reason to slam the disrespectful little bastard. After all, the other side has devoted all its efforts to enumerating them.

To avoid offending judges, lawyers will sometimes roll over, abandoning a legal point on which a judge is irrationally adamant, even when that point of law is important to their client's case. They figure it's better to lose the case than to blight their future careers—which is to say, they rank their duty to their own career over their duty to their clients. That conflict of interest can be rationalized in numerous ways, all of which come down to the absence of choice. It's an ugly moment when the judge leans over the bench and says, in so many words: "Nice little career you got here. Hate to see something happen to it."

Judges spend their whole careers tangled in unacknowledged conflicts of interest. Even beyond the obvious conflict posed by loathing a particular attorney or party, which good judges try hard to suppress, they must frequently choose between following the law and changing or "interpreting" it. Law exists to restrict the powerful, and judges are among the most powerful of government workers. It's natural for them to chafe against their restraints.

Democracy poses another built-in conflict of interest for judges. A judge who enforces a legislative enactment is doing the legislature's will, which in democratic theory means the will of the people. By contrast, a judge who declares the enactment unconstitutional, or interprets it to mean something different from what it says, is enforcing his or her own will. That means judges are routinely parties to the cases they decide. But you'll never hear them admit it.

Yet another conflict of interest for judges is known as "collegiality." This is a particular problem for appellate judges, who sit in panels of three, five, or seven, and who typically all have offices near one another or even next door. The rationale for having multiple judges deciding the same case is to allow for differences of opinion, but in practice a judge who expresses differences freely will make him- or herself an object of resentment and retaliation. Is intellectual honesty worth social ostracism? The conflict between honesty and comfort affects even staffers. I know of a judge's secretary who testified truthfully in a Judicial Standards Commission inquiry into her boss's fitness for the bench. Immediately after the hearing the court's chief judge told her that she needed to find another job. The court wanted only team players. Meanwhile, her former boss, the judge under investigation, was allowed to retire quietly on a full pension.

In New Mexico, the Court of Appeals employs a bizarre system to decide many appeals—between a third and half of the total—without briefing or argument. It's called the summary calendar, although it has nothing to do with calendars as most people use that word. As soon as a new appeal is filed, it's assigned to a staff attorney who chooses which side he or she wants to win. The staffer then drafts an opinion proposing to rule in that party's favor. A single judge signs off on the proposed opinion and the court sends it out, inviting the proposed loser to file a memorandum pointing out any errors in the court's reasoning, upon which a panel of three judges decides whether to adopt the proposed opinion as an official ruling of the court, that is, whether to side with their colleague or the outsider. In this way the staff attorney and the single judge effectively become advocates for one side or the other, and the disfavored party is placed in the position of simultaneously arguing to and against the court. The built-in conflict of interest makes the summary calendar system an ideal method for institutionalizing bias.

No other state is foolish enough to employ anything like New Mexico's summary calendar system. But every time any judge in any state goes off half-cocked, forcing a lawyer to file a motion for reconsideration, the lawyer faces a similar dilemma: How do I point out the error without making the judge dislike me personally? The judge likewise faces a corresponding conflict: Is it true that I made a mistake? If so, should I admit it? Many judges may be capable of answering the first question honestly in the privacy of their chambers, but few have the strength of character to give an affirmative answer to the second in public.

SOME DIFFICULT CONFLICTS of interest arise only from the necessity to suppress human feelings of sympathy toward sheep being shorn. I once represented a couple of businessmen who were caught in a cash crunch. They were unfortunate enough to owe money to a failed bank taken over by the government. The bank's receiver, appointed by the federal government, was an accounting firm, one of those then in the Big Eight, or Big Six, or whatever it was. The venerable name of that firm has since disappeared. Several other creditors also wanted money from my clients. Finally, there was a contractor who thought he was entitled to some fees for a project that had been discussed in some detail but never got as far as a contract being signed.

The resulting lawsuit was a mess, involving not nearly enough money and way too much law. Did the federal law displace the state law, or did the federal law not apply at all, or did they both apply, and if so, how? Who was entitled to how much of what money? Wouldn't it make more sense to complete the project than pull the plug after so much was already invested? And so on. The judge, perhaps despairing of straightening it out, ordered a settlement conference and ordered the lawyers to appear at it with "settlement authority," meaning the authority to agree to a compromise binding on their clients.

The bank was represented at the meeting by an accountant from the receiver. I remember asking him whether he had the settlement authority the judge ordered. He gave a big grin and said, "I have authority to accept one hundred cents on the dollar."

I should have turned right around and walked out with my clients. Partly, I admit, I shrank from the dramatic gesture—today I wouldn't be so timid. But it was easy to rationalize staying. After all, my clients owed a great deal of money, which made it inadvisable to get too high-handed. This meeting could be viewed as a confidence-building exercise. Besides, we could always complain later to the judge about the accountant's disobedience of her order. In the meantime we might as well see what he had to offer. And so on.

One or two of the smaller creditors were also present, but they understood that they had to stand behind the government as represented by the grinning accountant. What puzzled me is that the contractor and his wife had shown up with their attorney, an older man with white hair. They were the only clients at the meeting, other than my own. But the contractor hadn't loaned any money. He hadn't even signed a contract. His legal claim was weak to begin with. I didn't think he had more than maybe a 5 percent chance of prevailing, at best. But even if he prevailed, he wasn't going to get any money. He would be in line behind the minor creditors, who were behind the government, and none of them was going to get anything like what it was owed. The contractor's odds of actually getting any money weren't any better than, say, 5 percent of 5 percent. In a zero-sum game such as a lawsuit, that's the same as nil. Why were he and his wife wasting their time? Why were they throwing away the money they were undoubtedly paying their white-haired lawyer, who obviously hadn't taken the case on a contingency fee basis?

Before the meeting got underway I wandered over to chat with Whitehead, curious to figure out what was going on. He was a pleasant enough fellow. Before long he was telling me how he planned to retire soon. He was building a retirement home on an island off the New England coast—the sort of cold, damp place from which people more commonly retire to the sunshine of the desert rather than vice versa. By this time next year, he said, he hoped to have saved up enough to call it a career.

During the conference, Whitehead, who had been so affable with me, was offensively aggressive toward my clients. I remember noticing the back of one of my clients' necks getting red. Several times I tried to get things back on track with the accountant, but Whitehead kept interjecting himself. His three clients sat behind him, looking grim and determined. After an hour or two of this we had accomplished exactly nothing, except that some of us had acquired a good reason to be angry. I was mainly angry with myself for not having protected my clients. I had stayed within my comfort zone by not storming out, only to subject them to that.

Whitehead's switch in personality, from chatty friendliness with me to insinuating nastiness around the conference table, was obviously an act. He was rather overdoing the role of the indignant champion of the ill-used. But what I remember most distinctly was the hard eyes and set mouths of the contractor and his wife. They really, honestly believed they were owed money. They really thought they were going to get it.

That's when I realized that the purpose of Whitehead's act wasn't to impress me, or my clients, or the accountant, but his own clients. They were paying him a couple hundred dollars an hour because he had promised to recover the money that was rightfully theirs.

I saw in their grim faces that they were paying for Whitehead's retirement home.

Whitehead was acting under a conflict of interest, but there was nothing unethical about it. He was just doing what his clients wanted. Of course, they wanted it only because he had assured them it was theirs for the taking, but that didn't enter into the ethical calculation. The contractor and his wife looked on me with loathing but I felt sorry for them, the way a New Yorker feels sorry for the tourist suckered into three-card monte. But, like the New Yorker, I didn't interfere. By the standards of the profession, it would have been unethical in the highest degree for me to have done so. A lawyer may not communicate with a party represented by another lawyer. One attorney may not seek to undermine a client's faith in another attorney. The only ethical course of action open to me was to participate in something that bore an unpleasant resemblance to a con game.

I've always been curious to know when the contractor and his wife woke up. I'll bet they kept throwing good money after bad until they were too embarrassed to tell anyone about it. But by then Whitehead was relaxing to the sound of waves lapping against his private pier.

CHAPTER 16

Bieganowski Cellars

THE LAWYERS IN the Pogue firm's torts department handled much more interesting cases than those I worked on, but often it seemed to me they were on the wrong side. I never said it out loud, but emotionally I identified with the injured people. Dr. Arthur Bieganowski of El Paso, Texas, helped me to understand that the injured person and the person who caused the injury were only two points on a compass. The legal system dealt with their encounter by surrounding it with many other encounters, involving not just the lawyers on both sides but the insurance companies and the pain doctors. Dr. Bieganowski was a pain doctor.

He was trained as a psychiatrist and neurologist, but by this stage in his career he used those skills against his patients, rather than for their benefit. He set up a series of five ostensibly separate clinics to treat pain. Next he hired runners to obtain copies of accident reports filed with the El Paso Police Department, and had a Spanish-speaking telemarketer target injured people. The telemarketer was given a quota of patients he had to bring into the clinics. Once a patient showed up at one clinic, he or she was rapidly transferred through the other four. Although Dr. Bieganowski's office was the size of a small grocery store, he was the only MD on staff. But the various clinics also hired chiropractors, acupuncturists, therapists of all kinds, and even specialists in folk medicine such as cupping—using heated cups to draw bad spirits out of a patient's body. They kept Dr. Bieganowski's X-ray and thermoimaging machines busy, and the doctor gave his nurses quotas for administering facet block injections—injections of painkillers directly into the spine—regardless of whether the patients cared to undergo that experience. Before the bewildered patient stepped out in the west Texas sunshine again, many thousands of dollars in bills had been racked up.[1]

Once payment was received from an insurance company, Medicaid or Medicare, workers' compensation or the military, Bieganowski funneled the money through a succession of shell corporations with bank accounts in El Paso, across the border to Ciudad Juárez, and to the Turks and Caicos, before finally depositing it in the Cayman Islands.

According to newspaper articles dating from his heyday, Bieganowski was "an oenophile who delights in sticking his nose in a glass and inhaling the wine's aroma, then slurping a small mouthful to savor the spectrum of taste." He was "said to have the largest private collection of Champagnes in Texas."[2] Given the oil wealth in Texas and the state's fondness for superlatives, that must have been a lot of bubbles. For a time Bieganowski even owned his own winery, called Bieganowski Cellars, bottling wine—including the only merlot bottled in Texas, or so it was said—from grapes grown in New Mexico's Mimbres Valley.

In 1995, Bieganowski ranked third among physicians receiving money through the Texas Workers' Compensation system. His board-qualified specialty made him stand out on the top-ten list. There were seven orthopedists, one chiropractor, one general practitioner, and "Arthur Bieganowski neurology $760,435."[3] When his operation was finally shut down by federal authorities, he was sent to prison for fraud and "ordered to pay a staggering $23,000,000 in restitution and to forfeit the net proceeds from a real estate sale plus an additional $11,000,000," according to a Health and Human Services Department administrative law judge.[4]

I became acquainted with Dr. Bieganowski years before the feds were on his case. He filed a civil lawsuit in New Mexico federal district court against a whole bunch of insurance companies, accusing them of entering into a conspiracy to cut down his bills. The Pogue firm was hired to represent one of them. He filed in New Mexico rather than Texas because so many of his patients were from north of the state line. El Paso, which is many hundreds of miles distant from other major Texas cities, is only a short drive from Las Cruces, New Mexico's second-largest city. Historically, El Paso was the link between Old and New Mexico, and it remains the dominant metropolitan area of southern New Mexico. Residents of Las Cruces get their news from El Paso TV.

Filing the lawsuit was, in many ways, a crazy thing for Bieganowski to do, because he was picking a fight with corporations with the resources to fight him. He was also giving them a motive to spend that money on lawyers. In the short term, they had no desire to pay Bieganowski's bills. Bieganowski did such things as bill them for hydrotherapy in a Hubbard tank—a full-body immersion tank—even though his clinics didn't have access to such a tank. In the long term, the insurance companies wanted to dissuade other doctors who might otherwise be inspired by the oenophile's conspicuous consumption. Just as drug dealers would rather give their money to their lawyers than to the government, the insurance companies preferred to pay us instead of him.

Bieganowski apparently thought the insurance companies' cost-benefit analyses would lead them to a different conclusion—that it would be cheaper to cave than litigate. If that was his goal, he would have been better served suing them one by one. Going after all of them at once practically begged them to collude on their defense, as he accused them of colluding on the denial of the claims his various clinics submitted. All of the defense lawyers did, in fact, meet regularly to plan strategy. (A couple of the small fry sold out on us, but most kept the faith.)

I attended depositions in El Paso attended by at least ten attorneys, all of them, I'm confident, being paid by the hour. The attorneys' fees for a single day of discovery probably cracked the $25,000 mark. When Dr. Bieganowski himself appeared in Albuquerque to be deposed I was struck by his feminine appearance, an impression produced by ostentatious over-grooming. His nails were manicured, his hair sprayed, his clothes a palette of coordinated pastels. He wore a sweater draped over his shoulders, the two sleeves hanging down in front with their cuffs perfectly aligned, like a model in an old *New Yorker* ad. He was then around 45 years old.

During the morning he was questioned by a pugnacious little pepperbox of a lawyer, who barked out rapid-fire questions, drawing frequent objections from Bieganowski's attorney. The doctor's attorney, who had a shady reputation that may have been only partially deserved—in his younger days he was associated with some decidedly sketchy characters, but he had broken with them—was then about 55, though he looked older. Then came lunch. In the afternoon, a different insurance defense lawyer took over the questioning. This was a calm man named Lyman Sandy with a wonderfully resonant voice. Lyman had the voice of an overnight deejay on a 1970s FM station. He should have been hired to do the voice-mail messages for suicide hotlines—just hearing "your call is important to us" spoken in his voice would have made callers feel better. It was restful to listen to Lyman.

I had the impression that the oenophile's attorney might have joined him in a glass or two of wine with lunch. Or maybe he was just lulled by the relative peacefulness of the afternoon after the battles of the morning. At any rate, the lawyer's eyes began fluttering, then stayed shut, and his head began to loll. Lyman, never once raising his voice or changing his pace, began asking wildly objectionable questions, prying into Bieganowski's private conversations with his attorney—what are called lawyer-client confidences. If Bieganowski's attorney was awake enough to listen, he heard only the soothing music of Lyman's voice. He never objected, as the rest of us struggled to keep from laughing.

OF COURSE I KNEW in a general way about the fraudulent lawsuit industry. I'd read newspaper stories about gangs staging car accidents for the insurance. Then there was the clever shyster from New York who had a miniature ruler marked as though it were the normal length, so that by laying it on the pavement next to a two-inch crack in the pavement he could take a photograph "proving" the city had shamefully neglected to patch the eight-inch pothole that broke the axle on his client's car. But Bieganowski's scam was different. His patients had, for the most part, really been in car accidents. Many of them were actually injured. The point of running the patients through the five clinics wasn't merely to inflate the bills—Bieganowski could have, and did, inflate bills without all the bother of actually providing treatment—but to create a defensible legal claim. He was only incidentally in the business of treating patients. Principally he was in the business of manufacturing *evidence*. His medical practice was geared toward serving the needs of the legal system.

In the classic scenario, pain doctors who solicit automobile accident victims require the victim to see a lawyer, choosing one from a list of approved vendors. The pain doctor then requires the lawyer (if he or she wants to remain on the approved list) to sign a "letter of protection" promising to pay the doctor's bills first out of the proceeds of any settlement. The lawyer's job is to deal with the insurance company. When money is recovered, the lawyer first pays off the doctor who was responsible for the evidence that made the insurance claim possible, then subtracts his or her own fee, and finally gives the patient/client whatever is left over.

The three-way split naturally gave rise to a "three times meds" rule of thumb. If the medical costs are $5,000, the rule of thumb says the case is "worth" $15,000. Getting that much out of the insurance company allows the lawyer to recover a fee equal to the doctor's with a like amount going into the pocket of the injured person. If Dr. Bieganowski's operation conformed to this general business model, and the doctor really did pull down the tens of millions of dollars he was ordered to pay in restitution, how much did the lawyers on his approved list make? However much it was, they weren't ordered to pay it back.

I came to think of the name of the doctor's winery as a metaphor for the dank and dark cellars of the legal system. Bieganowski was a parasite. His hosts were injured people, most of them poor and uneducated, many of them living in a foreign land with imperfect command of the language. He used his knowledge of psychiatry to identify and exploit their vulnerabilities. He succeeded as long as he did, and as conspicuously as he did, only because the legal system provided the perfect environment for parasite to colonize host. Bieganowski ran a legal scam, not a medical scam.

I never knew what prompted him to file suit against the insurers. Hubris, I suppose. It was a catastrophic mistake. By filing suit, he imposed discovery obligations on himself. He should have known that the insurance companies' defense would be that they denied only claims they determined to be fraudulent. By suing, then, Bieganowski invited his worst enemies to prove he was a fraud. They succeeded. I'd be curious to know how much of the evidence used by the federal prosecutors to send him to prison first came to light during discovery in the civil cases he himself filed.

CHAPTER 17

Meat Market

WHEN I WAS in Ireland, I had my palm read by a middle-aged man from India. He was dressed traditionally in loose, colorful garments and was burning incense inside the incongruous modern hotel room in which he'd been installed, I think as part of a cultural exchange program. He refused to accept any money, which impressed me. He told me not to even think about women until I was 25, advice that would have saved me a great deal of emotional turmoil had it been hormonally possible to follow it. (I was 25 when I met Carla.)

He also remarked on a particular bump at the base of one of my fingers—I don't recall which one—and said, "Your father must have been a professor."

It would have been easy to guess I was a university student, and it would have been fairly safe to guess that my father was also college-educated or at least had intellectual interests. But putting a name to his profession struck me as a pretty bold stab in the dark, unless, of course, it wasn't a stab in the dark.

My father, who grew up in an immigrant community in Minnesota, was the grandson and son of railroad men. He was the first in his family to attend university. He kept at it all the way through his PhD in metallurgy. For several years he was on the geology faculty of the University of Kentucky. He left teaching for a job in industry as the kids kept coming, but later in life served as an adjunct faculty member at colleges in both Ohio and New Mexico. He loved teaching and passed that love on to his children. His oldest son became a professor while the two youngest, which includes me, have taught night classes at community colleges in two states.

When I was in my third or fourth year of practice I decided to pursue the goal of becoming a law professor. Attending three different law schools, with three very different philosophies of legal education, had given me the opportunity to think seriously about different approaches and the relative effectiveness of each. I thought that would translate into something of value to students.

I paid a fee to the American Association of Law Schools, the trade association / cartel responsible for organizing the annual convention at which the law schools do almost all of their hiring of new professors. As part of the registration I filled out a checklist that the AALS called a résumé. The checklist sought only two types of information, which was apparently all the schools needed to make their rough cuts. First, it asked about my demographic profile. Since the 1980s, law school faculties have become particularly sensitive to the diversity issue. That's because, until then, they had been so extremely un-diverse. Law school faculties remain largely clubs of aging white guys desperate to prove they aren't the sort of aging white guys who hire only younger white guys. The senior professors of today are, in fact, so deeply appalled by the systematic discrimination responsible for their professional rise that they want to make sure the ladder is pulled up after them. While I don't doubt the sincerity of their wish to see a more culturally diverse and inclusive faculty, I've also noticed that they don't adopt the most efficient means for achieving that goal, mass resignation. It's almost as if those in charge seek to salve their consciences by making outsiders pay for their institutions' sins. It's another example of baby boomers having it both ways, sternly declaring the fruit off-limits as the juice dribbles down their chins.

A friend applied to the AALS the year after me. She was a three-fer, being female, Hispanic, and lesbian. She received personal letters begging her to come interview from more than 180 law schools. Those 180-plus law school deans were shouting in chorus that they didn't care anything about her but were extremely anxious for the nip and tuck she could give their faculties' demographic profile. Unsurprisingly, her aspiration to become a professor evaporated. (I still think she should have licensed schools to use her name, likeness, and stats in exchange for a reasonable royalty. She could have been on the faculty of a couple dozen without even having to move house.)

The AALS checklist wants a second type of data, too. It wants information about the applicant's law school career. It fishes for verifiable facts establishing the faithfulness with which the candidate lives up to the stereotype of the ideal candidate. This part wasn't any more helpful to me. Honors degree? Nope. Order of the Coif? Nah. Law review? Uh-uh. Editor of law review? See above. Class ranking? Northwestern didn't rank its students. Law clerk to a judge? Nix.

Even I could see that I had nothing to offer any hiring committee. Nonetheless a handful of schools invited me to interview, probably because the interviewers had empty slots on their schedules and filled them randomly. The meat market—the inevitable name for the cartel's hiring fair—took place in Washington, D.C. I probably wouldn't have bothered attending had it not provided a good excuse to visit my oldest brother, who lived just across the river in Arlington, Virginia. The site was the Wardman hotel, near the zoo, said to be the District's largest. It was a Sheraton then but has since changed chain affiliation.

The meat market proved to be a disturbingly surreal experience. The hotel lobby was almost inconceivably massive, and everywhere you looked there'd be another young lawyer dressed in courtroom clothes wandering around with a slightly dazed expression. Each of the various law schools rented a hotel room where they conducted their interviews. The applicant would be seated on the edge of a bed or, if lucky, a chair facing six or eight faculty members, and hit with random questions. Some professors wouldn't say anything, just stare. Others would go off on weird tangents or start gossiping when I mentioned the names of my professors. Particularly memorable questions included "Why hasn't UNM hired you?" and "Which approach for teaching Article 2 are you most in sympathy with?" Possibly these were clever tests to see how the applicant responded to absurd and unanswerable questions. Then again, maybe not.

Each interview lasted, I think, 20 minutes. Then each well-dressed young person would be shown out of the room into a corridor where he or she would find similarly well-dressed young persons being shown out of adjacent rooms. The committee would take a few minutes to give a preliminary thumbs-up or -down while the applicants (or at least the popular ones among them) scurried to their next appointments. Each committee would conduct interviews all day. The most popular applicants did nearly as many. The second day was the same.

The AALS organized a reception for interviewers and interviewees after the end of the first day and I made myself attend, though I can no longer remember why. Maybe I was just attracted by the free drinks and food. I happened to see a young professor from the University of Oklahoma who'd been among my interlocutors that afternoon and said hello. His eyes darted wildly around the room as he tried to figure out some way to pretend he didn't recognize me. When he finally acknowledged me he immediately started making excuses about why he couldn't stay, although no one had asked him to. The next time I read a description of Asperger's syndrome this young professor came immediately to mind. But his gaucherie was charming in its way—he was incapable of dissembling.

I found it odd, then, that the rejection letter I received from Oklahoma a week or two later told me that "at this time" they couldn't offer me a position but were I to receive an offer from somewhere else, please do not accept it before notifying them. I spent a couple of days puzzling about what the letter was trying to get at before several nearly identical letters arrived from the other schools I'd interviewed with. Finally I realized that was the formulaic way law schools phrase their rejection letters. To this day I don't know if the words meant anything at all. Would the schools really reconsider hiring a rejected applicant if another school—particularly, one imagines, a school ranked higher than themselves—made an offer? It makes sense, in a way. A job offer from a more prestigious law school is just the sort of item that would fit on the AALS checklists.

The law schools use the meat market approach because they can. Lots of lawyers aspire to the comfortable life of a law professor. ("It's a good gig" is how one professor—not an interviewer—described academia to me.) For interviewers and interviewees alike it's convenient to be together in one place. But the meat market is more than just a facilitator of hiring. It influences hiring decisions in ways that, I suspect, most interviewers don't even realize. Given the volume of applicants, law schools must make the first cut based solely on the AALS checklists. That means not only that they consider an extremely narrow range of qualifications, or rather marks of past distinction—none of which qualifies a person to teach—but they're all considering exactly the same ones. The AALS checklist defines the ideal candidate. The law schools that use the checklist commit themselves to uniformity. It's a checklist in more ways than one, because fundamentally it asks whether the applicant has checked off each box in his or her life. The successful applicant will have begun conforming long before applying.

Law schools today have a very strong preference for hiring very young lawyers, just a year or two out of law school or even directly out of law school. I think it's partly financial—snag 'em before they get used to a big income. Partly, too, I think professors without much experience in the actual practice of law feel threatened by those who have that experience. The professor knows a lot more than the practitioner, but vice versa, too—and students are far more interested in learning what the practitioner knows. That can't be a happy thought for someone who's devoted 20 years to educating the ungrateful little shits.

Moreover, if a practitioner can step in and do a professor's job, doesn't that mean the professor hasn't been doing anything that requires special academic expertise? That, I think, taps into a deep anxiety for law professors, who worry about not being viewed as *real* academics. They don't, by and large, do research, and what little they do never amounts to much. They never advise PhD candidates. They don't have post-docs working in their labs. Their professional journals aren't even peer-reviewed. Law schools began as vocational schools—they were the 19th century's version of the car mechanic classes at the community college. I suspect many law schools seek academic respect by aping the practices of traditional academia, where the brightest stars move seamlessly from student to professor. If law is going to be taken seriously as an academic subject, shouldn't law schools hire the same way as serious academic subjects?

The difference, of course, is that biology professors and their students actually practice biology in their labs. Law professors and students, by contrast, don't practice law in their lecture halls and seminar rooms. A legal academy that treats itself as the norm and the practice of the profession as a deviation doesn't deserve to be taken seriously as an academic subject. It doesn't deserve to be taken seriously, period.

After I'd been home from the meat market for several months, I received a phone call from a professor at a law school classified by *U.S. News and World Report* in the third tier (out of four). He wanted me to fly out for an on-campus interview. From time to time I wonder how my life would have been different if I'd accepted the invitation. I would have enjoyed the teaching, but not the moving around that would have come with climbing up the hierarchy to a tier-two school and then—who knows?—maybe cracking the top 100. Carla would have been cut off from her family and network of friends; Alex would have grown up without grandparents and great-grandparents in the same town. No, it was the right decision to decline the invitation, even though I had a terrible reason for declining it: the misplaced loyalty I felt to my new boss. By that time I had dumped the Pogue firm and thought it would be rotten to leave my new start-up firm so soon after starting up.

Also, when I went to the meat market it was with the idea that I would teach Contracts. Contracts was what I knew, but it wasn't anything I ever cared about. Becoming a Contracts teacher would have meant extending the period in which I lived someone else's life. The sense of unreality that had hit me at the Biltmore in Phoenix never entirely went away during my four years at the Pogue firm, when I dressed in suits and knotted ties to my chin because, as everyone knows, that's what young associates at big firms do.

CHAPTER 18

Start-up

I WOULD HAVE ENJOYED teaching law. I suspected it at the time and now know it for sure, because I've taught for many semesters in the paralegal studies program at Central New Mexico Community College. I teach evening classes, one or two per term, which in many respects is ideal: I get only the students motivated enough to attend class after a full day of work, and I'm spared all the administrative hassles of a full-time faculty member.

Nonetheless, the real spur to my attendance at the AALS meat market was that I didn't much enjoy my life at the Pogue firm. I wanted to do something different. But while the unhappiness itself was unmistakable, I found it hard to diagnose its cause. Objectively, I had nothing to complain about. I liked my colleagues. The pay was good, and in New Mexico terms even qualified as excellent. I loved the first-amendment work, though unfortunately that was never more than perhaps 25 percent of my workload. I didn't love the rest of my work, but then, who does? Besides, the work was generally far more challenging than I've made it sound so far. A lot of my time was spent researching the law and writing legal briefs. I was acquiring a reputation in the firm as someone who was particularly good at the pen-and-ink stuff. But that reputation, the managing director was at pains to tell me, was a negative. Research and writing is what summer clerks do, after all. A *real* lawyer delegates that kind of thing to the junior associates.

The managing director was the partner elected by fellow partners to serve as CEO of the firm. During my Pogue firm career the managing director was a stout, white-haired man whose suits were always a little bit too tight, like Oliver Hardy's, as if they'd all been bought 20 pounds earlier. He walked with his toes turned inward, yet the overall effect wasn't comical. His eyes, small and narrow in his fleshy face, were cold, at least when he directed them at me. He was firmly committed to secrecy, rumor, and innuendo as the firm's official communication policy. He got where he was by playing hardball office politics, knocking off the previous managing director after a single two-year term rather than permitting him to reign for the customary two terms. That happened before I arrived. But I was there when he was elected to an unprecedented third consecutive term, the significance of which was entirely lost on me at the time (*see* official communication policy, above).

I'll call the managing director Cheney after the politician whose style most closely resembles his. Once a year he met with each of the associates to provide a performance evaluation, and I rarely talked to him on any other occasion except to exchange greetings. The evaluation he gave me in my fourth year was almost verbatim the same evaluation he'd given me the year before: I was spending too much time researching and writing and not enough time doing the work of a *real* litigator. The criticism wasn't very practical, since the work I did was assigned by the partners. Cheney was criticizing me for not being treated better by his partners.

One partner handling a big products liability case split up associates' duties by having me do all the motions and another associate (my fellow AALS applicant, as it happens) do all the depositions. The partner thought it made sense to have each of us doing the thing we were particularly good at, but it made both of us feel we were being denied the opportunity to develop the other skills. It hardly made sense to criticize me for being treated like that.

When Cheney repeated the nonsensical criticism after the passage of a year, I understood he was hinting at something that wasn't expressed in the literal meaning of the words he used. (*See* official communication policy, above.) By that time, my fourth year at the firm, I'd been able to pick up just enough background information to hazard a guess as to what. In a way that was almost wonderfully apt, it had to do with something that I had no control over and that, in fact, I hadn't even known about for my first couple of years at the firm.

When I arrived to work full-time at the firm I was given an office next door to a partner I'll call Silas. Silas had a slightly oversized head, or a slightly stumpy body, depending on which way your glance traveled. His hair was receding from his broad forehead. He affected the preppy look of the era with round tortoiseshell glasses, which inevitably gave him the nickname—behind his back—of Tweety Bird. But he was also known as one of the firm's best lawyers. He was formidably smart and ruthless. (Come to think of it, so was Tweety Bird.)

I'd first encountered Silas during my clerkship summer, soon after I was given permission to set up in an otherwise-empty office. To brighten up the bare walls I brought in one of those Landsat maps, a false-color satellite image, and hung it on one of the nails left over by the office's last full-time occupant. The map showed New Mexico in reds and greens, the central ridge of the mountains providing a pleasing symmetry. Once as I was sitting at the desk with the door open, Silas flew into the office and quickly walked right up to the map. He then stood there facing the wall, his hands in his pockets, pretending to be enraptured by the image. He stayed like that for awkward seconds as I stared at his back, wondering what it was all about. He started talking randomly about the map, but soon relaxed enough to turn and look at me. We talked for a few minutes, though I don't remember what about.

I thought I'd caught a glimpse of Silas's vulnerability—an unexpected shyness that made him lunge so awkwardly for an excuse for coming into the office to greet the summer clerk. It wasn't until many years later that I realized how wrong (and sentimental) I'd been. It would have been contrary to Silas's nature to put out the slightest effort to make a summer clerk feel at home. That wasn't because he lacked social skills; he just didn't exercise them without a good reason. He had remarkably little desire to make people like him, which was good, since most people didn't.

His reason for coming into my office had nothing to do with greeting a summer clerk. As I learned much later, he'd spent the previous few months campaigning to have an associate assigned full-time to him. It wasn't that he lacked for assistance; he could always draw on the corps of associates at the firm. But he wanted to have someone on constant call who was familiar with his cases and clients. Without my knowledge—without my least inkling—I'd been offered to him as a likely candidate.

He was in my office to check out whether I'd be acceptable as "his" associate. That's why he was so awkward. He would have been awkward in exactly the same way at his first slave auction in the antebellum South, wondering how to begin the pre-sale inspection. He was contemplating a decision that he knew would have important consequences for himself. He'd never made a decision of that type before and wasn't sure how to proceed. I had no clue what was going on, which made it the most *relaxed* interview I ever underwent in my life. But it also meant my first impression of Silas was a wrong one.

When I started work full-time at the Pogue law firm I was assigned the office next door to Silas. I thought that was because it happened to be empty. He had a couple of superb clients—the newspaper and TV station—so I was happy to work for him. But I also worked regularly with three other partners and sporadically for still others. No more than a third of my caseload, if that much, involved Silas's clients.

We worked well as a team, falling into a natural good-cop / bad-cop routine with opposing counsel. It wasn't that I was such an exceptionally good cop as that Silas was such an exceptionally bad one. I've never met anyone so indifferent to the impression he made on others. Silas didn't care that most people described him with unflattering anatomical references. In the course of every litigation there would come a time when opposing counsel was too angry with Silas to talk to him. They would talk to me instead, and by that point I sounded to them like the voice of purest reason—they were *grateful* to talk to me.

Looking back, I can't imagine why no one at the Pogue firm thought it worthwhile to inform me that I was assigned to Silas. Maybe the idea of informing me about my career at the firm just never arose, lack of communication being the distinguishing feature of Cheney's management. But being assigned to Silas meant that I started my tenure at the firm in a bad position, without knowing or even guessing it. While Cheney had a strong set of allies, he also had his detractors. And chief among them was Silas.

The relationship between Cheney and Silas was oddly asymmetrical. Cheney was a power in the firm while Silas, the ever-impolitic, was barely tolerated. Cheney, whose primary concern was maintaining his position, had very strong feelings about Silas, whom he correctly perceived as a threat. But the intensity of feeling wasn't reciprocated, because Silas just thought Cheney was a bad businessman—not the sort of thing to get all emotional about. I talked with Silas nearly every day, and with Cheney once a year, so it took me a long time to understand, or even suspect, the much different ways each man regarded the other.

Cheney was, in fact, a bad businessman, or rather not a businessman at all. During my last year at the firm, 1989–90, the firm had to decide whether to upgrade its VAX system of dumb terminals connected to a mini-computer kept in a climate-controlled, glass-walled closet—a setup that was very futuristic in a retro way. Cheney was strongly in favor of pouring money into the VAX. Silas was equally strongly in favor of establishing a network of personal computers. Both made their cases to the assembled partners. When Cheney realized Silas commanded the votes of a majority, he pushed through a face-saving compromise: pay a consultant $50,000 to study the issue and prepare a report (which, of course, recommended a PC network). The other partners went along with the obvious waste of money because it spared them from having to side with Silas against Cheney.

Cheney may have assumed Silas had poisoned my mind against him, turning me into another viper who, should I ever be given the opportunity to slither into the boardroom, would join Silas's reptilian cabal. (In fact, Silas never gossiped about office politics with me. He compartmentalized his life, and anyway we were never close on a personal level.) Or maybe Cheney just disliked me in the same way he disliked everything else about Silas. From his point of view, I was Fletcher Christian's cabin boy.

But those explanations occurred to me only in retrospect. During my first years at the Pogue firm I perceived only the coolness-verging-on-hostility of the managing director. All I knew was that, for some unfathomable reason, the most powerful lawyer in the firm had taken a settled dislike to me.

Silas didn't confide in me, but by my fourth year at the firm the people he *did* confide in passed along his developing plans to leave the firm and strike out on his own. That became yet another source of anxiety for me. All of the clients I most enjoyed working for, and the only ones with whom I'd developed any kind of personal relationship, were Silas's clients. The first-amendment work on behalf of the newspaper and TV station never amounted to more than 25 percent of my caseload, but if those clients went out the door with Silas, the percentage of my work that I truly enjoyed would drop from a quarter to zero.

That was a pretty grim prospect, so I went into Silas's office and asked him point-blank if he was planning to leave the firm, and in his blunt way he said he was. He'd already been out looking for office space. I asked whether he might need an associate to help his new firm get off the ground.

Starting up a new firm is exciting. Better yet, as an associate I didn't have to put up any money. The secretary we'd shared at the Pogue firm came with us, so it was as if our little triangle of the corridor had been beamed up and transported to the new site. We set up for business without proper furniture, just some odds and ends from home. The suite Silas rented was twice too big for us and had odd bamboo wall hangings left over from the last tenants. For some reason most of the telephone jacks weren't working, so I ran out to Radio Shack to buy 50-foot extension cords for our brand-new phones. Phone cords snaking across the floor remains my strongest visual memory of those early days. There were endless tasks to be done, from deciding whether to go with legal- or letter-sized filing cabinets to selecting insurance plans. It was fun. As I'd expected, the newspaper and TV station became the firm's first clients. Soon we were representing a second newspaper as well, so even a bit more than 25 percent of my day was taken up by enjoyable and meaningful legal work.

I'm not quite sure how Silas acquired a certain chiropractor as a client. We'll call him Dr. Marty. Dr. Marty looked like a TV evangelist. He was tall with thick blond hair and a wide, toothy grin, and he handed out copies of a paperback book that had turned his life around. It was a book about salesmanship, dressed up in self-help language. Dr. Marty was a salesman first, a chiropractor second or third. He once told me that he admired the trade name used by another chiropractor in town. He checked the records and discovered the competitor had registered the trademark only in New Mexico. Dr. Marty promptly registered it everywhere else. His dream was to use the name to franchise his concept, providing chiropractors around the country with detailed plans for building their own money-making machines in exchange for a royalty.

Dr. Marty came to us with a "commercial speech" matter. For years he'd been hiring a runner to obtain copies of accident reports filed with the police. His runner would get in line before the police station opened in order to be the first to receive copies of the overnight reports. That same day Dr. Marty would send solicitations through the mail to every accident victim, offering a free visit to his clinic to anyone covered by health insurance. Other chiropractors and several lawyers sent out similar solicitations, and many accident victims were infuriated by them. It was bad enough that their cars were totaled and their bodies in pain—they also had to deal with a flood of fake-sympathetic advertising while adjusting to the knowledge that traumatic events in their lives were public information.

On the other hand, many people responded to the mailings by making appointments at Dr. Marty's clinic. If that hadn't been the case, the practice wouldn't have been profitable for him. Obviously, then, a sizeable percentage of people who received the solicitations weren't offended by them.

The state's Board of Chiropractors proposed a new set of regulations intended to shut down Dr. Marty and the other chiropractors who ran operations similar to his. I was given the task of explaining to the board why the first amendment forbade it from proceeding as proposed. Prior to 1976 the regulations wouldn't have raised any constitutional issue, but in that year the Supreme Court rechristened advertising "commercial speech" and declared it subject to the first amendment's guarantee of free speech. By a process familiar to lawyers, once the Supreme Court declares something to be a constitutional issue, lower courts rapidly proceed to construct an entire elaborate edifice of case law atop the pronouncement, so that a field that had been left to the democratic branches of government for the first 200 years of national existence becomes subject to judicial veto on the basis of an elaborate set of improvised commands announced by judges in a wide series of unrelated cases.

A lawyer's job isn't to question authority but to manipulate it to the advantage of his or her client. I found a lot of fairly recent constitutional authority to support my argument that the proposed regulations "had an impermissible chilling effect on commercial speech." I also made the obvious, commonsense point that if addressees were offended or irritated, they were welcome to laugh with derision, throw the circulars away, and make a mental note of never, ever patronizing Dr. Marty. If enough people followed that course, the problem would soon take care of itself. But, I argued, the first amendment didn't give those who were offended the option of preventing others from receiving mailings they evidently appreciated. For someone immersed in first-amendment law, as I was then, it was an easy argument to make.

Dr. Marty was pleased as punch at our success in getting the regulators to back off their proposal. (I don't know whether we convinced them that our constitutional arguments were correct, but we certainly convinced them that it would be costly to defend the regulations against a constitutional challenge.) Dr. Marty was *so* pleased that he wanted to do something for Silas and me and our new firm. He wanted to send us patients. All he asked in return was that we sign letters of protection, promising to pay him first out of any proceeds recovered.

Dr. Marty, it turned out, was Dr. Bieganowski. Not as smart or educated as Dr. Bieganowski, and not nearly as successful—I doubt I'll ever see a Dr. Marty wine—but he worked the same way. As soon as a patient came in for the free visit, Dr. Marty ordered X-rays and thermograms and blood tests and urine tests and every other diagnostic tool he could think of, whether or not any of them was medically indicated. If he'd known what a Hubbard tank was, he would have prescribed that, too. That way, while the initial visit itself was free to the patient, the insurance company could still be billed for many hundreds of dollars. The diagnosis, I gathered, tended to be as uniform as the sequence of diagnostic procedures that produced it: with your severe misalignment you need to come back at least three times a week for the next 12 weeks.

From a financial standpoint, there was no reason for Silas to reject Dr. Marty's offer to start sending us patients. Dr. Marty was offering Silas the next thing to free money. Besides, developing a basic competence in handling personal injury cases couldn't be a bad thing. There was a lot of money to be made in that field. Silas accepted the offer on my behalf.

I told myself it was business. Lawyers all over town were making money doing this kind of thing for Dr. Marty (he had a stable of half a dozen lawyers he kept happy), and many others were doing the same for other chiropractors and pain docs. There was nothing remotely unethical about it. After all, if the insurance companies didn't cough up, our new clients would be responsible for Dr. Marty's entire inflated bill, so in a way we were protecting them from him. Any way you looked at it, taking these cases was *normal*. It was the way of the world.

But I kept thinking of excuses not to call the adjuster, not to start moving on any of the claims. The sticking point was Dr. Marty himself. I couldn't help thinking of him as a small-time Bieganowski, a parasite on injured people. And that made me a parasite of a parasite.

There are many reasons why all those studies find that lawyers suffer from depression at a rate two or three times that found in the general profession. The dilemma I found myself in at Silas's start-up firm was one of them. In a way, the situation with Dr. Marty was a crystallization of my entire legal career, which was then five years old. I'd been trained to think like a lawyer. When I did so, I concluded that Dr. Marty was giving me a valuable opportunity to learn how to do plaintiff's work while providing a financial prop to a new firm. There was no downside. I wouldn't even have to defend Dr. Marty's treatment decisions. I'd be representing the injured people whose insurance companies had accepted their premiums but now refused to pay their claims.

When I thought about it as a lawyer—logically and systematically, accepting the profession's frames of reference—the only possible conclusion was that I was doing the right thing. Then again, it was equally obvious that I'd been doing the right thing at the Pogue firm, too, enjoying one of the most prestigious positions that can be enjoyed by a freshly minted New Mexico lawyer, doing some of the most sophisticated legal work around at the state's highest starting salary. For five years I'd been on a lucky streak. I had nothing at all to complain about.

Of course, this way of thinking only contributed to my sense of dislocation, of living someone else's life and wondering where mine had gone. I gave Silas four weeks' notice.

I thought it was considerate to give twice the usual advance warning. That was enough time to allow him to hire my replacement, whom I could help train, ensuring a smooth transition. Besides, Carla was seven and a half months pregnant with our second child. I'd continue with Silas until a week or so before the due date, then take off a month or so between jobs, making up a little for my absence during the first month of Alex's life.

But when I broke the news to Silas, he instantly accused me of trying to get paid for a whole month without working. From his way of looking at the world, it was inconceivable that I could possibly have any purpose in providing so much advance notice except to cheat him. I packed up all my personal things that evening and left the office, never to return.

Silas retaliated by withholding my last paycheck, the one I'd earned for the two weeks before I left. I had to take him through mediation. The mediator himself was useless, so I took charge. I knew that a man featured in a recent TV newscast had threatened to sue the station. His lawyer had sent a copy of an unfiled civil complaint, hoping to shake loose a little money from the station without all the trouble of actually filing and serving it. I told Silas I would write one last motion to dismiss and supporting memorandum brief, which he could show to the other lawyer to convince him that, if he filed the suit, the station would not only fight back but win. It took me just a couple hours to bang out the brief, but that was face-saving enough for Silas to mail me my check. I never talked to him again until more than a decade had passed, when we met at a memorial service for a Pogue partner.

I told a friend of mine from law school days about the rupture with Silas. He, in turn, told a friend of his about the position. Silas quickly hired the friend of the friend to take my place. I'd met my replacement once or twice before. He came from another of the city's big firms and was distinctive-looking, with thick, wavy red-blond hair and prominent teeth of an unusual color, as if the top layer of enamel had been scraped off.

One day after a windstorm I was out walking with little Alex, who was then two or three. We customarily walked around the block together every day, but on this weekend morning we went an extra block, attracted by the spectacle of a fallen tree. It was a big, mature cottonwood, ripped right out of the ground by the wind. Luckily it had fallen toward the street, which its branches now blocked. Alex and I walked over to see the sight, joining a small knot of neighbors. The homeowners were in their yard with their own small children, chatting with everybody who stopped by to wonder and commiserate. The dad was wearing a T-shirt, shorts, and sandals. Something about him looked familiar. The thick, wavy red-blond hair, the prominent teeth ... It was strange to discover we were such close neighbors.

After that we ran into each other from time to time. We were always friendly in a neighborly way but avoided talking about the thing we had in common. I wondered what, if anything, he'd heard about me. Maybe Silas spoke about me as little as he ever spoke to me about Cheney.

Then I heard through the grapevine that he'd quit Silas's firm. The next time I saw him, I broke our tacit taboo and asked what had happened. He started to answer, paused, and then said, "I'm not ready to talk about it yet." Shortly afterward he moved out of state. Upon doing the arithmetic I realized he'd been with Silas for five years, the same number of years I'd lasted as "his" associate.

CHAPTER 19

Do-gooding

THE 16 PERSONALITY types of the Myers-Briggs test are a good 33 percent more discriminating than the 12 sun signs of astrology. And classification based on test-taking certainly *feels* more valid than classification based on day of birth, though there's a part of me that rather resists the idea that we come in only 16 flavors. Still (and I hope I don't offend anyone by saying this), both Myers-Briggs and astrology strike me as more substantial grounds on which to base life decisions than Chinese restaurant place mats.

I suppose Myers-Briggs doesn't so much classify one's personality as one's self-conception. At some point, wasting time on my computer at work, I took an online version of the test. It came out differently from the score I'd received when I'd taken it away from work. At work, with my attorney head screwed on, I got a T for "thinking." Away from work, operating with the head I was born with, I got an F for "feeling."

That much of the typology seemed exactly right—my work personality is different from my actual personality, because working in the law requires a rigid analytical technique. The conclusion of any legal dispute should, in theory, be pre-ordained—literally, because it's ordained by the law. Legal analysis, ideally, is a mechanical process. It makes use of only a very narrow range of human perception and intelligence.

Almost all legal argument is just a dispute about the proper category in which to slot a case. The lawyers on the opposite sides of the case are in the position of apple sorters arguing across the conveyor belt at the packaging plant: "Fancy!" "No, Extra-fancy!" Just as an apple's grade implies nothing about its taste or crispness, legal sorting doesn't necessarily imply anything about morality, or even justice, but only technical correctness.

A lawyer's role is amoral. That's not bad, but it's also not good. That's the point—it's value-free. The civil cases I worked on, with the exception of the media cases, were also generally value-free. One party may have broken the contract, but unless fraud was involved, the breach of a business contract is almost always a financial rather than moral matter. In practical terms our cases were all about what the legal system should do to replace a defunct contract. For anyone not directly involved, it didn't matter. Business litigation generally served no larger purpose—not even that of economic efficiency, since the lawyers were barnacles on the streamlined hull of commerce.

All that neutrality got to me. It was like living one's entire life inside a beige room. There's nothing wrong with beige. Beige has much to recommend it. But it's ... beige. It wasn't that I felt superior to the work. If anything, the opposite was true. I felt there was something not quite right with me. Why didn't I share the apparent contentment of the lawyers I most respected?

Thinking it through with the analytical tools of a lawyer was useless because legal analysis proceeds from first principles; and the first principles I had absorbed in law school and at the Pogue firm were prestigious is better; higher-paying is better; civil law is both more prestigious and higher-paying than criminal law. That led to the conclusion that I *was* happy, which somehow didn't convince me.

And yet destiny had been pounding on my door for years. In my first year at UNM, criminal law was my favorite subject. I remember mentioning that to my father. He said, "You wouldn't have the highest class of client." It was a wisecrack, not career advice, and he would have been mortified had he known how much I took it to heart. I told myself I liked the class so much only because the professor, Luis Stelzner, was so good. Later, at Northwestern, my favorite class was Constitutional Criminal Procedure. Again I ascribed my enthusiasm to the excellence of my professor, James Haddad, who gave me an A-plus. On the Multistate Bar Exam, my highest score was in Criminal Law, which I put down to the fact that I'd just taken that class with that great teacher. While researching the civil law in the Pogue firm library I'd run across criminal law opinions and feel guilty about reading them, like a little boy primed to hide a dirty book if Mom should come into the room. Except my "mom" was the dutiful, dissatisfied, tie-wearing part of me.

My first book, begun while I was still working at the Pogue firm, was all about society's response to criminal violence: *Such Men as Billy the Kid: The Lincoln County War Reconsidered.* The frontier wasn't lawless, as the cliché would have it. There was no shortage either of law or lawyers. But Billy lived in a time when the criminal law was used for purposes other than protecting citizens from harm. (All of us do to some degree, but it was particularly shameless then.) He would have told you the killings that earned his reputation were justified, morally and also legally. He systematically went after men named in an indictment for murder whom the sheriff protected from arrest. He knew the men were guilty, because they had almost killed him on the same occasion. In his day, the law prescribed only one penalty for murder. Many people in Lincoln County agreed with Billy, even if they were willing to go only as far as approving that which he actually did. The themes I dealt with in that book were all the themes that would dominate my subsequent professional life as a prosecutor. Writing the book was like peering through a portal into my own future. But I didn't understand what I was seeing.

The criminal law—society's response to violence—fascinated me. So I heard the pounding on the door, all right, but I kept convincing myself it was the wind. I made the mistake of thinking about my legal career with my lawyer's head.

DURING THE EARLY YEARS of the Reagan era, two of the Pogue firm's smartest partners filed a plaintiff's antitrust case in federal district court. For all their combined smarts, they'd picked the worst possible time in 20th-century American history to seek to enforce the antitrust laws. I don't doubt that the defendant's acts were antitrust violations at the time of their commission, but the law was changing faster than the partners could get the defendant into court. Judges are very susceptible to fads, and hostility to anything smacking of the regulation of business was a fad in the Reagan years. The defendant won summary judgment—the case was thrown out of court without a trial. That left the Pogue partners with only two options: accept the decision, abandoning their client, or else appeal the decision, seeking to get it overturned by a higher court. There are 13 federal courts of appeals. One hears only claims against the federal government. The other 12 are distributed geographically. New Mexico is included in the Tenth Circuit, headquartered in Denver. The Tenth Circuit hears appeals from the southern Rocky Mountains plus the tornado alley states of Kansas and Oklahoma. The Pogue partners appealed to it.

Then one of the partners left the Pogue firm to join another. He took half the lawsuit with him, agreeing to do half the work in exchange for half of the eventual payout, should it ever come. But the odds of winning an appeal are never high. You don't even acquire the right to appeal until you lose in the trial court. That's why, as the old saying goes, it's better to have a bad judgment than a good appeal. The appeal wasn't hopeless, exactly, but the two partners were smart enough to read the writing on the wall. They delegated work on it to their associates. I handled the Pogue firm's half of the appeal. It was my introduction to appellate practice, which soon became my specialty.

Mary Kay McCulloch handled the other half of the appeal for the other firm. Mary Kay and I spent months working together on the appeal. She was a delightful person, a nurse who had switched to law in mid-career, bright and engaging with a cracked voice and just a lingering trace of a singsong Minnesota accent.

Appeals begin where trial court proceedings end. Our first task was to familiarize ourselves with the trial court record, which was relatively easy because there'd been no trial. Then we researched the law, which turned out to be challenging indeed, not only because there was so much of it but because it was changing so rapidly. Cases from the previous decade were already obsolete even though the antitrust statutes they interpreted hadn't changed.

The name "antitrust" is antique, referring to the great monopolies of the Gilded Age—the tobacco trust, the copper trust, the sugar trust, and so on—which were organized on the same legal principles as a rich kid's trust fund. They took that structure only because the law of corporations was so undeveloped. (Until the 20th century, it generally required an act of the state legislature to charter a corporation.) The first antitrust statute, the Sherman Act of 1890—named after the brother of the Union general, a senator from Ohio—was defanged by reactionary federal judges who refused to enforce it. But Congress came back with the Clayton Act of 1914, telling judges it was serious. This time the judicial fad was for enforcing it.

From then until the Reagan era, antitrust was used to regulate a lot of anticompetitive practices, among them the practice of using a lawful monopoly in one product—such as the temporary monopoly provided by patent protection—to force customers to accept a second, less desirable product by offering them together on a take-it-or-leave-it basis. The highly publicized but ultimately anticlimactic antitrust case against Microsoft involved the accusation that it extended its "natural" monopoly in one product, its operating system, to a second product, its Internet browser, by bundling them together. Mary Kay and I were fighting a similar but much lower-tech version of that, involving farm equipment.

But we were litigating in the Reagan era. The Coase Theorum, as taught by Professor IT, explained the faddish orthodoxy: if enforcing the antitrust laws had any economically beneficial effect, players in the marketplace would have already enforced them, which means that antitrust enforcement is economically inefficient, and economic inefficiency is ultimately bad for consumers, and only a moron could fail to understand that. (The federal courts' refusal to enforce antitrust laws during the 1980s and 1990s allowed the growth of corporate colossi that, Americans discovered in 2008-09, were "too big to fail," allowing them to extort massive bailouts from taxpayers.)

The source of judges' authority in our society is that, as phrased by Justice Ruth Bader Ginsburg, they "neutrally apply legal principles" to resolve disputes.[1] That makes opposition to judges opposition to the law itself. But judges can neutrally apply legal principles only if the principles have an existence independent of the judge's decision. Remember Dean Langdell's case method of teaching law. It emphasizes study of the "leading cases" of the common law, in which judges announce new legal doctrines, diverting the flow of the common law from its accustomed channels. The case method, by its nature, directs the law student's attention to the power of judges to change the law, as opposed to neutrally applying it. When fads sweep through the judiciary, as with the anti-antitrust fads of the 1890s and 1980s, judges become almost childishly eager to exercise their power to change the law. Practitioners argue a case based on long-existing legal principles only to have judges decide the case on replacement principles. It's not at all unusual for the new law to come into existence in the very opinion that announces the practitioner's (and client's) loss. And there's nothing neutral about making such a switch.

Mary Kay and I were trying to research law that hadn't yet come into existence. We guessed that the Tenth Circuit judges would feel a kind of peer pressure, not wanting to be the only federal appeals court to buck the tide. And so when we came to write the appellate brief, we tried to anticipate what the judges might think in order to head them off at the pass.

An appellate brief is a legal argument in writing — the impassioned oratory beloved of screenwriters flattened into 2-D, with the actor's throbbing voice replaced by uniform gray lines of Times Roman. An entire trial is reduced to 30–50 double-spaced pages, with close examination of everything that went wrong (or, from the other side's point of view, didn't). The lawyer's audience is no longer a panel of jurors hurried along by the pace of trial but appellate judges, typically middle-aged or older, with all the time in the world to sit and ponder. Their decision-making is no less emotional than the jurors', but they generally demand that it be justified by legal abstractions. The somewhat-paradoxical job of the appellate lawyer is to arrange abstract ideas into their most emotionally-appealing sequence. Logic is much less important than persuasiveness, and the two are only sometimes the same. To be a good appellate advocate you have to know as much psychology as law and combine both with a certain literary deftness — unless, that is, you can arrange to make your arguments to biased judges, in which case any old thing you throw down on paper will vanquish even the most gifted foe. That leads to the other quality you'll need to cultivate in order to enjoy your career as an appellate practitioner: Zenlike detachment. Otherwise you'll find yourself repeatedly muttering phrases like "casting pearls before swine" as you read the opinions prompted by your briefs.

Mary Kay and I spent weeks working on the brief together. Such close collaboration produces a kind of intellectual intimacy. I knew essentially nothing about Mary Kay as a person but quite a bit about the way her mind worked and how she wrote. She and I were almost wholly responsible for the brief, and also for the reply to the other side's response (generally the party with the burden of proof gets to go both first and last), but neither of us got to argue the case before the Tenth Circuit in Denver.

Mary Kay flew up to Denver to watch the argument and came back with a bad feeling. As the two smart partners had implicitly predicted when they delegated the case to us, we lost the appeal. We went through the exercise of trying get the Supreme Court interested, which required preparing another brief and printing it in the format of a paperback book. That was an even more intensive collaboration. But the case ended with no damage award to split between the two firms and many unbillable hours. (Frustratingly, the Supreme Court ruled in favor of the plaintiff in a similar antitrust action just a year or two later, returning the law to something nearer its pre–Reagan era state.[3] Not only were we too late, but we were too early, as well.)

Mary Kay is one of those outgoing people with an endlessly wide circle of acquaintances. She seemed to be friends with everyone. For instance, she'd long socialized with Tom Udall, scion of the political family from Arizona. I knew Tom from the Bieganowski case; he had represented another of the insurance companies. When we were down in El Paso for depositions, I tagged along as Tom and a couple other attorneys walked across the bridge. We shared a delicious dinner in Juárez. During the 1980s Tom ran twice for Congress, once in Santa Fe (where he lost to Bill Richardson, later a presidential candidate inexplicably taken seriously by 2.11 percent of Iowa voters) and again in Albuquerque. He didn't get to Washington on either attempt but he built up formidable name ID. When he ran for state attorney general in 1990 he won handily, and hired Mary Kay to be director of the office's criminal appeals division.

As the name implies, the division does appeals, but it worked exclusively in the criminal law (although the division also handles habeas corpus cases, which are effectively appeals from unsuccessful appeals but for obscure reasons are usually classified as civil cases, although they aren't, really). The prosecution isn't permitted to appeal from a judgment of acquittal, so all posttrial appeals involve criminals whose guilt has been established beyond a reasonable doubt, in the unanimous opinion of 12 jurors. The division also handles pretrial appeals brought by the prosecution after a judge dismisses charges or suppresses evidence.

Mary Kay's arrival at the AG's office incensed one of the more experienced attorneys in the division, who had applied for the director's position for herself. She quit, giving Mary Kay an opening to fill almost immediately after assuming the directorship. Instead of publishing an ad and waiting for résumés to come by mail, Mary Kay asked herself whether she knew any relatively young attorneys (because the salary wasn't much) who had the skills and temperament for appellate work. I'll always be deeply, deeply grateful to her.

WHEN I INTERVIEWED at the Attorney General's Santa Fe office, Mary Kay set me up to talk with three women who already worked there. Only much later did I realize why she chose those three to conduct the interview: I was being hired at a higher salary than any of them received, since I was inheriting the salary of my predecessor, a relatively senior member of the division. The three women who sat down with me had all been hired during the administration of the prior attorney general, Hal Stratton (later to gain immortality on the cover of a *New Republic* issue dedicated to the "hacks" of the second Bush administration, which he served as head of the Consumer Products Safety Commission, indulging his ideological opposition to the regulation of consumer products). As attorney general, Stratton took the dogmatic free-marketer's view that a fair salary was the lowest salary that anyone was willing to work for, and so he customarily made low-ball offers to applicants to see if they would bite. These three bit.

A year or two after I started, a fourth woman in the division told me—apropos of what, I no longer recall—"Joel, all the women in the division were devastated when you were hired." Let me pause right here to say that remarks like that have a way of sticking in a guy's memory. There are even guys out there who might have their feelings hurt. But by then I knew enough about the salary situation to understand what she meant. For once in my life an appropriate response came immediately to mind: "I'm underpaid. You're underpaid more."

My interview with the three women apparently helped them get used to the idea of my insertion into their ranks. At least, they hid their continuing devastation from me. All three became friends as well as colleagues.

A secondary attraction of the new job was the opportunity to specialize in appeals. I enjoyed the research and writing, so similar to a historian's work. It was the legal work I was best at and enjoyed the most. In those days the research had a tactile quality missing today, as I spent much of my time at libraries—either the UNM Law School library in Albuquerque or the New Mexico Supreme Court library in Santa Fe—pulling down books from the shelves and writing careful notes on legal pads. We used online research only sparingly, since it was extremely expensive. Also, although I wasn't yet familiar with phrases like "user-friendly interface," neither Westlaw nor Lexis had one. (Those online databases were on to a good thing until the World Wide Web came along, when suddenly they had to learn phrases like "legacy system.")

By the conventional standards of the profession, there's no doubt I was climbing down the career ladder when I joined the Attorney General's office. "Climbing" isn't quite the right verb. It was more like a fireman's pole. I was taking a big (more than 20 percent) cut in pay and sharply limiting my future earnings potential. I was going to work for the government, with all that implied about stodgy bureaucracy and shabby offices. (And, indeed, some of the furniture in my windowless L-shaped new office came from prison woodworking shops, although I kind of liked the yard-sale funkiness of the look and didn't mind the bookshelf's slight lean.) I was giving up sophisticated civil law for the disreputable criminal law. I was assuming a job title, assistant attorney general, traditionally bestowed upon baby lawyers for their first job out of law school. Being an AAG was the sort of thing an upwardly mobile lawyer might do for a year or two to make contacts before launching his or her career proper. In short, I was being *unprestigious.*

But I was also doing something that was socially useful. The satisfaction that comes from meaningful legal work is, in fact, one of the things that make it unprestigious. Employers don't have to bribe people with high salaries to get them to do things they care about. In the legal world, where prestige usually correlates to high pay and the highest-paying jobs are those no one would do for less, prestige is generally a marker of meaningless work. New Mexico is an extraordinarily violent place, perennially among the most dangerous states for women and children. Growing up in the state from age 11, it had long seemed obvious to me that the violence had a chicken-and-egg relationship to the state's chronic poverty. Not only does uncontrolled violence discourage economic activity at the macro level, but individual victims of violent crime—a category that includes witnesses and everybody living in violent neighborhoods—suffer physically and psychologically in ways that hold them down. Abused poor children, for instance, drop out of school at roughly twice the rate of non-abused poor children—and New Mexico, like other particularly violent states, has a very high dropout rate.[4] In rankings of the states, New Mexico has spent the past half-century becoming relatively more violent and relatively poorer. I didn't have any delusions that by becoming a prosecutor I could break the self-reinforcing cycle of violence and poverty, but I was strongly attracted to the prospect of doing something to help, leaving behind my old feelings of parasitism. I wanted, in short, to do good—which, to a lawyer, feels strangely like a confession.

The greatest attraction of the new job was the opportunity it provided to get out of the beige room. Judith Herman, in the afterword to her classic *Trauma and Recovery: The Aftermath of Violence—from Domestic Abuse to Political Terror,* wrote: "moral neutrality in the conflict between victim and perpetrator is not an option." When I began to work on cases involving criminal violence, I left moral neutrality behind. I entered a world of vivid and sometimes disturbing color.

CHAPTER 20

Do-badding

I N *TRAUMA AND RECOVERY,* Judith Herman documents the human
tendency to identify with the abuser over the abused. In evolution-
ary terms, it makes grimly practical sense to side with the winner. For
most of human history, siding with a beaten, suffering person was
dangerous. It remains emotionally painful. We can see the tendency
in the way boys on a schoolyard jeer at the bully's victim, and hear
it in the laughter that greets a mean girl's most cutting remarks. It's
also the secret of action films: How many depict anyone mourning
those killed by our hero? How often do you see someone scrubbing
down the crime scene after the police and morgue attendants have
gone? Arnold Schwarzenegger based his entire movie career on the
readiness of viewers to forget about characters as soon as they drop
out of the frame.

In her book, Herman allows survivors of violence to speak for
themselves. The reader discovers the parallels between the experience
of domestic violence victims and Holocaust survivors. The comparison seems over-the-top at first but self-evident upon reflection, because
of course the scale of the violence doesn't change the individual's
experience of it.

Most of my work at the Attorney General's office has involved violence. In my early years I did some drug trafficking cases, though not

significant ones. The big dealers were prosecuted by the feds, with the state system handling the leftovers. During the 1990s, however, rulings from our state appellate courts requiring the suppression of ever-more evidence drove even the little cases into the federal system. That's been a catastrophe for the accused people—federal drug sentences are insanely long—but a blessing for me, because drug cases were too much like the civil cases I wanted to leave behind. Like disputes between big companies concerning sums of money that are rounded away on their balance sheets, drug prosecutions rarely have any moral dimension.

(I realize that many of those imprisoned for drugs are dangerous people who have avoided punishment for their other, morally far more serious crimes. Drug and weapon charges, which are easy to prove once the prosecution has cleared the hurdle of a motion to suppress the evidence, sometimes serve as a proxy for other, more morally significant charges that would be difficult to prove. It's a mistake to think everybody imprisoned for a nonviolent offense is a nonviolent offender.)

Most of my cases involve violent crimes, and New Mexico is a very violent place. (A prosecutor friend says the state's motto really ought to be "Beautiful, but dangerous.") The FBI's Uniform Crime Reports are far from complete, since the bureau counts only crimes reported by local law enforcement agencies, and even if the law enforcement agencies aren't sloppy in their record-keeping or playing games with the numbers to make themselves look more effective, they forward data only on crimes reported to them.

But statistics that remain constant over many years are probably significant, and New Mexico consistently ranks second among the states in the rate of what the FBI calls "forcible rape," a term that sounds redundant but is used to exclude what is sometimes described as statutory rape, the sexual exploitation of minors by adults. Interestingly, though, New Mexico tends to rank near the middle of the pack in robbery and larceny. If you can trust the figures, we're no more criminal than people in other states, just more sexually violent.

Homicide is generally considered the most reliably measured crime, since bodies are hard to hide and most disappearances are reported. (Unreported murders typically involve drug-using prostitutes, the disposable people of our society.) Some states, including Hawaii, the Dakotas, and the New England states, have homicide rates right in line with those of Canada, Australia, and Western Europe. But others—the Deep South, Maryland, Nevada, and New Mexico—have homicide rates four or five times as high.

New Mexico is also similar to the states of the Deep South in its poverty, although it's steadily becoming relatively poorer in comparison to them. Does poverty cause violent crime, or does a high level of violence suppress productive economic activity? The former is the conventional wisdom, even though the Census Bureau counts 37 million poor Americans and the country averages between 16,000 and 17,000 nonnegligent homicides a year. That's not what anyone would call a really strong statistical correlation.

Handling criminal appeals in a place like New Mexico has given me the opportunity to learn the amazing variety of terrible things people do to each other. One dreadful case would require only a few tweaks to become a Hollywood sick comedy. A young man named Kaydahzinne, who lived in the same apartment complex with his mother and brother but wasn't allowed into their apartment due to his long history of disturbed behavior, which was always exacerbated by alcohol, tapped at his brother's window during the small hours. His brother groggily looked out. Kaydahzinne reported, "I killed Joseph"—an albino friend who'd been staying with him. The brother said something like, "Get out of here," and went back to sleep. A few minutes later he heard another tap on his window. Beginning to lose patience, he looked out—and saw Kaydahzinne holding up Joseph's head by the hair.

Some other residents of the apartment complex were up late, drinking the last of the beer bought for their barbecue, and they saw Kaydahzinne walk to the Dumpster holding what they assumed was a plastic grocery sack of garbage. They idly watched him open the lid and toss his burden inside, where it landed with a thump. Meanwhile, Kaydahzinne's family called the police. When the cops arrived, the partyers reported what they'd seen. A couple of officers walked over to the Dumpster. The first one lifted the lid and shone his flashlight into its interior. Then he turned off his light, quietly replaced the lid, and said to his partner, "Look in there and tell me what you see." The second cop did.

A rookie cop was given the assignment of sitting in a patrol car with Kaydahzinne. Kaydahzinne confessed to him. He kept on confessing. The rookie first reminded him of his right to remain silent, then told him it would be a good idea to exercise his right to remain silent, then ordered him to shut up, and finally got out of the patrol car and closed the door, standing outside because he couldn't stand listening anymore.

That wasn't my only beheading case. In the other, a Santa Fe woman cooked breakfast for a couple of men who'd shared their methamphetamine with her. The men ate the eggs and bacon, then one of them killed and dismembered her, persuading the second that he was implicated and had no choice but to help dispose of the body. The next day, the first man went home to California. The second remained in Santa Fe. After about a week the police had learned enough to want to go talk to the second man. They arrived at his trailer just minutes after the first man did. He had returned from California armed with a pistol to tie up the loose end he'd left behind. Becoming a murder suspect saved the second man's life. After that, he really *did* talk to the cops, showing them the two places where the woman's body was buried.

I've also dealt with cases in which two toddlers were locked in a remote mountain cabin to starve to death, a fatal anal rape perpetrated by mop handle, and a rape-murder solved only because a Navajo man was curious enough to step out of his hogan to investigate strange noises in one of the most isolated areas of the continent. I've handled a case in which a person confessed to raping a five-month-old, and the habeas corpus petition of an obese woman who killed her baby by sitting on him. One infant, just ten weeks old, had 51 broken bones but lived. In another murder case, the defendant's wife gave one story whenever she was living with the defendant and an entirely different story each time she succeeded in fleeing to a shelter for battered women. Her husband later tried to hire a hit man to take care of her.

What all these cases have in common, besides the appalling violence, is the vulnerability of their victims. Victims of violence are the vulnerable by definition, of course, but each of these was peculiarly vulnerable even before the crime. Some were children. Of the two adult male victims, one was an albinistic Native alcoholic and the other mentally retarded. All the other victims were women victimized by men. Violence reinforces relations based on power, which makes criminal victimization a reliable marker of social status. The poor and disadvantaged are victimized many times more frequently than the better-off. That's why it's front-page news whenever a middle-aged white professional is murdered—it happens so rarely. The shooting death of a 20-year-old black male, by contrast, might get a mention in the roundup column on the third page of the metro section.

I've always seen my work in the terms outlined by Judith Herman: I take sides in the conflict between victim and perpetrator. But that's not how judges, or most lawyers, see the criminal law. They're used to thinking in courtroom terms. Inside the courtroom, the two parties are the government and the individual defendant. That sure looks like a tort case, which similarly involves an individual against a monolithic institution, the insurance company. In the conventional legal scheme of things (and lawyers are nothing if not conventional), criminal defense work and tort plaintiff work go hand-in-glove. When a judge is described as "liberal," it means that he or she is biased in favor of victims in tort cases and in favor of victimizers in criminal cases. Describing a judge as "conservative" implies the opposite pair of biases.

Good judges strive to eliminate bias from their rulings, of course. In one of the most frequently cited phrases from any Supreme Court opinion, Justice Robert Jackson, one of the few modern justices with a clear understanding of the day-to-day practice of law (Sandra Day O'Connor was another), wrote that judges should be "neutral and detached" when they rule in criminal cases.[1] Inside the courtroom, that means the good judge strives to be neutral as between the parties—the government and the defendant.

But more is at stake in a criminal prosecution than the fortunes of the two parties. The prosecutor's client is an abstraction. "The state" or "the United States" means the people who elected the representatives who enacted laws to protect the people from criminal violence—and to provide justice for those among them whom the government failed to protect. Judges aren't detached from the government, which they embody. Nor are they detached from the people, whose consent is the source of their power. But they can be neutral as between violence and safety, crime and law, injustice and justice, perpetrator and victim. They strive for this.

So I'm afraid Judith Herman is wrong. Moral neutrality between victim and perpetrator *is* an option. It's the option chosen by our government, or rather by those government workers put in charge of our society's attempt to protect its members from death, injury, degradation, and abuse.

I THOUGHT OF the criminal law as society's response to criminal violence. How much violence is too much? Who gets to decide, the people or their judges? The people have passed laws that say things like killing another person without justification or excuse is a crime that should be punished. When, if ever, should judges refuse to enforce such laws?

But I found myself appearing before judges who thought of the criminal law in much different terms, as a series of courtroom contests between mismatched contestants. I saw myself as representing (though not in the technical legal sense) the victim of the particular crime, and also the future victims of the perpetrator, should he be released to repeat his crime, and all the people whose lives are shaped by violent victimization or the fear of it. The judges perceived me as representing the victimizer. I was the courtroom bully, picking on the helpless defendant. Almost all developments in the criminal law since 1961 involve identifying new ways in which an accused criminal can be considered the victim of the government. In almost every appeal I've ever done, I've had to defend police officers and prosecutors against accusations that they obtained a fair and just verdict by despicable means.

For instance, in the 1970s the Supreme Court began using the melodramatic term "prosecutorial vindictiveness" to describe the situation when a prosecutor files criminal charges that are supported by the evidence but that the judge writing the opinion thinks shouldn't have been pursued. It's called a legal doctrine but in practice is really just an expression of the judge's emotion (which is not to say the emotion is never justified). One member of the New Mexico Supreme Court described prosecutorial vindictiveness this way: it "lays coiled and hidden inside the prosecutor's skull."[2]

It's strange to be a prosecutor in a court system whose highest officials define you as a person with a snake in your head. (It's not so strange to work in a system whose highest officials can't remember the difference between "lies" and "lays"—who can?) That particular justice, I know, thought of himself as a liberal, which meant in criminal cases that he absolutely opposed the death penalty and consistently favored the defense against the prosecution. He himself would doubtless deny any such prejudice at least in public—judges always do—but it was taken as a given by the lawyers who appeared in front of him. Once, shortly before an argument in the Supreme Court, I noticed that this justice's nameplate was missing from the bench. I asked the court clerk about it and she told me he was ill with pneumonia. I expressed my sympathy and wishes for a speedy recovery. My opponent, a public defender, said sotto voce, "Well, that helps you."

But I had a soft spot for this particular justice. He wore his heart on his sleeve: his demeanor during oral argument always told you how he was going to rule. He would sometimes slam shut his case file to illustrate how closed he thought the case was. He was also capable of writing clearly enough to allow lower-court judges to figure out what he wanted them to do (which is apparently harder than it might seem, given that no member of the current U.S. Supreme Court is consistently capable of it).

But liberalism based on courtroom roles, taking the side of the underdog against the system, isn't just sentimental. It's unreal. It ignores everything outside the courtroom, where the murderer proved himself anything *but* the scrappy underdog. Courtroom liberalism is the political equivalent of pulling the sheet over your head and ignoring the post-midnight sound of someone breaking down your kitchen door. The courtroom beneath the legal bedsheet is calm, but it isn't reality.

THE HUMAN PREFERENCE for emotionally identifying with the abuser rather than the abused, and the judicial tendency to view the criminal law as a courtroom contest, often combine in ugly ways. One of my cases involved an eight-year-old repeatedly raped by her mother's boyfriend (a common pattern—pedophiles romance single mothers to get at their children) and by his teenage sons (that's not such a common pattern). The girl's biological father assumed custody and, to protect her from the legal system, and possibly to protect them both from the defendants, refused to cooperate with the prosecution (a *very* common pattern, strongly encouraged by the Supreme Court in a 2008 decision).[3] The prosecution wanted to introduce statements the girl made to a nurse practitioner—in New Mexico, a nurse practitioner exercises all the privileges of an MD—who had been trained as a sexual assault nurse examiner ("SANE"). Under U.S. Supreme Court precedent, whether the jury could be permitted to hear what the girl said depended on the purpose for which she spoke to the nurse practitioner, Mary Ellen Lopez. The prosecutor elicited this testimony:

Prosecutor: And is the purpose of the SANE exams in your understanding—is the primary purpose, focus, on obtaining information pursuant to a trial or a prosecution?

Witness: No. It's to make sure the child is safe, and to examine for injuries, and to make appropriate referrals if injuries are found.

That uncontradicted testimony led three judges of the New Mexico Court of Appeals to conclude: "Objectively viewed, the primary purpose of Nurse Lopez's SANE examination was to develop and preserve evidence."[4] Therefore the jury couldn't be permitted to learn what the girl said. We'll never have a jury verdict determining whether the dad and his two boys were guilty. But assuming they were, the effect of the Court of Appeals' opinion was to give them official permission to move along to the next single mother of a little girl.

On the other hand, the scenery is beautiful and the weather pleasant.

CHAPTER 21

On the Public Dime

For my first day at the Attorney General's office, I dressed as I'd always dressed to go to work during my previous five years of practice. One of the senior attorneys, Bill McEuen—the best lawyer I've ever worked with—lifted up my tie and said, "First thing we have to do is get rid of that thing." That was only the first welcome change from private practice.

For five years I had kept a special pad on my desk to note the time I devoted to each case. Each hour of every day was divided into six-minute increments. (I was once instructed that I should never use any increment smaller than a .2, since even a short phone call should be followed up by a memo to the file documenting it, and how are you going to do that in less than six minutes?) At the Pogue firm, I'd total up the hours at the end of the day on a carbonless duplicate form, sending the pink copy to accounting and keeping the yellow one for my files. At the beginning of each month, accounting would send me a computer printout listing the amount to be billed to each client, providing an opportunity for corrections, alterations, deletions, or additions. At Silas's firm, we used a computer billing program that eliminated the paper but not the need for accounting for every minute of one's day. At the Attorney General's office, in welcome contrast, I was free. No more accounting for my time.

The time itself was different. It was regular. For the first couple of years I commuted to Santa Fe. It's just about 60 miles from Albuquerque and the drive takes just about an hour. When I began, I drove every day so I'd be able to return at once if Carla went into labor. But after Scott, our second son, was born, I joined a van pool. Fifteen or so of us would meet every morning at 6:30 and each afternoon at 4:30. I didn't stay late at work—I couldn't, without stranding myself in Santa Fe. I still sometimes brought work home, or worked on weekends, but only because it was less stressful to devote the time to the work than to stew about it. That kind of stress was natural, an aspect of the work itself and the pride I took in it. The pressure for billable hours, by contrast, was artificial stress, which is always worse because it's laced with resentment.

At the Pogue firm, the partners I worked for reviewed my work before it went out. They inevitably made changes, often petty stylistic changes—sometimes, I thought, just for the sake of making them, perhaps so they could feel justified in billing their time to the client. But I agreed that the review was warranted. The partners' names were on every pleading I ever filed (always above my own), so in a sense I was speaking in their voices. It was reasonable enough that they wanted to know in advance what their ventriloquist would make them say.

For my first few months at the AG's office Mary Kay read my briefs, but I don't recall her ever making any suggestions or changes. After that I was on my own. For someone who had spent five years as an associate, the responsibility was liberating. My cases were my cases. I wasn't implementing someone else's ideas about tactics and strategy.

I also wasn't juggling the demands of clients, or feeling guilty about sticking them with big bills for unproductive work. It wasn't that I had no clients. I represented the State of New Mexico in the direct appeals and various prison wardens in the federal habeas corpus cases. The first was an incorporeal abstraction and the others might as well have been—none of the wardens, my nominal clients, has ever contacted me about a habeas case. If a warden leaves office and another takes his place, we don't even bother changing the case name. It makes no difference who the respondent is, because the lawyer makes all the decisions anyway.

I enjoy being free of clients. That's not because they were so demanding or unreasonable—most of them weren't—but because they controlled me. At the AG's office, I found I could work on one case at a time, doing what needed to be done in a regular rhythm. I no longer had to deal with phone calls that made me suddenly drop what I was doing and start doing something else. I didn't have to accommodate sudden changes in budget or strategy.

Best of all, I could give up on a case. I didn't have to keep fighting in a losing cause, saying things that sounded stupid to my own ears. It frequently occurs that I give up on a part of a case, agreeing that a sentence should be shortened, or that two convictions for the same crime violate the double jeopardy clause, or whatever. More than once I've pointed out problems with a conviction that the other side hadn't spotted, in effect arguing against myself. And from time to time I'll tell the court that I don't oppose reversing the judgment and sentence altogether. The basic rule of thumb in the division is that if an argument can be made in support of the jury's verdict—that is, a legitimate argument, one based on legal authority—then it's our job to make it, no matter how weak. But sometimes there's no argument. The other side is simply right. I consider it one of the great perks of the job that I don't have to make an argument I think is legally unjustified, or would work an injustice. ("Unjustified" and "unjust" overlap, but they're not the same.)

WHEN ONE OF MY friends at the AG's office had a retirement reception I asked him facetiously, "What words of wisdom do you have for those of us who remain behind?"

Chris said, "Don't worry about what other people are doing and what other people are getting paid. It will just make you mad and you can't do anything about it." So much for my facetiousness. Those are indeed wise words for anybody working in the public sector.

As I see it, working for the government offers four advantages over private practice. Autonomy proved particularly important for me. I didn't know *how* important until I acquired it.

Second, the cases I've worked on since leaving private practice have all been interesting. That's true of the drug cases, too. It's even true of the one speeding case I did: an ex-cop who taunted a former colleague in plainclothes by conspicuously zooming past him on the highway, relying on a state statute that permits officers to issue traffic tickets only when wearing uniforms. Only someone with a real ax to grind would have taken a speeding ticket all the way to the Court of Appeals, but he ground away mightily. The stories of the criminal cases are interesting, and sometimes deeply affecting. Even more than that, they're meaningful. They have meaning for people other than those directly involved in the courtroom proceeding. Often they have more meaning than anybody should have to bear.

In the case involving the SANE examination mentioned in the last chapter, our appellate court went out of its way to change the law in a way that effectively decriminalized sexual relations with children too young to testify in court unless the perpetrator films himself, leaves behind sperm, or gets caught in the act. That's a distressing result, but it shows the stakes involved.

Third, I'm expected to work a 40-hour week, which is a lot less than big-firm lawyers are expected to bill although it's still just a little too much for anyone. (Who doesn't respond to greetings on Monday morning with some variation of "Good, but too short"?) Some of my colleagues have the discipline to arrive at 8:00, go home for lunch at noon, return at 1:00, and knock off at 5:00. I tend to be the sort who gets into a groove and wants to keep working until everything in my head is transferred to paper, which sometimes makes me the last to leave the office at night, which then (naturally) tends to make me the last to arrive the following day, until it feels like I'm living in a different time zone than the rest of the office. My eccentricity is tolerated, for which I'm grateful. But from my point of view, the most important thing is that the work dictates my hours rather than vice versa.

Fourth, I can retire after 24 years with a pension that pays 75 percent of my salary. If I hadn't wasted those first five years, I'd be planning to retire shortly after I turn 51.

But there is a downside. It's easily stated: $. My salary today, adjusted for inflation, is a little bit lower than my last salary at the Pogue firm, which I left 19 years ago.

CHAPTER 22

It's More Important to Have a Good Reputation than to Deserve One

O N THE NIGHT of May 29, 2004, Albuquerque police established a sobriety checkpoint on Menaul Boulevard, one of the city's main thoroughfares. As is customary, officers were stationed a block or two on either side of the roadblock to watch for motorists taking evasive action. On this particular night the spotters saw a sport utility vehicle make a sudden turn into a motel parking lot, then start turning around. Officers stopped the vehicle. A man was at the steering wheel and a woman in the passenger seat. The man was drunk and there was powder cocaine across the lap of his pants. More cocaine was found in the woman's purse.

The driver's mug shot was on the front page of the paper the following morning because he was John Brennan, for 20 years the chief judge of Bernalillo County District Court, by far the largest judicial district in the state. (Nearly one-third of the state's population lives in Bernalillo County, where Albuquerque is located.) His arrest and subsequent guilty plea were a political scandal and personal tragedy. They also raised a possibility that was only hinted at in the news coverage. For 20 years the person in ultimate charge of the court, the person with authority to assign felony drug cases to particular judges, was a person who might have had every reason—from friendship to blackmail to barter—to do favors for drug dealers.

One such favor might have been to use the fourth amendment, governing searches and seizures, to suppress evidence in the prosecutions of people working for the judge's supplier. Another possibility might have been to *not* suppress evidence in prosecutions against people working for his rivals. Since fourth-amendment law is both complex and subjective, with a dozen or more decision points in even the simplest case, it's an easy matter for any halfway-competent judge to accomplish either result on demand. For a drug dealer, it's hard to imagine a better friend than a judicial friend.

In the wake of the scandal, the papers reported that other district judges were also suspected of using cocaine. That prompted the state supreme court to issue a new rule governing the responsibility of lawyers to report judges' drug use. The new rule specified that lawyers were required to report a judge's use of illegal drugs to the Judicial Standards Commission—not the police. Furthermore, the Commission wouldn't accept anonymous reports: the first items of required information were the name, address, and telephone number of the person making the report. Moreover, the Commission didn't want to be bothered with rumors. It wanted to hear about judicial usage only if the person making the report had "specific objective and articulable facts or reasonable inferences that can be drawn from those facts"—a standard that I think could be satisfied by selling drugs to a judge, or being present when he does a line of coke, or listening to his confession. It's hard to imagine what else would qualify short of finding him blue in his chambers with the needle dangling from his vein.

So the meaning of the new rule was that lawyers *shouldn't* report suspicions that a judge is using illegal drugs (and is thus presumptively corrupt and subject to blackmail). Nor should a lawyer pass along even the most widespread courthouse rumor, although gossip within the legal community tends to be amazingly accurate. (Lawyers know how to evaluate evidence.) Only actual proof should be passed along, and then only if the lawyer doesn't mind facing retaliation from the judge and his friends on the bench. And, one last thing—the information will be evaluated in secret by the Judicial Standards Commission, which may or may not decide to do anything with it, depending on the particular judge's clout . . . er, depending on the strength of the evidence presented.

However, a much different standard applies so long as the lawyer doesn't do anything that might produce publicity. If the lawyer reports to one of a few officially recognized support groups, such as Narcotics Anonymous or the state bar's lawyer assistance program, evidence may be shared, not just proof. Evidence may even be shared anonymously. Similarly, a lawyer can participate in an intervention to help a drug-abusing judge without incurring a duty to notify the Judicial Standard Commission.[1]

That was the new rule issued in response to Brennan's disgrace, and the thinking behind it seems pretty plain. Alcohol or substance abuse by a judge is a personal failing that should be met with compassionate discretion. The goal is to restore the individual's health while avoiding unnecessary and destructive publicity that might shake public confidence in the judiciary.

That approach might sound familiar. It was previously adopted by the Catholic Church in response to reports of pedophile priests. The Church didn't ignore the priests' failings. On the contrary, it tried to help the fallen priests heal by providing compassionate, discreet treatment and spiritual support. One of the ways the Church sought to accomplish that end was to ship the sinners out to New Mexico, far from the major media centers, where a retreat for suffering priests was established in the remote Jemez Valley, just down the road from a couple of summer camps for children.[2] The retreat was run by the Servants of the Paraclete, which describes itself on its website as "a religious congregation of men dedicated to ministry to priests and Brothers with personal difficulties." The last two words are key: the church insisted on viewing the crimes of its priests as personal difficulties—the way the New Mexico Supreme Court prefers to view illegal drug use by its judges.

But it would be wrong to suggest there's anything unique, or even out of the ordinary, about the New Mexico court's commitment to discretion. So far as I've ever been able to determine, every court in the United States, without exception, is equally committed to the proposition that it's more important for the judiciary to have a good reputation than to deserve one. That's why, for instance, most states hear complaints against judges in black-hole secrecy. It's also why you never see video clips of the Supreme Court in session. Cameras are forbidden in all federal courts. That's a direct violation of both the first and sixth amendments (freedom of the press, public trials).[3] But as Dostoyevski's Grand Inquisitor observed long ago, the masses hunger for mystery and authority. The absence of cameras from federal courts helps satisfy both hungers.

In 2008 the Florida Supreme Court publicly reprimanded a judge of the state's intermediate appellate court, Michael E. Allen, for releasing an opinion critical of a fellow judge. Nothing in the opinion was false; the Florida Supreme Court's point was that the true information it contained shouldn't have been made public. Judge Allen should have reported it to the state's Judicial Qualifications Commission, an agency of the Supreme Court, so that his superior judges could decide whether to keep the information within the family. To clinch its case against Judge Allen, the Florida Supreme Court observed: "The proliferation of newspaper articles and public commentary statewide after the publication of [Allen's] opinion was a clear indication that the opinion did not 'promote public confidence' in the judiciary but instead had the opposite effect." That was the nub of the problem: by publishing truthful things, and allowing a reader to draw reasonable inferences from them, Judge Allen pulled back the velvet curtain. He gave the citizens of Florida information that allowed them to understand their court system a little more clearly. That was unethical.[4]

Michigan's best-known lawyer is Geoffrey Fieger, a wildly successful plaintiff's lawyer, onetime Democratic candidate for governor, and all-around newshound. The state elects its judges. Four Republican members of the Supreme Court won their seats by campaigning against Fieger, who wasn't a candidate but made an excellent bogeyman. According to a fellow Republican member of the court, one justice invoked Fieger in a campaign fundraising letter, another gave a speech to the Republican state convention bragging about how much Fieger hated him, and three of them ran a joint ad attacking Fieger by name. Those members of the court then presided over a disciplinary hearing against Fieger, in which he was condemned for announcing publicly that certain judges of the state's Court of Appeals had changed their names from Hitler, Goebbels, and Eva Braun. The four Supreme Court justices who were said to have used Fieger as a bogeyman in their campaigns all sat as impartial judges in his disciplinary hearing—and all four voted against him, providing the margin in an obviously unconstitutional 4–3 decision. When their fellow Republican wrote an opinion detailing the unseemliness of judges announcing their bias in public and then acting on it, the four rammed through an administrative order prohibiting her from publishing it. The order specified that information about the inner workings of the court may be released only to the Judicial Tenure Commission or, if it comes to that, the police—but not, repeat not, the public.[5] (That last part was only implied, but it was pretty unmistakable.)

In 2009, federal judge Samuel Kent, whom we met in chapter 13, pled guilty to lying to federal investigators looking into allegations that he sexually attacked women who worked in his office. When one of the women first complained about Kent to a supervisor, the supervisor replied that if she filed a formal complaint she'd be fired. When she finally did so anyway, the "judicial council" responded by investigating and verifying the complaint and then "punishing" Kent by sending him on a four-month paid vacation.[6] But then federal prosecutors charged the judge with sexual felonies. His case was assigned to a fellow federal judge from Florida, who demonstrated his solidarity by slapping a gag order on the victims, forbidding them from talking about their own lives. The judge—the one behind the bench, that is—kept the gag order in place even after ex-judge Kent pled guilty, when its only justification (to prevent potential jurors from learning about the case) lost whatever lame justification it had ever possessed.[7] I doubt whether the judge who issued the order thought it complied with the Constitution. Rather, I suspect, he thought the first amendment wasn't an issue. As the Supreme Court's rules about cameras in the courtroom demonstrate, compliance with the first amendment is optional for judges.

Each of these incidents captures the judiciary protecting its good reputation in order to avoid the more demanding task of living up to it. For most young lawyers, it's disillusioning—literally—to realize the extent to which the legal system relies on illusion to maintain its authority. Courtrooms are designed, decorated, and stage-managed to put people in the mood to submit. Judges solemnly present their opinions as records of their reasoning, when they're really just after-the-fact justifications prepared by law clerks and staff attorneys who fill in the blanks once the judge tells them how he or she wants the case to come out. And then participants in the judicial process, from victims of a judge's sexual assaults to members of state appellate courts, are forbidden from telling the people how their government actually works. Most state judicial discipline boards work entirely in secret, although "work" might give a misleading impression. Federal judicial councils likewise function as trash cans. These bodies exist to *prevent* accountability, by creating an illusion to the contrary.

When all the illusions are stripped away, we're left with bureaucrats treated like gods. They're treated like gods because lawyers know the price for perceived disrespect. The judge holds the lawyer's clients hostage. If the lawyer tries speaking truth to power, the clients suffer. That's why lawyers have no choice but to adopt a baseline obsequiousness in their dealings with judges. "Your honor" isn't a measure of respect but very nearly the reverse. It's American baksheesh, the emolument necessary to lubricate a transaction.

CHAPTER 23

The Laugh Barrier

I MAGINE THAT ON a humid morning in June you're taking in the sights of Washington, D.C. Just as you're admiring the elegant proportions of Maryland Avenue as it radiates northeastward from the Capitol to Stanton Park, an old man wearing a dress approaches you. The man's dress is black, floor-length, with a high neckline. Grabbing your arm, he shouts: "The Constitution changed today! That which was, is no more! The fundamental organization of our government is altered!"

Suddenly four more dress-wearing old men materialize out of the heat haze and surround you, all chanting the same unintelligibly apocalyptic things. I think you might justifiably conclude that the time for polite murmurs and discreet sidling had passed and the time to run away had arrived.

And yet, when five dress-wearing old men made just that pronouncement on June 19, 1961—admittedly, less pithily, and while they were inside the mausoleum-shaped building on the corner of First Street and Maryland Avenue rather than on the sidewalk outside it—they were taken completely seriously by . . . well, by everyone. The idea of not taking the Supreme Court completely seriously doesn't exist in American political life.

TV comedians are pitilessly funny about politicians who put themselves before the voters and tell us something of what they plan to do once they get power in their hands. But political appointees who refuse to tell us in advance what they have planned for us, who violate the first amendment by refusing to allow cameras inside their public buildings and penalizing criticism of themselves, and who institution-alize pomposity—somehow they're immune from ridicule (except for African-American justices' sexual proclivities and Italian justices' overly expressive hand gestures, stereotypes that prove the rule). Not even priests and the English royal family are too precious for jokes anymore. In America, only judges reside beyond the laugh barrier.

June 19, 1961, was the day the time-released 14th amendment, rati-fied in 1868, abruptly kicked in. On that day (or so the justices told us), the 14th amendment suddenly required that every state court in the country start hiding evidence from the jurors dragged out of their private lives to decide whether accused criminals were guilty. In some ways the most remarkable thing about the justices' performance is the way they sold it. By assigning to the 14th amendment a new meaning 93 years after its ratification, they were admitting that either (a) the 14th amendment really did say that but for the previous 93 years they had failed to enforce it; or else (b) the 14th amendment didn't really say that and they were just making it up. Either the court was incompetent or it was lawless. And yet the justices made that abject confession in such a way that it only increased their court's stature.[1]

I think their sales job was assisted by the indignation of their critics. The outrage of the reactionaries, still incensed about *Brown v. Board of Education,* decided just seven years earlier, allowed the liberals of 1961 to misperceive the court as the enemy of their enemy. The sheer non-sensicality of the court's ruling was paradoxically useful, too, because it allowed lawyers to adopt an attitude that lawyers always find congenial: that nonlawyers really can't hope to understand such things. Reporters have never had any difficulty locating law professors willing to say, in so many words, that three years of instruction are necessary to understand the profound mysteries involved in any court ruling.

Finding themselves taken seriously by everyone, especially their critics, the justices of the 1960s were emboldened to develop the doctrine of "selective incorporation," by which over a period of years various portions of the first eight constitutional amendments became, or didn't become, "incorporated" into the 14th amendment by an occult process discernible only to the justices themselves. The states originally enacted the first eight amendments to restrain the power of the federal government, but once they were selectively incorporated into the 14th amendment the federal government began using them to restrain the power of the states. Some portions of the first eight amendments became applicable to criminal prosecutions that had already become final, requiring the immediate release of the convicted, while other portions were incorporated only as of the day of the particular Supreme Court decision, leaving thousands serving time on convictions that, according to the Supreme Court, violated the Constitution. Still other portions of the first eight amendments weren't incorporated at all. For instance, every clause of the fifth amendment has been incorporated but the first. The seventh amendment remains entirely unincorporated.

Law professors took this stuff seriously because it was their job to teach and therefore to defend it. Students took it seriously because it would be on the final. Recent graduates took it seriously because it was on the bar exam. Practicing lawyers took it seriously because they had to deal with it in their professional lives.

But why did anyone else respond with anything but hoots of derisive laughter?

THOMAS CORBIN DRUNKENLY steered his car across a double yellow line on a road near Poughkeepsie, ploughing head-on into a car driven by Brenda Dirago. She died as a result of the crash. Corbin's blood alcohol content was tested at .19 percent, which translates into blasted. You can produce a similar BAC in yourself by knocking back ten drinks in rapid succession. At that level, those who haven't built up alcohol tolerance will be close to blackout. Corbin was injured in the crash and taken to the hospital, where officers gave him tickets for driving while intoxicated and crossing the center line. (I'm not sure whether Ms. Dirago was still alive then or whether the officers just didn't know she had died.) Corbin and his lawyer showed up at justice of the peace court on a day when the district attorney wasn't scheduled to appear. According to two judges of New York's highest court, writing much later, the attorney "actively misled a Justice of the Peace into believing that no accident occurred, and no one was killed." Four other members of the appellate court, however, concluded that the attorney's statements to the JP were "arguably truthful," which they considered good enough.[2]

The JP accepted Corbin's plea of guilty to the two minor traffic offenses, fining him $360. Then the district attorney indicted him for vehicular homicide. Corbin moved to dismiss the indictment, contending that under the double jeopardy clause of the federal Constitution he had fully paid his debt to society ($360), making him immune from punishment for Ms. Dirago's death. Writing for the Court, Justice Brennan agreed with him, declaring that "the Double Jeopardy Clause of the Fifth Amendment demands application of the standard announced today."[3]

Three years later, after Brennan's retirement, the Supreme Court reversed itself. After 1993, as before 1990, the Constitution permitted a drunk driver to be punished both for crossing the yellow line and for killing people.[4]

Lawyers are trained not to find anything strange about the Supreme Court zigging and zagging like that. Lawyers also find nothing peculiar about the idea that an amendment to the Constitution ratified in 1791, whose 108 words haven't changed since then, should suddenly change meanings, and then change again. Even the rhetoric sounds normal to lawyerly ears: not the justices but the fifth amendment itself demanded the new standard, as if it were an obtreperous piece of furniture in a Disney cartoon. The justices never explained how an amendment could go along for 199 years without making any demands not contained in its text, only to make contradictory ones in such rapid-fire succession. Did the fickle heart of a light-o'-love always beat beneath the amendment's placid exterior? Or do amendments get cranky as they age? Or—just maybe—should we picture Justice Brennan with a sock puppet on his hand, trying not to move his lips?

In 2004, Justice Scalia explained that the incompetents who preceded him on the Supreme Court had failed utterly in their constitutional task of interpreting the sixth amendment. Unable to take their bumbling any longer, he shoved them inside and told us what "the Framers" of the Constitution had meant all along but were too inarticulate to express in the words of the sixth amendment itself. Like a New Age channeler, the devoutly Catholic Scalia interpreted the psychic energy of "the Framers," passing along from the hereafter what they wanted us to know. It turns out that when the delegates to the constitutional convention drafted the sixth amendment, or the members of the various state legislatures voted to ratify it, or the people of the states voted for their legislators—any one of those groups might be Scalia's "the Framers"—not only were they all of one mind, but their one mind was focused on Sir Walter Raleigh, as revealed by the 19 mentions of Raleigh in Scalia's opinion. By the vision vouchsafed to Scalia in 2004, we now know that Raleigh's political show trial of 1603 disclosed the private thoughts of the Framers of 1791.[5]

In 1990, the justices evaluated Arizona's death penalty statute. After solemn deliberation, they found that it complied with the requirements of the United States Constitution. Twelve years later, they evaluated the same statute and declared it unconstitutional. Exact same statute, exact same Constitution, exactly opposite results.[6] Perfect poker faces, too.

It would be wrong to suggest there's anything unique about the U.S. Supreme Court's ponderous, consequential silliness. In 2008 the Mississippi Court of Appeals considered the appeal of Kenivel Smith, accused of shooting Andre Davis. In a videotaped statement to police given immediately after the shooting, Davis had no doubt Smith had shot him: they were face to face, just a few feet from each other. But Smith lay low and it was many months before he was arrested, and many months more before his trial got underway. When the prosecution called Davis to the witness stand, he had forgotten everything he once told police—a common occurrence when a witness is given sufficient time to contemplate the health advantages of memory loss. During cross-examination by Smith's attorney, however, Davis recovered his memory. It turned out everything he originally told the police was wrong. The Mississippi appellate court concluded Smith had been denied his right to cross-examine Davis precisely *because* Davis provided such helpful testimony on cross-examination. (In the following passage, the judges use "confront" as an exact synonym for "cross-examine.")

> It is undisputed that Smith did not have an opportunity to cross-examine Davis when Davis provided his statements. That Smith had an opportunity to cross-examine Davis at trial does not necessarily cure the constitutional confrontation problem. While the distinction may appear slight, the "Davis" who testified at Smith's trial was no longer the accusing witness against Smith. Smith's true accusing witness was the "Davis" of December 29, 2004. Therefore, Smith was unable to confront his accuser.[7]

So now you understand why cross-examining a person cannot be accepted as a substitute for cross-examining that person. I trust there will be no more confusion on that score.

I once saw a TV interview with Charles Addams, the great morbid *New Yorker* cartoonist, in which he talked about his classic cartoon of the skier hurtling down a slope, her parallel tracks going neatly to either side of a tall tree. Addams reported that psychiatrists use the cartoon to gauge a patient's reality testing: a patient who can explain how the skier made the tracks needs to be committed. Addams's remark gives me reason to worry whenever I think I might understand what the New Mexico Court of Appeals meant when, in the course of reversing the murder conviction of a state senator's nephew, it talked about "death caused by the exercise of nondeadly force."[8]

So Why Do It?

A TALL WELSHMAN NAMED Christopher Cullen, traveling across the United States, stopped at a youth hostel in El Paso. A young Englishwoman we'll call Sarah stayed at the same youth hostel. They didn't know each other before becoming part of an informal group of hostelers who took in the sights together, shared meals, and kept each other company on a visit into Mexico. After a few days, Sarah told the others she'd be continuing her journey. She planned to rent a car and drive up into New Mexico. Cullen asked if she could give him a ride to Deming, which was on her route and about halfway to his next destination, Phoenix. She agreed.

He navigated from the passenger seat and recommended that she visit City of Rocks State Park before dropping him off. She took his advice. The park is stunning—a landscape of giant boulders left vertical by unimaginable geologic forces—and extremely remote. Cullen pulled out a hunting knife and said he'd kill her. He raped her, then required her to drive into the Black Mountains, among the most rugged and remote areas in the lower 48 states. To discourage her from attempting escape, he took her shoes and made her drive with her pants pulled below her hips so they'd trip her if she tried to run. He used the neck cord from her sunglasses to tie her wrist to the shift lever. The cord wouldn't keep her tied up for long, but it only needed to give him time to use the knife. He made her drive a winding highway into the mountains and then along a dirt road to a cattle watering tank fed by a well on a windmill, where he raped her again. During the hours he kept her there she heard only one car pass by on the highway, half a mile or more away across the desert. Cullen wandered over and looked at the windmill, then came back and reported that it was inspected on a two-week schedule and the last inspection had been the previous day. He said, "I could kill you right here and no one would find your body for thirteen days."

But he didn't kill her then. He made her get back in the car and continue driving. As night fell he became hungry and had her drive into Truth or Consequences, the former Hot Springs, renamed for a radio show. He directed her into the drive-up window at a McDonald's. She placed the order for them, endorsing a cashier's check to pay for the meal. She thought about trying to write a message on the cashier's check but was afraid Cullen would see. When she passed the check to the cashier she mouthed, "Help me."

The cashier couldn't read her lips but could read the expression on her face. She said she had to ask her manager if they could accept a cashier's check. Really she wanted to say she thought something was wrong. The manager instructed her to say they'd be closing soon and had already turned off the fryer—which wasn't true—but that they would have the order out as soon as they could. That was to keep them from driving away. In the meantime he called 911. And because it's such a small town, the officers arrived within minutes.

Without the heroically resourceful McDonald's workers, Sarah would have died that day. The prosecutor, Mary Lynne Newell, now the district attorney in Silver City, was deeply committed to the case. Sarah was almost unbelievably strong. Cullen's counsel was reduced to suggesting she had used a hunting knife to slice off her own bra and leave it at the windmill in order to provide phony collaboration for her outlandish tale. While I was working on the appeal, Mary Lynne drove up to Albuquerque to meet with me. She said she had other reasons to make the trip to the big city, which I'm sure was true, but I'm equally sure she wanted to be certain I took the case as seriously as she did. She brought along a photograph of Sarah looking happy and relaxed, and told me Sarah's boyfriend had been a rock of support and that they would soon be married—a rare happy ending.

Shortly afterward Mary Lynne received a request from Interpol, the European police agency, for a DNA sample from Cullen. He was a suspect in crimes against women on the other side of the ocean, too.

My work on the appeal required the meticulous detailing of each separate offense he committed against Sarah during the ten hours he had her in captivity. The facts were such that the catalogue gained in power as I drained emotion from my written descriptions. I didn't need to use any colorful language. The Court of Appeals upheld his 140-year sentence and the federal habeas corpus court didn't give Cullen the time of day.[1]

That's one reason why I do what I do.

The prosecution of violent crime isn't a courtroom contest between the government and the defendant; it's the government's regulation of violence in the society. How much violence is too much? Who gets to decide what's too much, the people or their judges? For that matter, how much violence is too little? That last question sounds absurd, but I'm afraid it's not. The Arizona Court of Appeals, for instance, acted to prevent the level of violence in Tucson from slipping below the desirable minimum when it ruled that the Constitution prohibited a police officer from seizing a loaded handgun from an ex-con and current Crips gang member who had been riding in a lawfully stopped car, when the officer had no better reason to disarm him than a reasonable suspicion that he was dangerous—an immediate threat to her life. The U.S. Supreme Court unanimously reversed that decision, but the stunning thing is that it had to do so.[2]

The Arizona court's opinion talked about the gang member's rights, but that wasn't its only subject. It didn't acknowledge its other subject:

deciding how many murdered police officers are too few. I'm confident the judges kept themselves from becoming consciously aware that they were also answering that question. The conventional way of framing the legal issue would have spared them any such uncomfortable thoughts.

Much of my job consists of trying to get judges to accept responsibility for the real-world consequences of their decisions. Those consequences are the subject of the criminal law, not the words in the judges' opinions. Deciding whether to affirm the conviction of someone like Christopher Cullen affects many people, not just him. Releasing him would have meant condemning another woman, and probably more than one woman, to everything he did to Sarah, plus one thing more: violent death. Locking him up prevents that. It also provides justice, that complicated and indispensable thing, to Sarah. Cullen's prosecution wasn't primarily about him. It was a fulfillment of society's responsibility to its members, and especially the most vulnerable among them—people as vulnerable as Sarah had been at the windmill.

There's a vast difference between presiding fairly over legal proceedings, on the one hand, and adopting a stance of moral neutrality about another human being's suffering, on the other. In certain moods I think it requires three years of law school and extensive on-the-job training before judges can fully eradicate their ability to perceive that difference.

AND YET I PRACTICE LAW. I've done law professionally for 23 years, and for 3½ years before that as a student. I expect to do it six more years, until I can retire to write full time. The law has allowed our children (three now, since Benjamin joined us) to live their entire lives in a nice house in a good neighborhood within a few miles of both their grandmothers, attending pretty good public schools.

I started in the legal profession to earn a living. I had no desire to become wealthy but wanted some way to live independently without being eaten up by money worries. My preference was for brain work, out of the weather, in the company of intelligent and companionable coworkers. I've had all of that. But at some point I absorbed just enough of the sentimental oratory about the profession's noble pursuit of justice to begin asking how reality measured up. That was a mistake. The law can be of great service to individuals and even to mankind, but that's like saying music can be deeply moving and architecture inspiring. Who's disillusioned by a lousy song or cookie-cutter office building?

I teach paralegal studies courses at my community college. Many of my students work all day before attending classes that begin at 5:30. Often they have small children at home. Some have husbands in the military. (One student, the mother of a six-month-old, explained why her assignment was late: "My husband's in Iraq and he was hit by an IED over the weekend. He's okay, but I was a wreck until I heard from him. I didn't get the homework done.") The best reason to practice law, I think, is the same reason my students attend evening classes.

Just as you hope you're wasting all the money you spend on insurance, you hope your children's lives will be too pleasant and stable for them to be able to publish bestselling memoirs in their twenties. It's easy to lose sight of the modest nobility of that. I've never found earning a middle-class income enough, but I wouldn't want to be without it.

In would-be emulation of Chris, my retiring colleague who replied to my facetious request for words of wisdom by offering some, these are a few of the lessons I've learned, invariably the hard way, about reducing the oscillations between the poles of exaltation and cynicism described in the first paragraphs of the Introduction.

Don't think like a lawyer about your own life. The ability to disengage emotion and proceed logically is critical to lawyerly effectiveness. But when making life decisions, it's illogical to set emotion aside. Happiness itself is an emotion, and contentment is a whole bunch of them. It's doubtless a symptom of neurosis that I need to believe my law work contributes to a cause bigger than myself and more meaningful than a client's finances. But indulging the neurosis is, I've discovered, the only way to reconcile myself to my profession.

Beware the prestige trap. "Prestigious" is the technical legal term— a "term of art," as we in this most un-arty of professions call it—for the condition of having adopted someone else's values as one's own. Pursuing prestige is the single most efficient method for engineering your own misery.

Remember the variety. Because of the lack of a practicum, legal careers often follow nearly random courses. Law school graduates accept the job that's offered, and then their perceived career options narrow to the examples they encounter. There are always many more. Switching from litigation to an appellate practice, and from civil to criminal law, and from the private to the public sector, made my career one I no longer minded having.

Don't take it personally. This one is particularly hard to remember when judges or opposing counsel mean it personally. And they will, sometimes. But they can score points against you only by talking about themselves. They're saying, "I'm a jerk" and "I can't handle a judge's authority."

Avoid chronic cognitive dissonance. The old political saw says, "We live under a government of laws, not men." Naturally, some of the men would prefer it the other way around. Law exists to protect us *from* judges—as from all powerful people, whether elected, appointed, or violent. Power, including that of judges, will always tend toward the arbitrary. Lawyers are generally enthusiastic supporters of government by judges, believing it promises them a kind of reflective power: they can hope to influence policy by influencing the judge. Down that path lies cognitive dissonance. Lawyers who believe in the rule of law while encouraging its opposite—rule by judges—must maintain constant watchfulness to avoid becoming consciously aware of their own self-deception. Over time, the sustained effort causes the brain to shrivel.

Lead the horses to water. But don't take responsibility for making them drink. You can't stop a bad judge from being bad.

Be careful how you define victory. You might not win more cases that way, but you'll lose fewer.

AUTHOR'S NOTE

ALL OF THE stories in this book are true. With regard to publicly-known events, I've relied entirely on what I've learned from the news or judicial opinions and not on any private source of information. All expressions of opinion are, of course, my own, and none should be interpreted as making or implying any statement of fact. In several instances I've altered details to avoid revealing confidences or giving offense. As for the offense I give... If you can't count on judges to decide cases on the merits regardless of their feelings towards the lawyers involved, then the whole business of law becomes pretty absurd, doesn't it? It takes us right back to the clan elder enthroned in the darkness of the back of the cave, pounding the stone bench with a carved mastodon bone, his symbol of office, to punctuate his announcement of the will of the gods — if, indeed, the legal profession ever left that smoky gloom.

I'm deeply grateful to Claire Gerus, agent and guide; to many lawyer friends and colleagues, mention of whose names might not be to their professional advantage; to my boys, Alexander, Scott and Benjamin; and, always, to Carla.

ENDNOTES

INTRODUCTION

1 Address to the Suffolk Bar Association Dinner, February 5, 1885, quoted in Sheldon M. Novick, *Honorable Justice: A Life of Oliver Wendell Holmes* (New York: Little, Brown, 1989), p. 175.

2 John Hagan and Fiona Kay, "Even Lawyers Get the Blues: Gender, Depression, and Job Satisfaction in Legal Practice," *Law & Society Review* 41:51–78 (2007); Kennon M. Sheldon and Lawrence S. Krieger, "Understanding the Negative Effects of Legal Education on Law Students: A Longitudinal Test of Self-Determination Theory," *Personality and Social Psychology Bulletin* 33:883–97 (2007); Patrick J. Schiltz, "On Being a Happy, Healthy, and Ethical Member of an Unhappy, Unhealthy, and Unethical Profession," 52 *Vanderbilt Law Review* 871, 874–75 (1999); Connie J. A. Beck, Bruce D. Sales, and G. Andrew H. Benjamin, "Lawyer Distress: Alcohol-Related Problems and Other Psychological Concerns Among a Sample of Practicing Lawyers," 10 *Journal of Law and Health* 1, 18–31, 44–51 (1996); G. A. H. Benjamin, E. J. Darling, and B. Sales, "The Prevalence of Depression, Alcohol Abuse, and Cocaine Abuse among United States Lawyers," *International Journal of Law and Psychiatry* 13:233–46 (1990).

CHAPTER 1. THE DECISION TO APPLY

1 Noam Scheiver, "Republican Elitism," *New York Times* (Dec. 11, 2005).

CHAPTER 2. LAID-BACK U.

1 J. Loman, G. E. Quinn, L. Kamoun, G. S. Ying, M. G. Maguire, D. Hudesman, and R. A. Stone, "Darkness and Near Work. Myopia and Its Progression in Third-Year Law Students," *Ophthalmology* 109:1032–1038 (2002); Karla Zadnik and Donald O. Mutti, "Refractive error changes in law students," *American Journal of Optometry and Physiological Optics* 64:558–61 (1987).

2 Adam Liptak, "If the Law Is an Ass, the Law Professor Is a Donkey," *New York Times* (Aug. 28, 2005), reporting on John O. McGinnis, Matthew A. Schwartz, and Benjamin Tisdell, "The Patterns and Implications of Political Contributions by Elite Law School Faculty," 93 *Georgetown Law Journal* 1167–1212 (2005). Republican candidates achieved parity with Democrats at just one of the 18 highly ranked law schools included in the study: the University of Virginia. Comparatively Republican-friendly faculties were also spotted at Cornell, Vanderbilt, and the University of Chicago.

3 Bernard C. Steiner, *Life of Roger Brooke Taney: Chief Justice of the United States* (Baltimore: Williams & Wilkins, Co., 1922), pp. 509–11; Walker Lewis, *Without Fear or Favor: A Biography of Roger Brooke Taney* (Boston: Houghton Mifflin, 1965), pp. 463–64; William H. Rehnquist, *All the Laws But One: Civil Liberties in Wartime* (New York: Knopf, 1998), p. 34.

4 The quotation is from Connie J. A. Beck, Bruce D. Sales, and G. Andrew H. Benjamin, "Lawyer Distress: Alcohol-Related Programs and Other Psychological Concerns Among a Sample of Practicing Lawyers," 10 *Journal of Law and Health* 1, 4–5 (1996).

CHAPTER 3. THE BOGS OF PRESTIGE

1 Morgan Lee, "Writer Rewarded for Life's Work," *Albuquerque Journal* (Sept. 27, 2000).

2 Patrick J. Schiltz, "On Being a Happy, Healthy, and Ethical Member of an Unhappy, Unhealthy, and Unethical Profession," 52 *Vanderbilt Law Review* 871, 873 (1999).

3 David C. Lindberg, *The Beginnings of Western Science: The European Scientific Tradition in Philosophical, Religious, and Institutional Context, 600 B.C. to A.D. 1450* (Chicago: University of Chicago Press, 1992), p. 361.

4 Quoted in Thomas J. Ricks, *Fiasco: The American Military Adventure in Iraq* (New York: Penguin, 2006), p. 340.

CHAPTER 6. INITIATION BY LOTUS-EATING

1 James B. Stewart, *Follow the Story: How to Write Successful Nonfiction* (New York: Simon & Schuster, 1998), pp. 240–42 (quoting the author's 1983 front-page *Wall Street Journal* article); "Getting a Piece of the Power," *Time* (June 4, 1984).

CHAPTER 7. THE JUDGE'S GHOSTWRITER

1   G. Edward White, *Justice Oliver Wendell Holmes: Law and the Inner Self* (New York: Oxford University Press, 1993), pp. 311–313.

2   Douglas used the phrase in a congratulatory note to newly appointed Justice Rehnquist, who had once served as law clerk to Justice Roberts: "I realize that you were here before as a member of the so-called Junior Supreme Court." Bernard Schwartz, *Decision: How the Supreme Court Decides Cases* (New York: Oxford University Press, 1996), p. 48.

3   *Bush v. Gore,* 531 U.S. 98 (2000).

4   The case-selection process is detailed in H. W. Perry, Jr., *Deciding to Decide: Agenda Setting in the United States Supreme Court* (Cambridge, Mass: Harvard University Press, 1991), pp. 41–91. Anecdotal accounts, from differing points of view, can be found in William H. Rehnquist, *The Supreme Court: How It Was, How It Is* (New York: Quill, 1987), pp. 263–265; and Edward Lazarus, *Closed Chambers: The First Eyewitness Account of the Epic Struggles Inside the Supreme Court* (New York: Times Books, 1998), pp. 28–32.

5   David N. Atkinson, *Leaving the Bench: Supreme Court Justices at the End* (Lawrence: University Press of Kansas, 1999), pp. 48–55, 68–71, 93–94, 127–132, 164, and 174–175.

6   This legend is widely told. This particular phrasing is from Stuart Taylor, Jr., "Psst! Pass It On. The Successor to Rehnquist Will Be…," *National Journal* (April 28, 2001), p. 1211. With slight variations it can also be found in Richard Lacayo, "Marshall's Legacy: A Lawyer Who Changed America," *Time* (July 8, 1991), p. 24; and Stephen Chapman, "Octogenarian Justices Are No Asset to the Court," *Chicago Tribune* (July 4, 1991).

7   Atkinson, *Leaving the Bench,* pp. 156–160, 165; David G. Savage, *Turning Right: The Making of the Rehnquist Supreme Court* (New York: John Wiley, 1992), p. 73.

8   Terry Eastland, "While Justice Sleeps," *National Review* (April 21, 1989), p. 24; Max Boot, "Unrestrained," *National Review* (June 1, 1998), p. 30.

9   Lazarus, *Closed Chambers,* pp. 264–271.

10   David Plotz, "Mr. Efficiency," *Slate* (Jan. 11, 1998).

11   Tony Mauro, "Corps of Clerks Lacking in Diversity," *USA Today* (March 13, 1998).

12 Letter to the editor from Antonin Scalia, *Legal Times* (Oct. 2, 2000) (online edition). Scalia was responding to an article by Tony Mauro and Sam Loewenberg, "Who Really Wants to Lift Ban on Fees? Scalia's Frustration Seen as Factor for Reinstating Judges' Honoraria," *Legal Times* (Sept. 18, 2000). Scalia's letter confirmed the accuracy of the article.

13 Tony Mauro, "Chief Judge Won't Meet on Minority Clerks," *USA Today* (June 10, 1998).

14 Tony Mauro, "Rehnquist Blames Grad Pool for Lack of Diversity," *USA Today* (Dec. 8, 1998).

15 The figures are provided in Mauro, "Corps of Clerks."

16 Mauro, "Rehnquist Blames Grad Pool" (quoting Nov. 17, 1998, letter from Rehnquist to three unnamed members of Congress).

17 Mauro, "Corps of clerks." Selection to law review is the only clerk-selection criterion specifically mentioned by Rehnquist in *The Supreme Court: How It Was, How It Is* (New York: Quill, 1987), p. 262. For selection to law review, *see* Reinhard Zimmerman, "Law Reviews: A Foray through a Strange World," 47 *Emory Law Journal* 659, 671 (1998).

18 Karen D. Arnold, *Lives of Promise: What Becomes of High School Valedictorians: A Fourteen-Year Study of Achievement and Life Choices* (San Francisco: Jossey-Bass Publishers, 1995), pp. 17, 28–30.

19 Meg Greenfield, *Washington* (New York: Public Affairs, 2001), pp. 38–54.

20 Larissa MacFarquhar, "The Bench Burner," *The New Yorker* (December 10, 2001), p. 82.

21 Dahlia Lithwick, "Microsoft Dispatches: Microsoft Bad, Judge Jackson Worse," *Slate* (June 28, 2001).

22 *U.S. v. Knights,* 219 F.3d 1138, 1141, 1144, 1145 (2000), *rev'd,* 534 U.S. 112 (2001).

CHAPTER 8. CROSSING THE BAR

1 *Aleman v. Honorable Judges of Circuit Court of Cook County,* 138 F.3d 302 (7th Cir. 1998). The full story is told, with vivid detail, in Robert Cooley with Hillel Levin, *When Corruption Was King: How I Helped the Mob Rule Chicago, Then Brought the Outfit Down* (New York: Carroll & Graff, 2006).

2 Henry Clay Whitney, *Life on the Circuit with Lincoln* (1892) (Caxton Printers, 1940), pp. 61–88, chapter 2, "Life on the Eighth Circuit."

3   "[I]t was not until the 1820s that the average judicial age [on the Supreme Court] exceeded sixty." David N. Atkinson, *Leaving the Bench: Supreme Court Justices at the End* (Lawrence: University Press of Kansas, 1999), p. 11. The onerousness of circuit riding is reflected in many of the mini-biographies provided in Atkinson's chapter 2, "The Antebellum Court, 1789–1864."

CHAPTER 9. ROLL DEM BONES

1   Alison Grant, "BlockShopper.com Settles Suit Filed by Jones Day Law Firm," *Cleveland Plain Dealer* (Feb. 12, 2009).

2   These are preliminary figures for 2008, updated through February 11, 2008, available at law.com. The head counts are full-time equivalents as of August 31, 2008. The final 2008 *Am Law* 100 list will be published in May 2009.

3   Kennon M. Sheldon and Lawrence S. Krieger, "Does Legal Education Have Undermining Effects on Law Students? Evaluating Changes in Motivation, Values, and Well-Being," *Behavioral Sciences and the Law* 22:261–286 (2004).

4   Sheldon and Krieger, "Understanding the Negative Effects of Legal Education on Law Students: A Longitudinal Test of Self-Determination Theory," *Personality and Social Psychology Bulletin* 33:883–897 (2007).

CHAPTER 10. THE PRESTIGE TRAP

1   The Supreme Court spelled this out in 2009: "When the consideration for a contract fails—that is, when one of the exchanged promises is not kept—we do not say that the voluntary bilateral consent to the contract never existed, so that it is automatically and utterly void; we say that the contract was broken." *Puckett v. U.S.*, 556 U. S. 129 S. ct. 1423, 1430, 173 L.Ed. 2d 266 (2009). The "we" in that quotation doesn't include the judge at my first trial.

CHAPTER 12. DISCOVERING DISCOVERY

1   Brian Baxter, "Former Covington Staff Attorney Sues Firm for Racial Discrimination," *The Am Law Daily* (Feb. 25, 2009); Yolanda Young, "Law Firm Segregation Reminiscent of Jim Crow," *Huffington Post* (March 17, 2008).

2   Carmen DeNavas-Walt, Bernadette D. Proctor, and Jessica C. Smith, "Income, Poverty, and Health Insurance Coverage in the United States: 2007," U.S. Census Bureau, Current Population Reports, P60-235 (Aug. 2008).

CHAPTER 13. A TAXONOMY OF BAD JUDGES

1   John T. Dauner, "Memorial Celebrates Life of Judge, Wife," *Kansas City Star* (Dec. 4, 1998).

2   Lloyd Jojola and Jeff Proctor, "Judge, Wife Found Dead; Murder-Suicide Suspected by APD," *Albuquerque Journal* (Aug. 14, 2005).

3   Richard Espinoza and John T. Dauner, "Police Still Seek Answers in Deaths of Judge, His Wife," *Kansas City Star* (Nov. 30, 1998).

4   Rasheeda Crayton and John T. Dauner, "Judge, Wife Found Dead," *Kansas City Star* (Nov. 30, 1998). The paper was quoting Judge Kathryn Vratil.

5   www.10thcircuithistory.org/pdf_files/O%27Connor_bio.pdf (accessed Feb. 18, 2009).

6   Associated Press, "Police: Retired Judge and His Wife Found Dead," *Albuquerque Journal* (Aug. 13, 2005).

7   Richard A. Posner, "What Do Judges and Justices Maximize? (The Same Thing Everyone Else Does)", 3 *Supreme Court Economic Review* 1 (1993). The article has appeared in several versions, including the one found at www.law.uchicago.edu/Lawecon/WkngPprs_01-25/15.RAP.Judges.pdf (accessed March 31, 2009).

CHAPTER 14. PERSONALITY TESTS

1   Ray Dall'Osto, "Atticus Finch Was Wrong?" *Wisconsin Bar Journal* (April 4, 2008).

2   *State v. Knapp*, 2005 WI 127, 700 N.W.2d 899 (Wis. 2005); *State v. Armstrong*, 2005 WI 119, 700 N.W.2d 98 (Wis. 2005).

CHAPTER 15. SITUATIONAL ETHICS

1   "26-Year Secret Kept Innocent Man in Prison," CBS News (March 8, 2008); Sharon Cohen, "A 26-Year-Old Secret Could Free Inmate," AP Dispatch (April 12, 2008).

CHAPTER 16. BIEGANOWSKI CELLARS

1   *U.S. v. Bieganowski*, 313 F.3d 264 (5th Cir. 2002).

2   Holden Lewis, Associated Press, "Winery Sparks Revival of Industry in El Paso," *Dallas Morning News* (Jan. 29, 1989); Bob Lowe, "Texas Chardonnays Stand Tall Against French Wines," *Austin American-Statesman* (Aug. 24, 1991).

3   Bruce Hight, "Doctors, Panel Wrangle Over Workers' Comp," *Austin American-Statesman* (July 19, 1996).

4 *Bieganowski v. Inspector General,* Department of Health and Human Services, Departmental Appeals Board, Civil Remedies Division, Docket No. C-02-447, Decision No. CR1035 (April 30, 2003).

CHAPTER 19. DO-GOODING

1 *Republican Party of Minnesota v. White,* 536 U.S. 765, 804 (2002) (Ginsburg, J., dissenting). I changed "applying" to "apply."

2 Letter of May 26, 1911, in Melvin I. Urofsky and David M. Levy, eds., *Letters of Louis D. Brandeis* (Albany: State University of New York Press, 1971–78), vol. 2, p. 443. For the context of the remark, *see* Lewis J. Paper, *Brandeis* (Englewood Cliffs, N.J.: Prentice-Hall, 1983), at pp. 175–76.

3 *Eastman Kodak Co. v. Image Tech Services,* 504 U.S. 451 (1992).

4 C. Perez & C. S. Widom, "Childhood victimization and long-term intellectual and academic outcomes," *Child Abuse & Neglect* 18:617–633 (1994); National Center for Education Statistics, U.S. Department of Education, "Public High School Graduation Rates by State," nces.ed.gov/programs/coe/2008/section3/indicator21.asp (accessed April 1, 2009); "Dropout Rates in the United States: Compendium Report," U.S. Department of Education, NCES 2007-059 (June 2007).

CHAPTER 20. DO-BADDING

1 *Johnson v. U.S.,* 333 U.S. 10, 13–14 (1948). Jackson was writing specifically about ex parte warrant applications, when the defense is unrepresented. I think all he meant was that the judge should avoid getting caught up in the excitement of the police chase. But the phrase has acquired a much broader meaning with frequent repetition.

2 *State v. Brule,* 1999-NMSC-026, ¶ 4, 981 P.2d 782.

3 The reference is to *Giles v. California,* 554 U.S. 128 S. ct. 2678. 171 L.Ed. 2d 488 (2008).

4 *State v. Ortega,* 2008-NMCA-001, 175 P.3d 929 (N.M. Ct. App. 2007), *cert. denied,* 2007-NMCERT-12, 175 P.3d 307 (N.M. 2007).

CHAPTER 22. IT'S MORE IMPORTANT TO HAVE A GOOD REPUTATION

1 New Mexico Rules of Professional Conduct, Rule 11-803.

2 The history of the treatment center is detailed in Tom Roberts, "Bishops were warned of abusive priests," *National Catholic Reporter* (Mar. 30, 2009).

3　The Supreme Court has attempted to define away the sixth-amendment right to a public trial, describing it as a personal right of the accused rather than a public right. *Gannett Co. v. DePasquale,* 443 U.S. 368 (1979). But because any other result would have meant the Court itself was violating the sixth amendment, the Court's ruling was deeply self-interested. I can't think of any reason to consider it legitimate.

4　*In re Allen,* 998 So.2d 557 (Fla. 2008).

5　*In re Haley,* 720 N.W.2d 246, 259 n. 1 (Mich. 2006) (Weaver, J., concurring); *Grievance Administrator v. Fieger,* 719 N.W.2d 123 (Mich. 2006); Administrative Order 2006-8, Deliberative Privilege and Case Discussions in the Supreme Court (Mich. Dec. 6, 2006).

6　Michael A. Smith, "McBroom's Justice Swept Under Carpet," *Galveston Daily News* (Feb. 24, 2009); Brad Woodard, "Judge Kent Remembered for 'Rude, Crude' Behavior in Courtroom," KHOU (Feb. 24, 2009) (KHOU.com); Steven Lubet, "Bullying from the Bench," *The Green Bag* 2d Series, vol. 5 (Autumn 2001) (greenbag.org).

7　Mary Flood, "Media Ask Judge in Kent Case to End Gag Order," *Houston Chronicle* (Feb. 25, 2009).

CHAPTER 23. THE LAUGH BARRIER

1　The case being described is *Mapp v. Ohio,* 367 U.S. 642 (1961).

2　*Corbin v. Hillery,* 545 N.Y.S.2d 71, 543 N.E.2d 714 (N.Y. 1989).

3　*Grady v. Corbin,* 495 U.S. 508, 524 (1990).

4　*Grady v. Corbin* was overruled by *United States v. Dixon,* 509 U.S. 688 (1993).

5　The case being described is *Crawford v. Washington,* 541 U.S. 36 (2004).

6　*Walton v. Arizona,* 497 U.S. 639 (1990); *Ring v. Arizona,* 536 U.S. 584 (2002).

7　*Smith v. State,* So.2d, 2008 WL 4482521 (Miss. App. 2008).

8　*State v. Romero,* 112 P.3d 1113, ¶ 15 (N.M. App. 2005).

CONCLUSION

1　*State v. Cullen,* N.M. Ct. App. No. 14,254 (July 13, 1993).

2　*State v. Johnson,* 170 P. 3d 667, ¶ 26 (Ariz. App. 2007), *rev'd by Arizona v. Johnson,* 555 U.S. , 129 S.Ct. 781, 172 L.Ed.2d 694 (2009).